Psychiatry and Criminal Law

Illusions, Fictions, and Myths

Psychiatry and Criminal Law

Illusions, Fictions, and Myths

by

SOL RUBIN
*Counsel, National Council on
Crime and Delinquency*

Foreword by
Justice Amos N. Blandin, Jr.

1965
Oceana Publications, Inc.
Dobbs Ferry, New York

To Paula

Also by Sol Rubin

Crime and Juvenile Delinquency—
A Rational Approach to Penal Problems

The Law of Criminal Correction

Contents

PART I

Criminal Responsibility and Exculpation

PART II

Sentencing

FOREWORD

"Quarry the granite rock with razors or moor the vessel with a thread of silk; then may you hope with such keen and delicate instruments as human knowledge and human reason to contend against these giants, the passion and the pride of man."
Whether or not one agrees with Cardinal Newman, many thoughtful people, supported by substantial evidence, today believe that human knowledge and human reason are being worsted in the battle against crime. The reams of books and articles written on the subject of penology, the exaggerated claims and assertions of various individuals and groups as to how their latest techniques are producing "outstanding results," and the vast expenditure of public funds—all these offer little consolation to the victims of brutal crimes, nor do they reassure people who find the individual freedom and safety of law-abiding persons more and more invaded by lawless elements.

Amid the welter of confused and conflicting panaceas and their failure to produce satisfactory results, it is indeed encouraging to read a book which presents a sensible formula, and one which I believe offers more hope for improving a highly unsatisfactory and controversial field of criminal law than anything else I have read.

Sol Rubin states his thesis simply. As Professor Edward H. Warren, of the Harvard Law School, told our class many years ago, "all perfect things are simple." I realize that there are those who will react violently to this. The often overworked cliché, "But you *mustn't* oversimplify," has become a powerful fetish. While at times the cliché has merit, often it serves only to mask the failure to think a problem through. I believe the clarity and the good sense of the Rubin rule evinces that its author has thought his problem through.

In brief, his proposition is that the M'Naghten rule should be the test to determine the guilt, or innocence by reason of insanity, of the accused. If a verdict of guilty be found, then the question of sentencing—the degree of individual responsibility which the offender must assume for his crime—will be decided by the presiding judge after hearing all relevant psychiatric and other evidence which the parties may choose to offer. To me, this presents a principle comprehensible to lawyers and laymen alike, and one which has been successfully relied upon to do justice throughout the centuries by kind and wise men.

Dean Pound tells us that the fundamental purpose of the law is "to bring about and maintain an ideal relationship among men." I believe the Rubin rule meets this test. It combines the virtues of M'Naghten and those of the so-called Durham Rule rationale without the vices of either. It permits full scope for the play of humanitarian impulses and the best that psychiatry has or will have to offer. At the same time, by engaging the resources of the individual, it embraces a strong philosophy of individual responsibility rather than a weak philosophy of excuses, on the premise that no one, adult or juvenile, can ultimately be improved except by himself.

In short, I have an abiding conviction that the rule is so simple that it can be understood and successfully applied by laymen and lawyers, and so reasonable that it ought to be approved.

Amos N. Blandin, Jr.
Associate Justice
Supreme Court of New Hampshire

PREFACE

As the reader will presently note, the word "illusions" in the title refers to illusions, mainly about psychiatry, shared by some psychiatrists, judges, and lawyers. The word "fictions" in the text is a legal word-of-art meaning a concept which, acknowledged by all as false, serves certain purposes commonly agreed upon as desirable. It is to these "fictions" that the term "myths" is related.

I do not condemn illusions, fictions, or myths. None of us can live without them. We have them as children, thinking of our parents, and as youths, regarding our statesmen; it is perhaps well that their glamor, authority, and wisdom are accepted, temporarily at least. But maturity, the development of our own strength, and a sound relationship with authority require us to become aware of their failings and limitations. Even then the illusion is worthy and perhaps necessary, as long as it is not excessive. So also legal fictions and psychiatric illusions have their use, until we overdo them.

One way of overdoing our illusions or fictions is to pretend to believe, or actually believe, that they are real. This way lies either hypocrisy or neurosis. I have, in fact, once or twice used the word "hypocrisy" in dealing with the knowing use of an illusion or a fiction to achieve objectives that go beyond their functions. Such uses I oppose and have attacked and condemned.

Many people have helped, in many ways, in the writing of this book and in my work, too many to name more than a few. My deep thanks go to Justice Amos N. Blandin, not only for the generous foreword he wrote, but even more for his urging that ideas we talked about at meetings of the NCCD Advisory Council of Judges should be developed and published. The confidence of Judge Blandin, a critical, outspoken man, experienced with the New Hampshire rule (predecessor of Durham), was a valued resource.

I want to pay tribute to the memory of Judge John W. McIlvaine, federal district judge in Pittsburgh, who died July 1, 1963. He was a member of the Advisory Council of Judges of the National Council on Crime and Delinquency and chairman of its Committee on Narcotics. I keenly felt the loss of his experience and humane spirit. With a mutuality of philosophy toward offenders, he helped and advised me.

I want to thank Miss Armine Dikijian, NCCD librarian, and Joseph L. Andrews, reference librarian of the Association of the Bar of the City of New York, both of whom have been uncommonly generous not only in bringing material to my attention, but in granting without complaining that any request I made for material was perfectly reasonable.

Sol Rubin

PART I

Criminal Responsibility and Exculpation

Chapter 1

M'Naghten Versus Durham

Psychiatry pervades our culture. Not only is psychiatry responsible for the administration of the existing huge system of mental
hospitals, but history is being rewritten by psychiatrists (sometimes by psychiatric historians) and historical figures are
psychoanalyzed; job applicants are chosen by psychological tests;
soldiers are discharged on psychiatric recommendations. Marital
difficulty, low marks at school, a poor relationship with a boss or
an employee—each is a reason for visiting a psychiatrist.

Inevitably the wide influence of psychiatry affects the criminal
law, as it does other aspects of law and other social institutions.
Psychiatric knowledge—or, in simpler terms, the understanding
of people's behavior and motivations—affects the criminal law and
its administration in at least three ways: (1) in legislation defining
acts that are criminal; (2) in the trial and on the sentencing; and
(3) in the correctional treatment of persons who have been found
guilty and sentenced.

The use of psychiatry in determining whether a defendant
whose mental capacity is at issue shall be found guilty of the
charge against him has in recent years received a great deal of
attention. It is useful, in fact, to start with this part of the problem, because a thorough examination of it leads to and illuminates

the other phases. What rule of law, using what psychiatric information, should govern in deciding whether a defendant who is mentally disturbed shall be deemed legally responsible for his criminal acts?

What Rule for Criminal Responsibility?

It has been claimed that in almost all jurisdictions the rule of law by which a mentally ill person is adjudged legally responsible or not responsible is outmoded. The rule thus attacked is the one enunciated in M'Naghten's Case over a hundred years ago. It states that "to establish a defence on the ground of insanity, it must be clearly proved that at the time of committing of the act, the party accused was laboring under such a defect of reason, from disease of the mind, as not to know the nature and quality of the act he was doing; or if he did know it, that he did not know he was doing what was wrong."[1] The M'Naghten case did not make new law. It was a restatement of a legal proposition long followed;[2] but it is the most recent authoritative statement of the rule, and it is the case whose language is followed.[3]

---

[1] Daniel M'Naghten's Case, 10 Clark and Fin. 200, 210; 8 Eng. Rep. 718, 722 (1843).

[2] Coke, early in the seventeenth century, laid down no test for the degree of insanity necessary to excuse an offender from responsibility, but held that a madman does not know what he is doing and is lacking in mind and reason "and therefore he cannot have a felonious intent"—Beverley's case, 2 Coke's Rep. 571 (1603). Hale, in the second half of the seventeenth century, distinguished between "total insanity," which negatived criminal intent, and "partial insanity," which did not, and said that as regards total insanity, "the best measure that I can think of is this: Such a person as labouring under melancholy distempers hath yet ordinarily as great understanding as ordinarily a child of 14 years hath is such a person as may be guilty of treason or felony"—1 Hale, P.C. 30. A hundred years later Hawkins laid down a different test: "Those who are under a natural disability of distinguishing between good and evil, as infants under the age of discretion, ideots and lunaticks, are not punishable by any criminal prosecution whatever"—Hawkins, Pleas of the Crown (1824), I. 1: Royal Commission on Capital Punishment 1949-1953, at 397. Hall comments: "Psychiatrist-critics of the M'Naghten Rules assume that they were the creation of the legal mind of 1843, preceded only by such absurdities as the 'wild beast' test of insanity. Fantasy dies hard in the minds of historians out to prove a thesis; but it bears repeating that there was considerable understanding of mental disease centuries before Freud, and that the M'Naghten Rules, except for their emphasis on the particular criminal act in question, were a restatement of long-existing law."—Studies in Jurisprudence and Criminal Theory 281 (1958).

In 1954 a different rule was enunciated by the United States Court of Appeals in the District of Columbia. The defendant, Monte Durham, had been convicted of housebreaking. His history included imprisonment for crime and mental hospital commitments. On his trial the psychiatric testimony was that he was suffering from psychosis with psychopathic personality. He heard false voices and suffered from hallucinations and believed that other employees in the store where he worked watched him and talked about him. The psychiatrist also testified that "if the question of the right and wrong were propounded to him he could give you the right answer."

The Court of Appeals said:

The fundamental objection to the right-wrong test . . . is not that criminal irresponsibility is made to rest upon an inadequate, invalid or indeterminate symptom or manifestation, but that it is made to rest upon *any* particular symptom. In attempting to define insanity in terms of a symptom, the courts have assumed an impossible role. . . . The rule we now hold . . . is simply that an accused is not criminally responsible if his unlawful act was the product of mental disease or mental defect. We use "disease" in the sense of a condition which is considered capable of improving or deteriorating. We use "defect" in the sense of a condition which is not considered capable of either improving or deteriorating and which may be congenital, or the result of injury, or the residual effect of a physical or mental disease.[4]

The Durham case also, like M'Naghten, did not state an entirely new rule. It more or less adopted a ruling long the law in New Hampshire, whose Supreme Court had held in 1869 that an accused is not criminally responsible "if the [unlawful act] was the off-spring or product of mental disease."[5]

---

[3] The language may vary a bit, reading "nature and quality" in some states, "consequences" in others; "wrong" means "moral" wrong in one state, "legal" wrong in another.—Reid, Disposition of the Criminally Insane, 16 Rutgers L. Rev. 75 (1961); also Pieski, Subnormal Mentality As a Defense in the Criminal Law, 15 Vanderbilt L. Rev. 769, 774 (1962).

[4] Durham v. United States, 214 F.2d 862 (D.C. Cir. 1954).

[5] State v. Pike, 49 N.H. 399, 402 (1869). Perhaps they are not alike:

Although practically every case in the state courts since the Durham rule was pronounced has rejected it in favor of the rule in M'Naghten's case, and although the federal courts elsewhere have not adopted the rule,[6] the debate around which of these rules should govern is probably the most controversial issue in criminal jurisprudence today (aside perhaps from the question of capital punishment). Numerous articles and some books have been written about it.[7] The central difference in the effect of the rules is that more defendants come within the Durham rule (suffering from mental disease or defect that caused them to commit crime) than M'Naghten (so mentally diseased as not to know what they were doing or that it was wrong); that is, more mentally ill people are exculpated under Durham.[8] It has been asserted that, in

---

Mueller, Criminal Law and Administration, 36 N.Y.U. L. Rev. 111, 119-20 (1961). Maine, by statute, has adopted the rule, with additions; see ch. 3 n. 37.

[6] Anderson v. United States, 237 F.2d 118 (9 Cir. 1956); Sauer v. United States, 241 F.2d 640 (9 Cir.), cert. denied, 354 U.S. 940 (1957); Howard v. United States, 229 F.2d 602 (5 Cir.), revd. on rehearing en banc, 232 F.2d 274; Voss v. United States, 259 F.2d 699 (8 Cir. 1958); Wion v. United States, 325 F.2d 420 (10 Cir. 1963). But the Third Circuit enunciated a rule closer to Durham than to M'Naghten, in United States v. Currens, 290 F.2d 751 (1961), discussed infra p. 65. Rejections by twenty-two state courts are cited in Krash, The Durham Rule and Judicial Administration of the Insanity Defense in the District of Columbia, 70 Yale L.J. 905 at 906 (1961).

[7] Biggs, The Guilty Mind (1955); Glueck, Law and Psychiatry: Cold War or Entente Cordiale (1962). Many of the articles are cited herein. Since Durham, over 150 articles have appeared whose titles indicate that they deal with some aspect of the insanity-defense controversy; the Durham case itself has provided almost fifty law journal notes or extended discussions.—Goldstein & Katz, Abolish the "Insanity Defense"—Why Not?, 72 Yale L.J. 853 at n. 5 (1963).

[8] From July 1, 1954 (the date of the Durham decision) to November 16, 1960, 229 persons were found not guilty by reason of insanity and committed to Saint Elizabeths Hospital. In 1959 and 1960 the number of persons rose to 59 and 100, respectively.—Overholser, Criminal Responsibility: A Psychiatrist's Viewpoint, 48 A.B.A.J. 527, 530 (1962). But the increase in acquittals for mental illness is deceptive. "In the District of Columbia the last decade has seen an increase in acquittals by reason of insanity, but this has been largely offset by a decrease in the number of defendants found incompetent to stand trial, so that the total number of persons charged with crime who are eventually hospitalized instead of imprisoned has not changed very much. The combined total of those found guilty by reason of insanity and those found incompetent to stand trial in our District court was 61 in 1953, the year before the Durham rule was adopted, and this total was not reached again until 1959. Acquittals rose

this regard, Durham is a sounder rule ethically. The Durham rule, it is also said, facilitates the more effective use of psychiatric testimony when the defense of insanity is raised. These would seem to be desirable advantages. If they were, in fact, the true results, they would reflect a worthy reform. But these points are not well taken. In effect—and, when closely examined, in theory—Durham does not achieve its claims. Further, pursuing a new focus, particularly a sentencing reform, we arrive at the conclusion that M'Naghten (or something like it) is a better rule to be applied on the trial and that Durham (or something like it) is a rule better applied at the point of sentencing.

The Controversy Is Raised at the Wrong Place

Perhaps the debate over the advantages and weaknesses of the M'Naghten and Durham rules does not progress because the issue is being argued under misleading conditions.

First: in practice in most jurisdictions, the question of responsibility is generally raised only in capital cases.[9] Usually, therefore, the issue being fought is not the straight-forward one of legal responsibility, but rather the question of whether the defendant will be subjected to the death penalty. In effect, the prosecution argues for a finding of responsibility so that the defendant can be convicted and executed, and the defense argues insanity so that death can be averted.

A good deal of affinity is felt for the Durham rule by those who consider the application of the death penalty too harsh or want to abolish it altogether. Unfortunately, many mentally ill and mentally deficient people have been and are being executed.[10]

---

steeply, but findings of incompetency decreased proportionately. And acquittals by reason of insanity are still only a small proportion of our criminal verdicts. In 1963 there were 1,439 defendants in criminal cases filed in our District court. Of these, 983 were convicted and only 50 were acquitted by reason of insanity."—Bazelon, The Future of Reform in the Administration of Criminal Justice, the Edward Douglass White Lectures in Law (1964).

[9] Of 296 insanity pleas entered in California in 1962, 55 were in homicide cases, 51 in assault, and 38 in burglary. "It is generally thought that homicide is the offense which attracts most of the not guilty by insanity pleas; however, the data . . . would certainly indicate that there are many other offenses where this type of plea is employed." Crime in California 1962, at 120 (1963).

[10] See cases in the annotation, 69 A.L.R. 348.

I advocate abolition of the death penalty, but I do not thereby endorse Durham as a partial remedy. The only remedy for the wrongness of the death penalty is abolition. Here we come to the first instance of one of my main themes: that the Durham rule seeks to change a rule applicable on the *trial* in order to remedy errors in our penology—specifically, errors in our *sentencing* systems, of which the death penalty is a part.

Although the death penalty for murder has been abolished in nine states[11] and the number of executions has decreased steadily,[12] the issue of capital punishment cannot be ignored in the context of the rules of responsibility. In all jurisdictions where the death penalty is authorized, state policy has scruples about killing the insane. The law says not only that an insane man is not guilty, it also says that even if a man has been found guilty he may not be executed if he is insane. Governors frequently commute the death penalty on the ground of the defendant's mental illness even though that condition was not sufficient to exculpate the guilt. If we are looking for consistency and wish to ameliorate the death penalty while using a sound rule of responsibility generally applicable to noncapital cases—and if M'Naghten is that rule—the remedy is to apply something like the Durham concept to the issue of execution and not to the trial. Let us labor for a liberal rule—perhaps by statute—incorporating the mental illness concept of Durham as applicable to the issue of execution. Here again it appears that the place of the remedy is not on the trial but after conviction.[13]

---

[11] Alaska, Hawaii, Maine, Michigan, Minnesota, North Dakota, Rhode Island (except murder committed by a prisoner), South Dakota, Wisconsin.

[12] The annual average number of executions in the United States was 167 in the 1930's, 128 in the 1940's, and 72 in the 1950's; and in 1961 eighteen jurisdictions executed a total of 42 persons—the lowest number on record. Federal Bureau of Prisons, National Prisoner Statistics, Executions, 1961 (1962).

[13] Or, perhaps it can be done by a redefinition of the offense. The British Homicide Act of March, 1957, provides [§ 2(1)]: "Where a person kills or is a party to the killing of another, he shall not be convicted of murder if he was suffering from such abnormality of mind (whether arising from a condition of arrested or retarded development of mind or any inherent causes or induced by disease or injury) as substantially impaired his mental responsibility for his acts and omissions in doing or being a party to the killing." *Cf.* the "partial insanity" concept, American Bar Foundation, The Mentally Disabled and the Law 355 (1961). See Pieski, *op. cit. supra* note 3, at 790-94, section headed "Partial Insanity, Mitigation

This approach would have the advantage of saving some lives without fouling the whole issue of a proper rule for offenders generally. We should be looking for a rule that would be generally applicable to offenders who survive, and that would be useful in dealing with them constructively.

The Battle of the Experts

I have suggested that the Durham rule is seeking a reform "at the wrong place" because the rule of responsibility arises mainly —certainly in its most hotly contested form—in capital cases. The issue of capital punishment should be separately dealt with, through ameliorative rules (if we are seeking amelioration), covering who may be *executed* (rather than who may be convicted); although basically it is the issue of abolition that is involved. The argument on behalf of the Durham rule is that it facilitates the introduction of psychiatric testimony on the trial. It appears upon examination that this is not so— and again, we shall see, the substantial improvement in the use of psychiatric testimony comes at the postconviction stage, on the sentence.

Psychiatric testimony is not heightened by the change in the legal rule of responsibility. Both Durham and M'Naghten require that the psychiatric evidence be introduced in the context of a criminal trial, in the usual adversary procedure. The result is that a trial under the Durham rule is still a "battle of the experts";[14] and testimony under the M'Naghten rule can be, and generally is, admitted as liberally as under Durham.

Jerome Hall noted:

> Although the M'Naghten Rules are phrased in terms of cognition, they are generally interpreted broadly by the courts, with the result that all psychiatric evidence relevant to the defendant's mental condition is admitted. And not a few of the most experienced forensic psychiatrists believe the M'Naghten Rules function very well

---

of Punishment, and Diminished Responsibility"; Sparks, Diminished Responsibility in Theory and Practice, 27 Modern L. Rev. 9 (1964).

[14] "The most striking feature of the post-Durham insanity cases [in the District of Columbia] is the failure by nearly all the psychiatric experts to utilize the new rule for the intended purpose."—Watson, Durham Plus Five Years: Development of the Law of Criminal Responsibility in the District of Columbia, Am. J. of Psych., October 1959.

in practice, without miscarriages of justice attributable to the use of the Rules, and that no better substitute has been proposed.[15]

The Supreme Court of Wisconsin, which follows the M'Naghten rule, said:

We are of the opinion . . . that if the offered testimony, together with other expert testimony, had sufficiently tended to prove that at the time of the offense defendant was subject to a compulsion or irresistible impulse by reason of the abnormality of his brain, the testimony should have been admitted. Even under the right-wrong test, no evidence should be excluded which reasonably tends to show the mental condition of the defendant at the time of the offense.[16]

Other state courts have declared similarly.[17]

[In California] the immediate impact of the Gorshen decision[18] has been a sharp increase in the use of psychiatric testimony of this type in almost all murder trials . . . [Important] to the science and art of forensic psychiatry has been the shift away from static, diagnostic, and classification psychiatry toward dynamic description of the particular mental mechanisms which led up to the crime. Psychiatric examinations have had to be much more de-

---

[15] Hall, *op. cit. supra* note 2, at 282, citing East, an Introduction to Forensic Psychiatry in the Criminal Courts 73-74 (1927); East, Delinquency and Crime, 90 J. Mental Sci. 382, 391 (1944).

[16] State v. Carlson, 5 Wis. 2d 595, 93 N.W. 354, 361 (1958).

[17] State v. Di Paolo, 168 A.2d 401 (1961)—although adhering to M'Naghten, New Jersey permits a defendant to offer, with respect to whether the penalty shall be death or life imprisonment, the complete psychiatric picture unrestrained by the M'Naghten concept. People v. Gorshen, 51 Cal. 2d 716, 726, 336 P.2d 492, 498 (1958); see Comment, 12 Stan. L. Rev. 226 (1959). Pennsylvania v. Woodhouse, 164 A.2d 98 (1960).

[18] Evidence bearing on the defendant's capacity is admissible to show that he was incapable of harboring a particular mental state; "on the trial of issues raised by a plea of not guilty to a charge of a crime which requires proof of a specific mental state, competent evidence that because of mental abnormality not amounting to legal insanity defendant did not possess the essential specific mental state is admissible."—People v. Gorshen, *supra* n. 17.

tailed and many more hours have had to be spent with the defendants in order to uncover such psychological mechanisms and to interpret them in the psychodynamic framework of the defendant's life history.[19]

How is it under the Durham rule? Judge David L. Bazelon, who wrote the opinion of the court in the Durham case, has said:

> The psychiatrist is called upon to play a rigidly limited role when he testifies under a strict interpretation of M'Naghten; and . . . an open rule like Durham asks him for something the law has never consistently received, welcomed or appreciated—namely, profound insight into the nature and motivations of the defendant. Well, what happens? By and large the answer is—Nothing much. And that is true whether the psychiatrist is forced to testify within M'Naghten, or simply reluctant to expand within the framework of Durham. . . . In general, the *practice* under Durham is not yet decisively—or anything like satisfactorily—different.[20]

Judge Bazelon considers that the fault lies in the fact that the psychiatrists in the District of Columbia continue to use the old labels. He is seeking, therefore, the same reform that is already occurring—as we have just noted—under M'Naghten!

But the Durham scene is worse than it appears in Judge Bazelon's observation. It is not only the quality of psychiatric testimony that is a concern.[21] Even if the quality of the psychiatric testimony improved, the witness would still be subject to the very type of cross-examination—and equally expert witnesses with contrary opinions on the other side—that is the key problem. A rule of responsibility that operates on the trial cannot change this. Any trial rule continues the battle of the experts.

The worsening of the situation under Durham comes about in that the experts are dealing with a far more complex and speculative series of problems than are the psychiatrists under M'Nagh-

---

[19] Diamond, Criminal Responsibility of the Mentally Ill, 14 Stan. L. Rev. 59, at 81-82 (1961).

[20] Bazelon, Equal Justice for the Unequal, Isaac Ray Lectureship Award Series of the American Psychiatric Assn., U. of Chi. 1961, lec. 2, p. 2.

[21] See Jenkins v. United States, 307 F.2d 637 (1962)—inconsistencies in the testimony of the psychiatrists; three I.Q. tests, all with different results. See the opinion of Burger, J., concurring in Blocker v. United States, 288 F.2d 853 (1961).

ten. Compared with the simple issue in M'Naghten—did the defendant know his act was wrong?—the Durham rule opens up for the jury the difficult issues of mental illness and defect and their causative effect with respect to the crime committed. We shall discuss this in some detail in chapter 3; but it is obvious from the mere statement of the respective tests that Durham testimony is subject to interminable question, as compared with M'Naghten.

The Question Asked at the Right Place

The Supreme Court of New Jersey was one of the courts that was urged to abandon M'Naghten in favor of Durham. Like many others, the court remained with M'Naghten.[22] In a concurring opinion Chief Justice Weintraub declared:

> If we could think of conviction simply as a finding that the mortal in question has demonstrated his capacity for anti-social conduct, most of the battle would be decided. What would remain is the employment of such post-conviction techniques as would redeem the offender if he can be redeemed and secure him if he cannot.

And again:

> Until a basis for personal blameworthiness can be scientifically demonstrated, I would not tinker with the existing law of criminal responsibility. Rather I would permit the scientist's growing knowledge of human behavior to have a wider sway in the area in which it can safely be utilized with evident fairness to society and to the individual. I refer to the post-conviction disposition of the offender.

That is, the resolution of the problem would come not on the trial, but on the sentence. Another student of this problem, Dr. Bernard L. Diamond, expresses an ideological preference for the Durham rule—indeed, a longing for it—but nevertheless finds that it will not accomplish what its advocates hope for it:

> Harm is done . . . if psychiatry and the law divert their attention and limited energies from the urgent problem of the great mass of criminal offenders toward the peripheral issue of insanity. It makes more sense to focus

---

[22] State v. Lucas, 30 N.J. 37, 83 (1959).

reform efforts directly upon the total system of administration of criminal justice and thus attempt to cope with the bulk of anti-social deviation in constructive, humane, and effective ways.[23]

Unfortunately, the issue before the New Jersey court, as before every court that has to choose between M'Naghten and Durham, did not relate to postconviction disposition but rather to the question of criminal responsibility. In his concurring opinion Justice Weintraub suggested that the correct place under M'Naghten for considering the mental condition of a defendant who is not insane is in the postconviction procedure: on the sentence. Dr. Diamond came to the same conclusion. His reference to reform of the "total system of administration of criminal justice" is really to sentencing and correctional services:

> From such a viewpoint the solution is not to make new laws that will displace large portions of the prison population into mental hospitals, which then become prisons in disguise. Rather it would be better to transform correctional systems and prison institutions into fit places to which mentally ill persons may be sent for treatment, rehabilitation, and eventual restoration to a normal life in their families and communities.[24]

Unfortunately, heretofore no sentence procedure seemed particularly useful in the context of the M'Naghten-Durham controversy. However, a sentencing plan devised by the Advisory Council of Judges of the National Council on Crime and Delinquency provides the kind of sentence procedure that seems to resolve the issue successfully. The Advisory Council of Judges is a group of fifty appellate, trial, federal, and state judges that has been providing leadership on questions of sentencing, court and correctional services, and related matters. In addition to several guide books for judges,[25] it has produced the Model Sentencing Act, which bears upon the current issue.

We shall later discuss the Model Sentencing Act in detail. At the moment it is sufficient to note that the MSA establishes three

---

[23] Diamond, From M'Naghten to Currens and Beyond, 50 Calif. L. Rev. 189, at 205 (1962).

[24] *Ibid.*

[25] Guides for Sentencing; Guides for Juvenile Court Judges; Procedure and Evidence in Juvenile Court, a Guidebook for Judges.

categories of dangerous offenders, who may be subjected to long terms of confinement and treatment. For two of the categories the court, before imposing a long term, is required to find that the defendant is suffering from "a severe personality disorder indicating a propensity toward criminal activity." In order for necessary diagnostic material to be obtained, material upon which the judge may base a finding of "dangerousness," the Act provides that certain defendants shall be committed to a state diagnostic center for clinical study. (The two crime categories in which the defendant is subject to a long term if the personality pattern is found are (a) "a felony in which he inflicted or attempted to inflict serious bodily harm" and (b) a felony which "seriously endangered the life or safety of another," the defendant having been previously convicted of one or more felonies not constituting a single criminal episode with the instant crime. The third category of dangerous offender is the racketeer, for whose sentencing no finding of a personality pattern is required.)[26]

The work on the Model Act took several years. In March 1960, when the committee charged with the main work of drafting held one of its meetings and the statutory form of its sentencing idea began to take shape, the writer (who serves as counsel to the NCCD and to the ACJ) suggested to the committee that the M'Naghten-Durham question was, indeed, being asked "in the wrong place," but that upon the formulation of the sentencing plan which we have here sketchily set forth, a situation exists by which the question can be asked "in the right place." (Compare Durham—"unlawful act the product of mental disease or defect," with the MSA—"suffering from a severe personality disorder indicating a propensity toward criminal activity.") This was an unforeseen but valuable result of the Model Sentencing Act. The Model Act approach makes it clear that it is not so much the rule of responsibility that is behind the times—psychiatrically, if one wishes—but our penology; and this became evident because the model act visualizes a new penology.

As Judge Weintraub points out, neither M'Naghten nor Durham deals with the individual on the basis of what the community needs and what the individual needs. The defects in sentencing, particularly its hit or miss nature, have been pointed out many

---

[26] Model Sentencing Act § 6 (1963).

times. Neither M'Naghten nor Durham really helps solve this problem. The Model Sentencing Act not only provides a much more precise way of determining the dangerousness of offenders, but it also opens the way for a flexible, ample use of psychiatric evidence—*on the sentence consideration.* Under the Act the judge, if he is considering committing a defendant to a long term as a dangerous person, *must* obtain psychiatric evidence, developed at a diagnostic center, where the defendant is studied and out of which a report to the court is made. With other material in hand, particularly the presentence report of the probation department, the judge proceeds to sentence. A hearing must be held on the sentence, but it is not rigidly curtailed by the rules of evidence applicable on a trial, particularly the restrictive artificiality of the "hypothetical question"; and, because the trial rules of evidence are not applicable, the "battle of the experts" diminishes greatly, perhaps disappears.

The Model Act not only facilitates much more precise sentencing—more than does any existing or other proposed code—especially in detecting dangerous offenders and those who are mentally ill, but also envisages that such defendants shall be given special treatment, following clinical diagnosis, in a suitable therapeutic institution. It provides the postconviction procedure that Judge Weintraub said must exist for this riddle to be solved; it is the penal reform that fits the bill of Dr. Diamond. We will find in chapter 9, where we consider the MSA in detail, that it solves, astonishingly well, all of the problems we see in Durham as well as M'Naghten.

Let us continue to examine here the trial issues to see what the problems are.

The Legal Rule and a Therapeutic Orientation

If one grants the relevancy of an improved penology to our issue, particularly and specifically a sentencing plan that facilitates and encourages the use of psychiatric testimony in a fashion superior to that possible on the trial, the question still remains: Which rule—M'Naghten or Durham, or some other—is better on the trial? Does the Model Sentencing Act illuminate this problem? Part of the answer must wait until the last chapter, after this issue as well as some specific sentencing problems have been explored. We there suggest that in a jurisdiction that adopts the Model Sentencing Act, the M'Naghten rule is a natural and superior complementary trial rule. But even without that, some modern values in the M'Naghten rule are being overlooked by advocates of its change.

Part of the argument on behalf of a change in the trial rule is the humanitarian one that people who are mentally ill should be treated, not punished. The Model Sentencing Act has the same motivation (joined with, as is the case with Durham or any other rule, reference to the requirements of public protection). However, whereas substituting Durham for M'Naghten would affect only a small number of defendants, the recognition of mental illness on the sentence can affect many defendants. A sentence plan could treat mentally ill defendants who are not exculpated under M'Naghten; but many mentally ill defendants would not be exculpated under Durham, either, and a sentence could and should undertake to treat, not punish them.

At this point we face the question of whether the penal commitment can be therapeutic; we face the wish of the Durham advocates to enlarge the civil commitments, which, they say, represent treatment, and to narrow the criminal commitments, which, they say, represent punishment. Where is the therapeutic advantage in dealing with a mentally ill person who has committed a crime—in a civil or criminal commitment? Again, as noted more than once before, evaluation of the rule of responsibility from this point of view cannot help involving the sentence and correctional treatment.

The defendant who does not have a consciousness that he committed a criminal act is not at all helped by a conviction, and both Durham and M'Naghten agree that he should not be convicted. The M'Naghten rule declares that one who is so far removed from reality that he does not know the nature of his act does not have the mentality to be adjudged responsible. But the Durham rule would exculpate a defendant who is mentally ill but *does* know the nature of his act. For the law to tell him that he is not responsible for his act is likely to deter and complicate his rehabilitation because it contradicts commonsense fact. To declare that he *is* legally responsible, but because of his mental illness, is subject to special treatment on the sentence is more consistent with reality and more likely to support his rehabilitation. To say to him, "You are not a criminal, you are sick" (Durham), is much less realistic than to say to a mentally ill offender who is not within the M'Naghten rule—because he understands the nature of his act—"You committed a crime, but you are sick. Your sickness has something to do with your criminal behavior, and we will endeavor to determine how sick you are. You will be subjected to psychological and correctional treatment for your cure while you are serving your sentence." The latter would seem to engage the defendant's own resources much more than the former. (We must keep in mind that we are talking about a rule for dealing with persons who have committed antisocial acts, who will be dealt with by means other than execution.)

We have an interesting application of this approach as a therapeutic matter in the work of Dr. John M. Murray, Chief Consultant in Psychiatry of the U.S. Air Forces, at the Air Force Convalescent Hospital, at Fort Logan, Denver, Colo., during World War II. The hospital had 1,700 operational or flying fatigue cases under treatment, men who had been dealt with as deserving of freedom of the grounds. They had done a magnificent job overseas, were told they were not responsible for their condition, and were not subject to ordinary controls. The result was such extensive aggressive behavior by the patients that the administration was planning to shut down the hospital.

When Dr. Murray took over, he ordered courts-martial in three pending cases.

> They have gone against regulations—let them have the book. Then, after court has passed a sentence on them, I'll see each one of these boys individually. . . . When we tell them they don't need controls, we're wrong. They need controls, but as a result of their sickness they can't hold the controls, and they break down in defiance in these brawls. They have to recognize us as kindly and understanding individuals—not maudlin in any sense of excessive sympathy, but kindly and understanding. But —we are the exponents of adequate controls, and if they are not in such condition that they can maintain these controls, they are not ready to go out and mingle in society at this time. They are in need of further treatment.

In the course of the next five weeks they had five more court-martial cases, and after that, none.[27] These men had apparently come to recognize, among other things, that all their antisocial actions involved unpleasant consequences to themselves.

"People with severe mental illnesses continue to have a sense of responsibility," note Dr. Ernest M. Gruenberg and Dr. Frank G. Boudreau in presenting a striking report on how that sense of responsibility can be increased by methods of care, particularly the opening of mental institutions.[28]

A recent article entitled "A Quarter Century of Court Psychiatry," by Dr. Emanuel Messinger and Dr. Benjamin Apfelberg, draws exactly the same conclusion:

> Our distinct impression, gained from observing thousands of recidivists in the Clinic and elsewhere, is that stern penological measures usually have a more salutary and longer-lasting restraining effect than hopeful but misguided "psychiatric guidance." This impression is particularly true for psychopaths, who characteristically welcome the intercession of the psychiatrist or prison psychologist as a means of escaping or mitigating punishment or of manipulating their environment to evade responsibility.[29]

I should like to quote from several other psychiatrists who have commented on this phase of the problem. Dr. Seymour L. Halleck:

> The psychiatrist who serves as consultant in agencies concerned with juvenile delinquents is frequently asked the question, "Is this child mentally ill—is he sick?" The question implies that if he is seen as being ill he belongs in a special class necessitating disposition and treatment entirely different from that utilized in the customary approach to delinquency. A dichotomy is then set up creating constant conflict in the minds of many workers as to whether the clients they deal with are "bad" or "sick." The writer contends that this question is meaningless and that this kind of schizophrenic thinking has led to serious difficulties in understanding the delinquent. . . .
>
> Many people feel that if a person is sick he should not be held responsible for his behavior. . . . One view cur-

---

[27] Unpublished paper.
[28] Preface to Steps in the Development of Integrated Psychiatric Services, Milbank Memorial Fund, N.Y. (1960).
[29] 7 Crime & Delinquency 343, at 348 (1961).

rently emerging . . . states that every person is responsible for what he does and that if one is, indeed, to respect the basic dignity of human beings one must assume that they are responsible individuals, who, even in their sickest state, know right from wrong and retain some elements, however small, of choice. . . .

Treatment for a delinquent must begin with a clearcut realization on his part that he is a responsible person who has a considerable role in his own destiny. By the very implication that delinquents can change, they are assumed to be responsible. It is hard to conceive of any form of psychotherapy that can succeed *unless* the individual is regarded as a person who can assume responsibility for his acts.[30]

Dr. Bernard L. Diamond:

The arbitrary division of criminal offenders into the two classes of the sane and the insane no longer makes any sense. . . . Responsibility as a concept is losing its usefulness as a moral judgment and is acquiring a new, and much more valuable therapeutic meaning. Thus, with many mentally ill persons one may speak of their "extended responsibility." Extended responsibility means that mentally ill persons are to be treated as if they were more responsible for their actions than they really may be, simply because it is therapeutically and socially desirable to do so.[31]

Dr. Thomas S. Szasz:

Punishment is, in sum, a corollary of responsibility, based upon the concept of man as capable, within limits, of making free moral choices: a normal adult who is the author of harm to others should be punished for the reasons stated. . . . If human beings are in any degree free moral agents, then treatment cannot be wholly substituted for punishment; treating all criminals as ipso facto sick persons cannot be justified even on humanitarian grounds. A dogma that equates normal adults with helpless victims of disease is incompatible with respect for personality and distinctive human traits. . . . It seems

---

[30] Halleck, Juvenile Delinquents: "Sick" or "Bad"? Social Work, April 1962, p. 58.
[31] Diamond, *op. cit. supra* note 23, at 204.

to me the most dignified, and psychologically and socially most promising, alternative is not to consider mental
illness an excusing condition. Treating offenders as responsible human beings, even though sometimes they
may not be individually "blameworthy," offers them the
only chance, as I now see it, of remaining "human" and
possibly becoming more so.[32]

Others psychiatrists, also experienced in criminal law administration, with whom I have discussed this point, are in accord
with the foregoing statements. I know of no forensic psychiatrist,
or any psychiatrist, or any lawyer or judge, who has considered
this phase of the problem and is of a different mind.

Should M'Naghten Be Modified?

A number of writers and almost all of the appellate courts
prefer the M'Naghten rule, sometimes with the view that if it is
not altogether sound, the Durham rule does not resolve any of
the problems any better. We have thus far found advantage in
M'Naghten and shall find other comparative advantages. The
Durham rule stemmed from criticism of M'Naghten. Is some
modification of M'Naghten indicated? (As we shall see, in Chapter 3, Durham is *not* a modification of M'Naghten, but a replace-
ment of it with quite a different character.)

The critics of M'Naghten charge—and it is this that troubles
those who defend the old rule—that in some cases the seriously
psychotic individual who is obviously disoriented from ordinary
reality is held legally responsible for his crime, whereas in other
cases such a person is properly found not guilty by reason of
insanity. I suggest that nine-tenths—perhaps all—of the criticism
would vanish if there were no death penalty. To put it another
way: there would be little, if any, objection to convicting these
persons if they were not to be executed, because many would
presently wind up, by transfer, in a mental hospital anyway.
Besides, if they were not to be executed, the prosecutor would
not press as hard for their conviction as against acquittal by
insanity.

---

[32] Criminal Responsibility and Psychiatry, in Toch (ed.), Legal and
Criminal Psychology (1961). See also Glasser, Reality Therapy, 10 Crime
and Delinquency 135 (1964).

The interesting thing is that M'Naghten is not the rule that is used to determine whether a person already convicted and sentenced to death is insane. The rule governing that issue is hardly ever discussed; [33] it is badly in need of clarification or modification. As observed before, many mentally ill murderers are executed, and all agree that they should not be.

We come then to the one narrow, although important, remaining issue—that M'Naghten allows mentally ill murderers to be placed in danger of execution. Some defenders of M'Naghten assert that it works; that is, that if it is properly interpreted, it is not subject to this criticism. Professor Jerome Hall had this to say about the requirements and interpretation of the rule:

> The first wing of the M'Naghten Rules—the accused's knowledge of the "nature and quality of the act he was doing"—is an ordinary way of specifying what, in part at least, is meant by the psychiatrist's "reality principle." It concerns knowledge of ordinary actions and their everyday consequences. It is a plain way of defining an elementary criterion of rationality, simply stating the truism that a rational person is a sane person. . . . About the second clause of the M'Naghten rules—the so-called "right and wrong" test—sophisticates have said that it requires an ordinary person to do what philosophers through the ages have with dubious success been trying to do, namely, to distinguish right from wrong. But the assertion that the Rules require any such competence in abstract thinking is a mere strawman construction—which, incidentally, would hold most persons insane, whereas the complaint is that the M'Naghten Rules allow many psychotics to be found sane. What the clause stipulates is incapacity, due to serious mental disease, to make commonplace social valuations—to

---

[33] "To require suspension of the execution, . . . it must appear that the defendant is so unsound mentally as to be incapable of understanding the nature and purpose of the punishment about to be executed upon him."— Weihofen, Mental Disorder as a Criminal Defense 464 (1954). "The meager authority indicates that the common law test of insanity is whether the defendant is aware of the fact that he has been convicted and that he is to be executed."—Hazard & Louisell, Death, The State and the Insane: Stay of Execution, 9 U.C.L.A.L. Rev. 381 at 394 (1962). Meanwhile, many mentally ill people are executed; see the cases in the annotation at 69 A.L.R. 2d 348.

realize, for instance, that it is wrong to kill a human being or take his property.[34]

Elsewhere Professor Hall writes:

> A very important consequence of the integrative view[35] would be to give the word "know" in the M'Naghten Rules a wide meaning; and it is now generally admitted that this would meet the principal current criticism of the Rules. . . . The present narrow, intellectualistic interpretation of the word "know" by psychiatrists intent on adoption of the "irresistible impulse" test merely perpetuates the rationalist psychology of the M'Naghten era.[36]

Hall quotes Cleckley and Bromberg:

> When no longer dismembered and falsified in one-dimensional aspect, but considered in all that we sometimes imply by "appreciation," "realization," "normal evaluation," "adequate feeling," "significant and appropriate experiencing," etc., the term "knowing" does not restrict us solely to a discussion of the patient's reasoning abilities in the abstract.[37]

Professor Henry Weihofen writes:

> If the word "know" were given this broader interpretation, so as to require knowledge "fused with affect" and assimilated by the whole personality—so that, for example, the killer was capable of identifying with his prospective victim—much of the criticism of the knowledge test would be met.[38]

---

[34] Hall, *op. cit. supra* note 2, at 281.

[35] "Integrative jurisprudence has its immediate orientation in a persistent effort to correct the most serious fallacy in modern jurisprudence: the sophisticated separation of value, fact, and idea (form). This fallacy is manifested in the particularism of prevailing legal philosophies, i.e. in their restriction to, or concentration on, one of the above spheres of significance, with consequent exaggeration and error. The premise of this criticism is that the soundest measure of any legal philosophy is its 'adequacy.' " *Id,* at 25.

[36] *Id.* at 289.

[37] Cleckley & Bromberg, The Medico-Legal Dilemma, 42 J. Crim. L., C. & P.S. 729, 737 (1952).

[38] Weihofen, *op. cit. supra* n. 33, at 77.

Sometimes, at least, such a solution obtains in practice. Dr. Diamond describes a case in which he testified for the defense in the trial for murder of a mother who strangled her second child when he was eight weeks old:

> She knew the nature and quality of her act and that it was wrong. Nevertheless, at the moment of the killing she believed it to be the only course of action open to her. There was no difficulty in convincing the court that the defendant was legally insane and did not know right from wrong because of mental disease. . . . Four years earlier, with the birth of her first child, she had developed a severe post partum psychosis characterized by several weeks of overt delusions, hallucinations and psychotic behavior. Although she had had similar destructive thoughts toward her first baby, she was so psychotically disorganized that she was not able to translate these into action. Within a few weeks she had recovered, having experienced a delusional ecstasy of rebirth herself, and until the birth of her second child she had lived a relatively normal life with no obvious evidence of mental abnormality. . . . Psychological testing of the defendant shortly after the killing revealed that, despite the absence of any gross signs of mental illness, there was sufficient abnormality of thought and emotion to diagnose a still-existing schizophrenia, and all of the clinical facts taken together left no doubt that the slaying of her child was a direct consequence of her mental illness.[39]

The fact must be conceded that such an outcome will not always occur. In Dr. Diamond's case, the three court-appointed psychiatrists agreed with his testimony that the defendant was legally insane. In other analogous cases the state's psychiatrists do not agree, and other persons equally or more psychotic are found guilty.[40]

---

[39] Diamond, *op. cit. supra* note 18, at 61, 62. So also, Wertham, The Show of Violence (1949), the Albert Fish case.

[40] "The following persons failed to qualify for an exception under *M'Naghten* and to induce the court to change its test: (1) In California an ambulatory schizophrenic whose impulse to kill was not impeded by the actual presence of a police officer, and a 'wobbling,' bromide-consuming, 'mad' looking stick-up man whose 'head went in "circles"' and who

Such an outcome is obviously wrong. If a portion of the energy that has gone into the M'Naghten-Durham controversy were devoted to preventing, in the application of M'Naghten, a verdict of guilty when the defendant is grossly psychotic, a good legal solution would be found. In England, 40 per cent of those tried for murder are declared insane; in the United States the reported figures are from 2 to 4 per cent.[41] (Yet in England only .15 per cent are found guilty but insane of offenses other than murder.)[42] Even if convicted, these people should not be executed; M'Naghten does not govern on execution. But still they are.

There are some who believe in the death penalty but not for the mentally ill and who would, for the benefit of this group mainly, change the M'Naghten rule. I believe this is a very small force, indeed. It does not include the Durham court, for in the District of Columbia the Durham rule is applied in less-than-capital cases (although this application may lessen, since the insanity defense can no longer be forced on a defendant).[43]

I would join in *any* rule to diminish the application of the death penalty.[44]

The bigger question is this: In noncapital cases, which rule is best, for society and the defendants?

---

wandered around the victimized store 'with his arms outstretched and his hands dangling'; (2) in Florida 'laughing Willie,' the town moron, who had been civilly insane for twenty years, and who had killed his fifteen-year-old wife; (3) in Nevada an apparent paranoiac 'with a background of mental disorder and of psychiatric treatment'; (4) in New York a post-slaying suicide survivor who had to be institutionalized for four years before he recovered sufficient mentality to stand trial; (5) in Rhode Island a lad who raped and killed an 86 year-old retired school marm."—Mueller, Criminal Law and Administration, 34 N.Y.U.L. Rev. 83, at 85 (1959).

[41] Guttmacher, The Mind of the Murderer 8 (1962).

[42] Koestler, Reflections on Hanging 70 (1950).

[43] Lynch v. Overholser, 369 U.S. 705, 82 S. Ct. 1063 (1962); see ch. 2 *infra*, pp. 38-39.

[44] *Supra* note 13. It is difficult to determine whether the Durham rule reduced executions in the District of Columbia. It is true that between 1955 and 1962 there was only one execution, in 1950-1954 three, 1945-49—13, 1940-44—3, 1935-1939—5, 1930-34—15. But the precipitate drop since 1954 corresponds exactly with a similar drop throughout the country. The number of executions for the years 1962 and back to 1955 was 47-42-56-49-49-65-65-76. For 1950-54 it was 413; 1945-49—639; 1940-44—645; 1935-39—890; 1930-34—776. Of course the reductions in the states took place without any change in the rule of criminal responsibility.

Chapter 2

The Question of Punishment

Urged to abandon M'Naghten in favor of Durham, the Supreme Court of New Jersey remained with M'Naghten: "Until such time as we are convinced by a firm foundation in scientific fact that a test for criminal responsibility other than M'Naghten will serve the basic end of our criminal jurisprudence, i.e., the protection of society from grievous anti-social acts, we shall adhere to it."[1] This recognizes one purpose of the criminal law—the protection of society. But rehabilitation of the individual offender is acknowledged generally to be a concomitant goal of the criminal law. In his concurring opinion Chief Justice Weintraub likewise declared that "none will dispute that society must be protected from the insane as well as the sane. The area of disagreement is whether a civil or a criminal process should be employed when forbidden acts have been committed"; that is, what is best in the light of the defendant's mental condition, best for public protection and the offender's rehabilitation.

Both the M'Naghten and Durham rules separate persons who have committed criminal acts into two groups—those who should be dealt with through penal-correctional services, and those who should be dealt with in institutions for the mentally ill.

---

[1] State v. Lucas, 30 N.J. 27 (1959).

As observed previously, the Durham rule would provide for civil disposition of a number of defendants who under M'Naghten would be subjected to criminal conviction.[2]

Which Rule is for Punishment of Criminals?

Having this group in mind, the advocates of the Durham rule argue that the ethical issue of punishment is involved. They assert that the M'Naghten rule is punitive, because it convicts some persons who are mentally ill, whereas the Durham rule is not, because it does not convict those who are mentally ill (if the illness caused the crime). Judge David L. Bazelon, of the United States Court of Appeals, who wrote the opinion in the Durham case, urges this position. He writes:

> However much we may tell each other that it doesn't really matter whether we class a man as criminal or sick, as deserving punishment in a prison rather than treatment in a hospital—perhaps because there is so little difference between the custodial care offered by overcrowded mental institutions and by prisons—there *is*, at heart, a tremendous difference. Assignment to a mental hospital represents an act in a social affirmation that this man is not to be blamed. Classing the offender as "ill" is one step along the path towards community acceptance of some small share of the responsibility, with all this may imply for the commitment of resources in the future. In contrast, the sentence to prison with its assessment of "fault" or "blame" results in dealing with him in a manner assuring that he will repeat again and again the acts which bring him to blame and to prison.[3]

That is, the distinction is said to be between "*punishment* in a prison" and "*treatment* in a hospital." Punishment versus treatment—of course one chooses treatment. But there is something wrong with the distinction as made. The difference is between a civil and a criminal commitment. To say that it is also a difference between punishment and treatment begs the question, and it is that very question that should be examined.

---

[2] *Supra* ch. 1, at p. 4.
[3] Equal Justice for the Unequal, Isaac Ray Lectureship Award Series, American Psychiatric Assn., U. of Chicago, lec. 1, p. 8 (1961).

The present and past generation of penologists do not talk of prisons-for-punishment. Quite the contrary; they administer what they—and many laws—prefer to call correctional institutions. And, in fact, not many of the punishing elements of older prisons remain, except for (and the exception is important) the security features of many of the institutions, and, most important, the loss of liberty.

This is granted by Judge Bazelon, for he also writes:

> The 1931 report of the famous Wickersham Commission concluded with noble simplicity as follows: "The prison does not reform the criminals. It fails to protect society." Anybody familiar with these problems could carry on a similar recital interminably. And the same would be true with respect to conditions in mental hospitals—report after report after report from the day of Dorothea Dix to the most recent issue of one of our most learned journals. But not one public mental institution in the United States meets the minimum requirements of the American Psychiatric Association. . . .
>
> The basic similarities between the prisons and mental hospitals are: (1) both are essentially over-sized dumping grounds for unwanted human beings; (2) both are substantially structured as institutions by society's niggardliness, and its basic desire not to be bothered; (3) faced with their overwhelming problems of size and resource, both end up being run primarily for the convenience of the organization—that is, manageability and good order take precedence over concern for the incarcerated human beings.[4]

Judge Bazelon justifies the adherence to the civil commitment not because it makes a practical difference in treatment, but because he is hopeful that the noblest concepts of man's humanity toward man can be realized only by a sympathetic appreciation of man's personality and its warps, whereas punishment is an outmoded concept. We suggest that the Durham position and its interpretation is actually—perversely and paradoxically—the position that perpetuates the concept of punishment.

Judge Bazelon, who is an advocate of progressive reforms in penology, nevertheless insists on always attaching the term "punishment" to criminal conviction, and the term "treatment"

---

[4] *Id.* at 8, 10.

to civil (mental) commitment. This suggests acceptance of the idea that a commitment to a correctional institution is punishment. It is; in the same sense, so is a commitment to a mental institution—in both cases the inmate is compulsorily deprived of his liberty. Whether it is the prison warden or the mental hospital superintendent who interprets the commitment as treatment, to the inmate the commitment is punishment, deprivation of liberty because of his act or condition. Correctional authorities today reject the idea that the purpose of a criminal commitment is punishment. *The Durham decision does not.* It accepts the outmoded idea that the criminal commitment is punishment, and it hopes to expand the group excluded from criminal commitments.

Thus Judge Bazelon elsewhere writes, of the Durham decision: "Finally, it was our purpose to restore to the jury its traditional function of applying 'our inherited ideas of moral responsibility to individuals prosecuted for crime' under the historically sanctioned precept that 'our collective conscience does not allow punishment where it cannot impose blame.' "[5] The implication of this, the converse of it, is that where we *can* impose blame, we shall impose punishment. So when Sheldon Glueck writes, "Is he nevertheless to be deemed guilty, to be stigmatized a criminal and, if he commits a homicide, subjected to the death penalty or hopeless life imprisonment? Is not the pronouncement of such a doom by society's laws against a member suffering from mental illness contrary to elementary morality?"[6]—the converse is that if one is *not* mentally ill and commits a crime, he is to be "stigmatized a criminal"; if he commits a homicide, subjecting him to the death penalty or hopeless life imprisonment is not contrary to elementary morality.

This result was recognized by a judge of the Supreme Court of California, who said: "Is it not an inverted humanitarianism that deplores as barbarous the capital punishment of those who

---

[5] Bazelon, The Awesome Decision, Saturday Evening Post, Jan. 23, 1960. "The urge to punish is strong, and punishment is justly due if the individual is mentally responsible. Yet punishing the person who is in truth mentally disorganized is recognized as ill-advised and indeed immoral."—Special Commissions on Insanity and Criminal Offenders, July 7, 1962, California, p. 14.

[6] Glueck, Law and Psychiatry: Cold War or Entente Cordiale 79 (1962).

have become insane after trial and conviction, but accepts the capital punishment of sane men?"[7]

The meaning of the criminal and civil commitments is exaggerated in the Durham statements. The stigma of a criminal conviction exists; so does the stigma of a mental hospital commitment.[8] So the transfer of a prisoner under a penal commitment to a mental hospital without due process of law is invalid because such a transfer is a *worsening* of the prisoner's situation. Said the New York Court of Appeals: "The issue here is not whether appellant is insane, but whether the courts below may properly refuse to even inquire into the nature of his condition and the possibility that he may be illegally confined with deranged persons who are liable to harm and/or adversely affect him. . . . It seems quite obvious that any *further* restraint in *excess* of that permitted by the judgment or constitutional guarantees should be subject to inquiry."[9] In the criminal law a number of states have statutes for restoring the civil rights of criminals upon discharge, and even annulling the conviction itself.[10] A "hopeless life term" is not advocated by penologists; quite the contrary.[11] Wardens generally are strong advocates of abolition of the death penalty.[12]

Which Institution Represents Treatment?

The question of punishment is not answered as self-evidently as the Durham decision supporters suggest it is. As pointed out in the previous chapter, the criminal, even the mentally ill criminal, is being dealt with in therapeutically sounder fashion if he *is* legally convicted rather than legally exculpated; and, as indicated above, the way in which the argument on behalf of this aspect of Durham is made is actually an inverted acceptance

---

[7] Traynor, concurring, in Phyle v. Duffy, 34 Cal. 2d 144, 208 P.2d 668, 676-77 (1949), *cert. denied,* 338 U.S. 895 (1949).

[8] See p. 147.

[9] People ex rel. Brown v. Johnston, 9 N.Y. 2d 482, 174 N.E. 2d 725, 215 N.Y.S. 2d 44 (1961).

[10] National Council on Crime and Delinquency, Annulment of a Conviction of Crime—A Model Act (1962).

[11] Harrison, Why Michigan's Penal Code Needs Revision, 4 NPPA J. 122 (1958). Rigg, The Penalty Worse Than Death, Saturday Evening Post, Aug. 31, 1957—life sentence without parole.

[12] Lawes, Twenty Thousand Years in Sing Sing (1932); "The Bitter Debate Over Capital Punishment," Look, May 7, 1963.

—or, at least, exaggeration—of the punishment content of a criminal conviction.

Let us now get down to closer practicalities. In which institution does the mentally ill criminal get better therapy? In which institution does he make better progress toward cure and the ability to live lawfully in the community? Judge Bazelon says:

> Practically speaking, the legal term "insanity" can be defined by the consequences of its use. When pronounced "not insane," the accused is sentenced to prison as a punishment. When held insane, he goes to a mental institution for treatment. This is the practical aspect, what all the theoretical discussion boils down to—punishment or treatment.[13]

As to "the practical aspect," what actually happens? An alcoholic woman, otherwise respectable, tried to plead guilty to the minor criminal charge of alcoholism. Instead, she was acquitted for her illness (alcoholism) and civilly committed. She sought her freedom. After a year's confinement, she was freed in federal court, the judge saying:

> It may be that this petitioner needs hospitalization. *Obviously, she should not be among insane people.* There was a time when insane people were placed in jails, temporarily, at least. We looked upon this as a barbaric custom that has been pretty well eliminated. But we have reverted to it in reverse; we are placing sane people in insane institutions, which I think is even more barbaric.[14]

This defendant, like others acquitted for mental illness in the District of Columbia, was automatically committed to St. Elizabeths Hospital. Again as to "the practical aspect," what is St. Elizabeths and what is the penal alternative?

> The penitentiary at Lorton, Virginia, has facilities for psychotherapy which provide treatment for many prisoners who need that type of help, whereas St. Elizabeths, despite the new John Howard Pavilion, still houses some of its patients in buildings which are 100 years old, and in some units of the hospital 1000 patients

---

[13] *Op. cit. supra* n. 5 at 56.
[14] Tremblay v. Overholser, 199 F. Supp. 569, 1961; our ital.

are cared for by only two psychiatrists. . . . The possibility that the expected treatment of the absolved defendant may not be available at St. Elizabeths is a matter which bears heavily upon the probable length of the period of confinement in St. Elizabeths. . . . Whether the treatment in lieu of punishment which the proponents of the Durham rule advocate is, as a practical matter, actually being rendered at St. Elizabeths is the subject of much debate.[15]

The current "non-medical, social rehabilitation techniques are just as desirable for the mentally ill offender as they are for the offender who shows no evidence of mental disease," says Dr. Diamond.

And paradoxically, specific psychiatric techniques, such as group therapy, are just as useful for the normal offender as they are for the mentally ill offender. By and large, it has already been demonstrated by prison hospitals, such as the California Medical Facility at Vacaville, California, that just about any type of psychiatric treatment that could be given at a mental hospital can also be given in a prison, providing properly trained psychiatric personnel are available. . . .

There is a danger that liberalization of the rules of criminal responsibility, as is achieved by *Durham* and *Currens*,[16] may inadvertently subvert the basic principles of humanitarian penal reform. Large numbers of offenders can, under these laws, be labeled as insane, then confined for indeterminate periods up to life in institutions called mental hospitals, which are really prisons in disguise, with only a pretense of treatment and with a gross disregard of civil liberties and due process. . . . The institutions in which these insane offenders are kept may be worse than a prison. The social stigma of the label "criminal insane" may be more degrading than the label "convict" alone. The custodial officers, although called "doctors" may be more punitive and anti-therapeutic in their attitude than true correc-

---

15 Halleck, The Insanity Defense in thes District of Columbia—A Legal Lorelei, 99 Georgetown L.J. 294 at 315-16 (1960) and citing Transcript of Proceedings of the 21st Annual Judicial Conference of the District of Columbia Circuit 60, May 26-27, 1960. See Fact Digest, Overholser v. Lynch, no. 27a.

16 *Infra*, p. 65.

tional officials. . . . Precisely this has already happened
in the usual hospital for the criminal insane, the psychopathic delinquent, and the sexual psychopath.[17]

Elsewhere Dr. Diamond refers to the California correction department facility at Vacaville:

> The California Medical Facility at Vacaville is an in-
> tegral part of the correctional system and is able to pro-
> vide excellent psychiatric treatment for at least a limit-
> ed number of prisoners. The doctors who work in this
> hospital need not concern themselves as to who is sane
> or who is insane. Treatment can be provided accord-
> ing to the needs of their patients without regard for
> legal technicalities. This hospital represents a pilot or-
> ganization of very high order. I do not hesitate to say
> that Vacaville provides a higher standard of psychiatric
> treatment than does the corresponding hospital for the
> criminally insane at Atascadero, California, which is op-
> erated by the Department of Mental Hygiene. So there
> is no doubt that good psychiatric treatment can be given
> within a department of corrections. Of course, their lim-
> itations are severe because of restricted budgets, lack
> of bed space, and too few trained personnel. But these
> limitations are even worse for many hospitals for the
> criminally insane which are outside a correctional sys-
> tem. What is still worse, such hospitals for the insane
> may often be only prisons in disguise—barbaric institu-
> tions operating under a false front of medical respec-
> tability in which there is not even a pretense of ade-
> quate therapy.[18]

Other statements may be quoted. Sheldon Glueck, for example:

> As to the state of public mental hospitals, many such
> institutions fall far short of even a modest standard; in-
> deed, some can be more accurately described as huge
> modern survivors of eighteenth-century English "gaols"
> or "bedlams." Last year the results of a wide-ranging
> five-year investigation of American mental hospitals
> was made public by the Joint Commission on Mental

---

[17] Diamond, From M'Naghten to Currens, and Beyond, 50 Calif. L. Rev.
189 at 199-203 (1962).
[18] Diamond, Criminal Responsibility of the Mentally Ill, 14 Stanford L.
Rev. 59, at 85 (1961).

Illness and Health, under the direction of Dr. Jack Ewalt, an experienced psychiatrist and hospital administrator, aided by a carefully selected staff and by impressive advisory and consultative committees. The survey disclosed widespread abuses, including the fact that the great majority of state mental hospitals are little more than "convenient closets" for the storage of the mentally ill and that "more than half the patients in most State hospitals receive no active treatment of any kind designed to improve their mental condition." Only recently, too, a special committee on psychiatric services in New York City, headed by Dr. Lawrence C. Kolb, reported conditions in the mental institutions of America's largest city that can only be designated as shocking.[19]

Dr. A. Warren Stearns:

Although traditionally the insane have been found not guilty, and thus free from punishment, they have been incarcerated in hospitals for insane criminals where for the most part the regime has been less desirable, less medical, certainly less therapeutic than in well-run prisons. It is not unusual for a person with some degree of mental impairment to be willing to plead guilty to second degree murder and take a life sentence rather than be incarcerated in a hospital for insane criminals.[20]

Dr. Jerome D. Frank:

Although the traditional mental hospital is rapidly changing, it probably still represents the dominant pattern of care for hospitalized patients. . . . The basic assumption underlying its structure and organization is that mental patients are irresponsible and therefore liable to harm themselves or others. Furthermore, most patients are viewed as suffering from chronic illnesses that are unlikely to improve, so that they will require lifelong care. These assumptions have led to the building of mental hospitals in rural settings at a distance from the communities they serve, where patients are cared for behind locked doors, economically and out of harm's way. . . . Once in the hospital he perceives him-

---

[19] Glueck, *op. cit. supra* n. 6 at 159.
[20] Stearns, Concepts of Limited Responsibility, Federal Probation, December 1954, p. 20.

self as entirely dependent on the treatment staff for release. He is completely immersed in the hospital world, and his sense of personal identity is weakened through the hospital routines. These are based on *an unshakable assumptive system according to which everything that happens to him is treatment.* . . . The isolation, highly simplified life, authoritarian atmosphere, and impersonality of the hospital enable certain patients to mobilize their recuperative forces, but for many who do not respond promptly, these features may retard recovery.[21]

Dr. Robert C. Hunt:

Much of the unnecessary crippling of the mentally ill must be laid at the door of the state mental hospital both from the standpoint of how it functions internally and how it is used by the society it serves. . . . Commitment to the state hospital continues, in most cases, to represent to the patient and to his family major social surgery by 'putting him away.' . . . All but a tiny minority spend their lives behind locked doors and barred windows with their occasional airings strictly guarded by watchful attendants. In 1792, Philippe Pinel removed the chains from the lunatics in the Bicetre and dramatically demonstrated that most of the mad behavior was an artifact, a reaction against the brutal methods of control imposed upon the mentally ill. . . . In our enlightened times, . . . beyond question . . . much of the aggressive, disturbed, suicidal, and regressive behavior of the mentally ill is not necessarily or inherently part of the illness as such but is very largely an artificial by-product of the way of life imposed upon them. . . . Our modern standard practices may be almost as brutalizing and degrading as those which Pinel abolished.[22]

These statements have not been selected to support a particular viewpoint. Few descriptive-evaluative statements go the other way. The statements in support of mental hospital commitment for mentally ill offenders are not descriptive or evaluative. They are

---

[21] Frank, Persuasion and Healing 192, 205 (1961); our ital.

[22] Hunt, Ingredients of a Rehabilitation Program, in An Approach to the Prevention of Disability From Chronic Psychoses: The Open Mental Hospital Within the Community, Milbank Memorial Fund 12-14 (1958).

theoretical statements, the net impact of which is that mentally ill people, even if criminals, should be treated like sick people, hence should be treated in mental hospitals, which should be effective, therapeutic places for mentally ill people.[23]

Even Judge Bazelon wrote:

> Most of the phychiatrists who testify in court are oriented toward the administration of large mental institutions. I say "institution" advisedly, rather than "hospital," because the public mental hospital, as most of us know, is much more often concerned with custody than with treatment—and perhaps necessarily so, having in mind the lack of facilities, personnel and funds, to say nothing of knowledge.[24]

I do not hold any brief for prisons. They have many shortcomings. Some are good places for the right people; some are bad, and some are horrible. *All* of them hold some people who should not be in an institution. The same things are true of mental hospitals. In both types of institutions inmates are held too long.[25] In general, prisons have good vocational and educational programs, probably better than the correspondings programs in mental hospitals. The people in them are, phychologically, a much more normal community than are those in a mental hospital. Probably as much progress has been made in "opening" prisons as in opening mental hospitals.

Any notion of the superior "treatment" aspect of the civil commitment must vanish in the many jurisdictions where the civilly committed person may be transferred to a penal institu-

---

23 This point is elaborated in chapter 4.

24 Bazelon, *op. cit. supra* n. 3, lec. 2, p. 4.

25 Judge Bazelon quotes from a letter from Donald Clemmer, director of the Department of Corrections of the District of Columbia, as follows: "Whereas there are many exceptions, depending on personality variables and environmental conditions, it is my impression that after 14 months or so the *overall* reformative process declines to the point where it is practically ineffective. . . . After 12 to 16 months or so another process, the process of 'prisonization,' moves in and controls the inmate in such a way that *overall* reformative assets become negligible."—*Id.* at 2. Compare Lehrman, Do Our Hospitals Help Make Acute Schizophrenia Chronic? 22 Diseases of the Nervous System 489 (1961)—"At times some of our psychiatric hospitals may inadvertently have an antitherapeutic effect on patients, thereby tending to make some acute schizophrenic reactions chronic." And Lehrman, Follow-Up of Brief and Prolonged Psychiatric Hospitalization, 2 Comprehensive Psychiatry 227 (1961).

tion and where the mentally ill defendant who is committed on a penal conviction may be placed in or transferred to a mental institution.[26]

One more note on the question of which commitment is punitive: When an accused person in the District of Columbia is acquitted on the ground of insanity and confined in a mental hospital, he and his estate are charged with the expense of his support there.[27] This does not happen when a defendant is committed to a penal institution.

Automatic Mental Commitments

The Durham decision in the District of Columbia was soon followed by an act of Congress providing for mandatory commitment of those found not guilty by reason of their mental condition.[28] There seemed to be a fear that exculpation of mentally ill offenders would result in their freedom.[29]

Obviously, a commitment is punishment in the same sense that imprisonment is—it is deprivation of liberty. As Judge Bazelon says, "It is institutionalization itself that is wrong."[30] And from the point of view of public policy, it is a bad punishment particularly when it is automatic. No criteria of dangerousness or of the defendant's inability to care for himself are required.

---

[26] "In 27 states, the 'criminal insane' . . . are confined in a separate ward or unit in the state hospital; in five, they are unsegregated in the hospital. In two, they are kept in a ward or unit in the penal institution; in Texas, Oklahoma and Mississippi, some are retained in the penal institutions while others are sent to the hospital. Nine states provide separate institutions for the criminal insane."—Weihofen, Institutional Treatment of Persons Acquitted by Reason of Insanity, 38 Texas L. Rev. 849, 850 (1960).

[27] D.C. Code § 24-301 (f).

[28] D.C. Code § 24-301 (d).

[29] "The enactment of § 24-301 (d) in 1955 was the direct result of the change in the standard of criminal responsibility in the District of Columbia wrought by Durham v. United States."—Lynch v. Overholser, 369 U.S. 705, 82 S. Ct. 1063, 1070 (1962). The court cites Krash, The Durham Rule and Judicial Administration of the Insanity Defense in the District of Columbia, 70 Yale L.J. 905, 941 (1961), that there was apprehension lest it result in a flood of acquittals. It notes, 369 U.S. at 716, 82 S. Ct. at 1070, that previously "it had been customary for the court and the appropriate executive official to order the confinement of all those who had been found not guilty solely by reason of insanity." The chairman of the Congressional Committee, at least, did not like the Durham decision—Halleck, op. cit. supra n. 15 at 306.

[30] Bazelon, op. cit. supra n. 3, lec. 2.

Even if the criminal charge was a trifling one, absolutely no discretion is left to a court to exercise independent judgment as to whether a particular defendant should be committed to St. Elizabeths Hospital or is even in need of psychiatric treatment at the time of trial. The defendant is denied any opportunity to be heard upon the subject of his mental health and is subject to such automatic commitment even if he is capable of showing that he is (a) no longer mentally ill, (b) not dangerous to himself or others, and (c) that, even if mentally ill, confinement in a mental hospital is contra-indicated under accepted standards of psychiatric treatment.[31]

A sizeable number of other jurisdictions also have a mandatory commitment on acquittal for insanity; others place the issue before the jury, or allow discretion to the judge.[32] It should be observed, however, that the harm in these jurisdictions is less than in the District of Columbia. First, the other jurisdictions operate under the M'Naghten rule, and the automatic commitment is applicable to fewer people; second, a defendant excul-

---

[31] Statement of Lawrence Speiser, representing the American Civil Liberties Union, to Subcommittee on Constitutional Rights of the Committee on the Judiciary, U.S. Senate, May 2, 1961.

[32] "At the time the mandatory confinement amendment to the District of Columbia Code was passed, it was the rule in only ten states and in England that the court is required forthwith to commit to a mental hospital any person found not guilty of crime by reason of insanity. In England, under the Trial of Lunatics Act of 1883, the jury returns a verdict of 'guilty but insane' if it acquits a defendant on that ground. Such a verdict represents an affirmative finding by the jury of the insanity of the accused. In four of the ten states with mandatory commitment laws, the accused must prove his insanity as an affirmative defense. In three of the ten states, the accused has the burden of introducing enough evidence to raise a reasonable doubt of his sanity; merely introducing some evidence of insanity will not suffice. While the remaining three states resemble the District of Columbia in that the introduction of evidence, although not necessarily enough to create a reasonable doubt, nevertheless shakes the presumption of sanity, they differ from the District in that they follow the right and wrong test. In none of them will merely some evidence of a mental disease or defect such as the naked, self-serving speculation of the defendant suffice to raise the issue. . . . In New Hampshire, the only state which has a test for criminal insanity like the District of Columbia's Durham rule, there is no mandatory confinement after an acquittal on the ground of insanity. Commitment is discretionary with the court."—Halleck, *op. cit supra* n. 15 at 309-10. See references and list of states in dissenting opinion of Justice Clark, Lynch v. Overholser, *op. cit. supra* n. 29 at 107.

pated under the M'Naghten rule probably meets the criteria for civil commitment because his condition, usually psychosis, is much more severe than the "mental illness or defect" required by the Durham rule.

But the greatest contrast is not between exculpation under Durham and exculpation under M'Naghten, but between Durham-plus-mandatory commitment and *penal conviction*. For, it is argued, Durham results in "civil commitment=treatment," whereas otherwise the defendant would receive "criminal conviction=punishment." The fact is, of course, that not every conviction of crime is followed by commitment to a penal institution. Far from it. In some jurisdictions (Rhode Island, for example) two-thirds or more of offenders are placed on probation, and the courts avoid committing many defendants by using suspended sentences and fines. Mentally ill offenders are suitable for probation supervision.[33]

The Durham court is misled by the concept of "civil commitment=treatment, not punishment." it says:

> If [the defendant's] violent act . . . sprang from mental disorder—if, indeed, he has a mental illness which makes it likely that he will commit other violent acts when his sentence is served, imprisonment is not a remedy. Not only would it be wrong to imprison him, but imprisonment would not secure the community against repetitions of his violence. Hospitalization, on the other hand, would serve the dual purpose of giving him the treatment required for his illness and keeping him confined until it would be safe to release him.[34]

Peculiarly, this says that the hospital is a more *secure* place

---

[33] Wallinga, The Probation Officer's Role in Psychiatric Cases, 50 J. Crim. L., C. & P.S. 364 (1959); Yepsen, The Mentally Deficient Probationer and Parolee, Federal Probation, December 1942. "We have a cultural tradition in our society of almost automatically hospitalizing psychosis, as well as a tradition (and current practice) of not using community psychiatric facilities for the seriously ill. Hospitalization as such is among the causes of disability. This is especially true of the traditional, highly security-conscious hospital, and is probably equally true of the best of the open hospitals."—Dr. Robert C. Hunt, in Steps in The Development of Integrated Psychiatric Services 88, Milbank Memorial Fund (1960).

[34] Williams v. United States, 102 U.S. App. D.C. 51, 250 F.2d 19, 26, (1957).

than a prison, hardly the contrast that is typically made, or that a hospital superintendent would boast about. It is true that *security* is here a combination of treatment and incarceration, but so also does a penal commitment involve treatment plus incarceration. The statement says, in effect, that the hospital may hold him longer than under a penal commitment. Yet, says the Durham court, "it would be wrong to imprison him." It says, in effect, that the hospital is holding him more securely, longer, but is not imprisoning him. The fact is that a majority of offenders are not violent people; the majority commit property offenses, violations of the peace, or affronts against morals. And many—drug addicts, vagrants, alcoholics—simply have a *status* to which the law attaches criminality. Thus the alcoholic woman who would have gotten a small fine or a few days in jail was subjected to an indeterminate commitment when the court refused to accept her plea of guilty because of her mental illness —alcoholism.[35]

Even if the crime is a violent one, the routine assumption that an indeterminate commitment must follow is unwarranted. Sheldon Glueck, writing about the Massachusetts law requiring mandatory commitment for life upon acquittal on the ground of insanity in the case of manslaughter, says:

> This harsh provision has meant virtually life imprisonment; and in fact until very recent years the institution involved was more a prison than a hospital. Such a disposal of an acquitted person is in direct contradiction to the fact that mental illness has resulted in legal exculpation because of blamelessness.[36]

The lengths to which the Durham court would go in its adherence to its viewpoint is best illustrated by its ruling on whether the defense of mental illness may be imposed on a defendant who does not wish to plead it. The Durham court said it could,[37]

---

35 *Supra*, page 28.
36 Glueck, *op. cit. supra* n. 6 at 120.
37 Overholser v. Lynch, 109 U.S. App. D.C. 404, 288 F.2d 388 (D.C. Cir. 1961). Before Overholser v. Lynch was reversed by the Supreme Court of the United States the defendant—not a dangerous person; he had overdrawn his bank account by $100—"was then confined to St. Elizabeths Hospital in a ward containing more than 1,000 patients and cared for by no more than two psychiatrists. No treatment beyond the random and mechanical application of drugs was available. Psychotherapy was not even thought of in that context. The defendant, instead, received the boon of

in a check writing case. The United States Supreme Court said it could not;[38] but until then, this is what the Durham court had approved:

> In a number of recent cases involving troublesome misdemeanants, *or where the evidence of guilt is slight,* the government introduces "some" evidence of the defendant's insanity. Without attempting to carry its burden of proving that the defendant was sane, the prosecution requests the insanity instructions. The court then instructs the jury that they must return a verdict of not guilty by reason of insanity unless the government has proved beyond a reasonable doubt that the defendant was sane. . . . In the District of Columbia, verdict of not guilty by reason of insanity does *not* represent an affirmative finding by the jury that the defendant was in fact insane. It merely means that the government failed to sustain its burden of proof. Since it is mandatory that a defendant who raises the issue and is acquitted by reason of insanity be committed to a mental hospital, the result is a possible long-term confinement without any determination that the defendant was or is actually insane.[39]

In perhaps nine out of ten cases in which the issue of insanity was raised, it was the prosecution that introduced it.[40] Thus, in the District of Columbia the Durham decision and its interpretations became a weapon of prosecution rather than a method of securing the best disposition of the defendant.

In spite of the Supreme Court's ruling preventing the prose-

---

being permitted to work upon a vegetable patch within the hospital grounds. His illness, depressive in character from the start, did not show any improvement within these surroundings for many months. Upon his conditional release from St. Elizabeths Hospital almost a year after his incarceration by these means, the defendant appeared a broken man, shunned by his friends and erstwhile neighbors and incapable of persuading any prospective employer that he was worthy of any but the most menial and routine of jobs."—Statement of the American Civil Liberties Union before the subcommittee on Constitutional Rights of the Committee on the Judiciary, U.S. Senate, March 29, 1961.

[38] Lynch v. Overholser, 369 U.S. 705, 82 S. Ct. 1063 (1962).

[39] Calif. Special Commissions, *op. cit. supra* n. 5 at 80; our ital.

[40] "In perhaps 9 out of 10 cases in which insanity . . . is the factor, it is the prosecution which first introduces it by moving for a trial and commitment to a state hospital." Reid, The Working of the New Hampshire Doctrine of Criminal Insanity, 15 U. of Miami L. Rev. 14, at (1960).

cution (for the time being)[41] from imposing an insanity plea, the Durham decision still is a chess piece in prosecution-defense strategy rather than a searching out of the defendant's mental condition on behalf of his welfare. In a noncapital case in a jurisdiction that authorizes automatic commitment upon establishment of the defense of insanity, the defense will weigh the alternatives—the probable penal sentence and the indeterminate insanity commitment. In the many cases carrying a maximum sentence of a year or perhaps a few years it will be more interested in submitting a guilty plea. Thus the state's interest in knowing about and dealing with mentally ill offenders is defeated.[42]

Under the M'Naghten rules the problem is resolved—if correctional services contemplated and made possible by the Model Sentencing Act, including the state diagnostic center, are available. If the defendant is seriously disturbed, it is to the interest of the state to have this known to the court at the time of sentence. Under the Model Sentencing Act the court can proceed with a diagnostic study without the defendant's consent, upon plea or conviction. Also, under the MSA, a defendant who is mentally ill but not dangerous may be committed (*if* com-

---

[41] Lynch v. Overholser, cited *supra* n. 38, was put not on constitutional grounds but on statutory interpretation. The prosecutor's influence in raising the question of competency to stand trial is related; see the statement of Judge Bazelon, cited ch. 1, note 8.

[42] "Not infrequently an attorney who defends a person accused of crime in the District of Columbia may be faced with the difficult and unusual task of preventing the prosecution and the court from learning that his client has a valid defense. This anomalous situation arises by virtue of a series of recent judicial interpretations of the mandatory confinement provision of the District of Columbia Code which provides that all defendants acquitted of crime by reason of insanity shall automatically be confined to a hospital for the mentally ill. Because this provision may now so operate as to impose upon acquitted defendants sanctions far more severe than those attached to conviction, the defense attorney may believe that . . . he will better serve the interests of his client by avoiding the insanity defense entirely. . . . The election by the attorney and his client not to raise the defense of insanity, even where it might succeed, is morally and professionally justified in light of the post-trial procedures now in effect in the District of Columbia. . . . It is no secret that the insanity defense is seldom raised by defendants in municipal court, even in cases where it could be. The prospect of a relatively light sentence upon conviction of a misdemeanor—the only type of crime tried in municipal court—is much less foreboding than the possibility of indefinite confinement in a mental hospital."—Halleck, *op. cit. supra* n. 15 at 315.

mitted) for only a relatively short term—not over five years—the same term applicable to a defendant who is not ill. So a property offender, never deemed dangerous under the Model Sentencing Act, would not be deterred from submitting evidence of mental illness. Defense counsel therefore need not fear an indefinite commitment if he helps the court understand and deal with the mentally ill defendant. It is our penology that requires reform; again, it is the existence of a plan like the Model Sentencing Act that "modernizes" M'Naghten: M'Naghten is better adapted than Durham to such a sentencing system.

Meanwhile, the punitive automatic commitment in the District of Columbia and elsewhere[43] ought to be revised, to accord with the rule in a majority of jurisdictions where the civil commitment following acquittal for insanity is not automatic. In some jurisdictions the defendant acquitted for insanity may go free;[44] in the federal courts he is freed, and nothing untoward appears to have happened as a result.[45] Furthermore, the discretion to commit should be based on relevant criteria, such as the dangerousness of the offender who has been acquitted,[46] or—since he has not been convicted of crime—in accord with the civil commitment procedure for persons who have not been accused of crime.

Commitment for Incompetency; Discharge

The question of mental competency to proceed before the trial or on the trial is not involved in the debate over rules of

[43] Colorado, Georgia, Kansas, Maine, Massachusetts, Michigan, Minnesota, Nebraska, Nevada, New York, Ohio, Wisconsin, Virgin Islands; in these the mandatory commitment applies only if the defense raises the plea of insanity. Lynch v. Overholser, cited *supra* n. 38 at n. 8.
[44] If found by the jury to have recovered—Illinois, Maryland, Mississippi, Missouri, Oklahoma, Texas, Washington; Weihofen, *op. cit. supra* n. 26 at n. 3 and 4. Jurisdictions in which discretion is exercised,—Reid, Disposition of the Criminally Insane, 16 Rutgers L. Rev. 75, at 105 (1961).
[45] See Sauer v. U.S., 241 F.2d 640 (1957), a rather dispirited upholding of M'Naghten, based principally on the argument that under it fewer defendants are acquitted to go free than would be freed under another rule.
[46] "The question that arises upon the defendant's acquittal is whether he is presently a substantial risk to society. If he should be found not to be such a risk, we recommend that he be released subject to such orders regarding his conduct, including submission to therapeutic treatment, as in the circumstances seem appropriate. Some offenders will fall into this category, and we can see no point in requiring them to be institutionalized." —California Special Commissions, *op. cit. supra* n. 5 at 33.

responsibility for the criminal act. At various stages of a criminal proceeding prior to trial, incompetency on the part of the accused usually results in a commitment. The commitment may follow automatically upon a finding of incompetency to proceed or to stand trial.[47] In general the test is the ability of the alleged (or convicted) offender to understand the proceedings and to assist his counsel in them.[48]

Considerable thought has been given to the method of detecting such incompetency, particularly where serious offenses have been committed. The best known of these approaches is the Massachusetts Briggs law, under which a routine psychiatric examination is had of all defendants in capital cases and all recidivists.[49] In all jurisdictions procedures for testing certain defendants are used.[50] Sometimes the procedure is quite informal, and it has been criticizd for the violence it does to due process of law. Richard Arens and Harold D. Lasswell write:

> There are grave dangers developing that "medicine" can be used as punishment without strict observance of due-process requirements. In the phrase of a recent legal publicist, we see the increasing infliction of "medicine . . . [as] punishment *sans* due process of law." The danger is indicated by such statutory authority as that which permits summary, though temporary, mental commitment of an individual answering a "criminal" charge, when the prosecuting officer initiates the motion. No other evidence is required than courtroom observation.[51]

Dr. Szasz speaks of "the right to trial"[52]:

> The most serious abridgment of a person's civil rights may result from circumventing the proper legal deter-

---

[47] E.g. Indiana States. Annot. § 9-1706a.

[48] See the citations listed in Note, Compulsory Commitment Following a Successful Insanity Defense, 56 N.W. U. L. Rev. 409, at n. 28.

[49] Mass. Ann. Laws (1942) ch. 123 § 100A.

[50] Kentucky, examination of those indicted as habitual criminals; the Michigan law, modeled on the Briggs law, repealed in 1951.—Tenny, Sex, Sanity and Stupidity in Massachusetts, 42 Boston U.L. Rev. 1 (1962). Tenny finds fault with the Briggs law.

[51] In defense of Public Order, the Emerging Field of Sanction Law 46 (1961); the quotation is from De Grazia, The Distinction of Being Mad, 22 U. of Chi. L. Rev. 339, 355 (1955).

[52] The title of ch. 13 in his Law, Liberty and Psychiatry (1963).

mination of his "guilt"—that is, of whether he has in
fact violated any of the laws—by finding that he is
mentally too ill to stand trial. For if thereupon he is
"imprisoned" in a mental hospital, he is *ipso facto*
being "punished." This procedure also effectively
deprives him of the opportunity to clear himself of the
criminal charges which were brought against him.[53]

A defense may exist which is not affected by the defendant's incompetency—the statute of limitations; or any affirmative defense, in fact, which could be established without the
defendant's testimony. "Frequently an affirmative defense is
jeopardized by the passage of time. Memories fade, witnesses
die or move away, and documentary records may become
unavailable. In many cases the defense will be that of non-
responsibility—here the longer trial is postponed, the more difficult it is for the defendant to make such a defense."[54]

John H. Hess, Jr. and Herbert E. Thomas studied 1,484
defendants committed in Michigan for incompetency to stand
trial, and 200 on "parole." In six years only 105 of those committed had been returned to the committing courts. "Our findings indicate," they reported, "that well over one-half of the
individuals committed as incompetent will spend the rest of
their lives confined to the hospital." They cited a man committed as incompetent pending trial on a charge of gross inde-
cency in 1926 and still under treatment thirty-six years later,
at which time he was said to be showing signs of simple psychosis.

The issue of incompetency, say Hess and Thomas, "was most
frequently raised not on the basis of defendant's mental status
but rather was employed as a means of handling situations and
solving problems for which there seemed to be no other recourse
under the law."

It was our opinion that many persons were committed to Ionia State Hospital who were not in fact incompetent to be tried. Also, it was our judgment that with
existing treatment methods and facilities, the majority
of individuals committed as incompetent could be read-

---

[53] Szasz, Politics and Mental Health, 15 Am. J. of Psych. 508, 509 (1958).
[54] Hess, Pearsall, Slichter, & Thomas, Comment, Criminal Law—Insane
Persons—Competency to Stand Trial, 59 Mich. L. Rev. 1078, 1094 (1961).

ied for trial within a matter of weeks or months. . . . When intervention on behalf of a patient by the court or lawyer (or even continued interest by the family) did occur, closer attention was invariably paid to the patient's return to court for trial. . . .

In a strictly legal sense, many persons are deprived of the constitutional guarantee for a "speedy trial," and hence deprived of the opportunity to be found innocent, not guilty by virtue of being not responsible, or at the very least, guilty with an earlier start on a prison term. (Time spent as incompetent in the hospital is "dead time" in terms of any future sentence.)

The authors are highly critical of the doctors' reports, most of which either were confused as to the mental criteria being called for by the court or lacked any useful psychiatric information for the court.

To put the matter bluntly, in many cases a prison sentence would be preferable to the presumably more compassionate act of committing an individual as incompetent . . . Many of the patients committed as incompetent . . . do not consider it a hospital but rather a prison, and an extremely undesirable prison at that. For the majority it is a prison to which one is committed on an incomprehensible basis and one in which concepts of parole, treatment, or discharge gradually shift from unlikely possibilities to forlorn hopes, to psychotic delusions.[55]

We have attempted to show that the mandatory commitment on acquittal for insanity or mental illness contradicts the anti-punishment position. It is more punitive than penal dispositions: that is, it commits a person to an institution involuntarily for a term which is potentially and often actually longer than a prison term and from which release is often more difficult than from a prison. The same would appear to be true of mandatory commitment of an accused who is found incompetent at some stage before the trial.

If not a mandatory commitment, what else? It is not enough to say that commitment shall be discretionary rather than

[55] Incompetency to Stand Trial: Procedure, Results, and Problems, 119 Am. J. Psych. 713 (1963).

automatic. In the cases we are now discussing, there is no conviction; in fact, no more than prima facie evidence of crime has been introduced. There has been, in effect, only an accusation. Again, the most natural criteria to turn to would be those governing civil commitment unrelated to criminal accusation, but these too are vague and in need of more precise definition.[56] Should not dangerousness be a principal criterion? And should not dangerousness refer to dangerousness to the person? Very likely.[57]

An interesting, sensible decision in the United States Court of Appeals holds that a test of commitment at the point of incompetency is whether the commitment would be likely to lead to competency. There is no presumption that it will, and (at least in that case) the burden seemed to be on those seeking the commitment. Said the court:

> We feel that the record does not furnish sufficient grounds for commitment. . . . Where a defendant . . . is receiving extensive psychiatric care and there is no question as to the integrity and high professional competency of his personal psychiatrist, we do not consider 18 U.S.C. § 4246 as intended to compel the District Court to determine which of two equally reputable methods of psychiatric treatment would prove most efficacious in a particular case. . . . In a case such as this, where a man's life may literally hang in the balance [a reference to the testimony of the defendant's psychiatrist] a judge ought not undertake the hazardous venture of changing the course of psychiatric treatment without, at the least, a much fuller hearing and a far greater preponderance of expert testimony than existed here.[58]

If the criteria are not met, the accused should be released

---

[56] "Of the thirty-seven jurisdictions which now provide some form of judicial hospitalization, only five phrase the sole criterion for hospitalization in terms of whether the individual is dangerous to himself or others. Twelve other jurisdictions augment this provision by stating that the need of the patient for care or treatment may serve as an alternative basis for hospitalization. Seven states, on the other hand, provide no other basis for hospitalization than the patient's need for care or treatment."—Lindman & McIntyre (eds.), The Mentally Disabled and the Law 17 (1961).

[57] Infra, p. 175.

[58] United States v. Klein, 325 F.2d 283 (2d Cir. 1963).

(as he was in the case cited immediately above) pending his fitness to stand trial, just as though he were free on bail or on his own recognizance.

If the accused is, in fact, committed for incompetency, what happens upon his recovery? He is subject to trial and penal commitment. If he is committed, time in the mental hospital is not credited on the penal commitment. Certainly we are being harsher with the mentally ill offender than with the one who is not mentally ill if we subject him to more than one proceeding—one for his illness, one for his offense. If we are reaching for an ethic that says that we should not punish the mentally ill, we ought at least to avoid duplicating punishment for him. There should be no prosecution following release after commitment for incompetency. There is existing precedent for this suggestion.[59]

Presumably the defendant who has admitted the crime but has been acquitted for insanity is adjudged as having committed the criminal act, whereas the incompetent is not condemned. No matter how serious the crime committed by the defendant acquitted for insanity, he is entitled to discharge upon recovery. Why should the situation of the defendant whose prosecution has been interrupted for his incompetency and who has then been committed and has recovered be in a worse position than the defendant acquitted for insanity? The only purpose served, it would seem, is to complete the record by determining whether he committed the act or not.

For purposes of commitment the state usually argues that the defendant who interposes the defense of insanity when the crime was committed must be presumed to be insane at the time of

---

[59] John Reid points out that in Rhode Island it is left to the discretion of the judge as to whether the defendant shall be remanded for trial. In New Jersey, if there is recovery within a reasonable time, the trial judge may exercise his statutory authority to determine the issue of past insanity at a second hearing and, if it is found that the suspect was insane at the time the crime was committed, the criminal charge is dropped. Maine provides that the defendant is to be set free if the court is satisfied the defendant will not endanger the community. Vermont has held that the status of such a person is not that of a criminal but of an insane person confined under civil commitment.—Reid, *op. cit. supra* n. 44 at 79-80 (1961). No doubt other jurisdictions have similar rules, e.g., New York—see, Mental Illness and Due Process: Report and Recommendations on Admission to Mental Hospitals Under New York Law 230 (1962).

the trial. It is at least as reasonable to consider incompetency at the time of trial to relate back to the time of commission of the act. (The question of "release of dangerous people" is treated elsewhere.[60])

Perhaps the argument against this disposition is that the commitment for incompetency at the procedural stages is for a less serious mental condition than the insanity test on the trial (at least in the M'Naghten jurisdictions). But the difference in the rules may be used positively and not only to support the renewal of the trial on recovery. If the rule were that on recovery after commitment the trial would not be resumed, (1) the prosecution would not be as quick to argue for incompetency, and the shaky aspects of due process that we have referred to would be strengthened; (2) additional support would be given to our urging that on incompetency the defendant's treatment without institutionalization be considered—e.g., as was done in the case discussed at page 44. I do not argue that in a case such as that—where the incompetent defendant is not committed—he ought not to be tried on recovery. I suggest that the criminal trial be barred only if there has ben a commitment, that is, deprivation of liberty—like the commitment on acquittal for insanity. (It is somewhat analogous to statutes that provide that time spent in jail awaiting trial shall be credited on any sentence of commitment after trial.)

And so it is possible to suggest, as I do below, the writing of a statute that takes account in this way of exactly such a disposition, commitment for insanity or mental illness, in relation to a criminal charge.[61]

Duration of Commitment; Release

Another way of judging how "punitive" the civil commitment of the mentally ill offender is in practice is to compare the duration of his custody with that of the criminally committed offender. A longer commitment might be justified by a higher success rate—that is, a lower recidivism rate; but there is no evidence that the longer term, whether in the prison or mental hospital, is more successful.[62] All criminal commitments, except

---

[60] *Infra*, chs. 8 and 9.
[61] *Infra*, pp. 168-170.
[62] Lehrman, *op. cit. supra* n. 25.

those for the crimes that carry life terms—are of limited duration. Jerome Hall writes, "From a medical viewpoint, it may be absurd to relase an offender at a fixed time that in fact has no relation to rehabilitation. But if no law fixed an upper limit, there is no adequate protection for any convicted person against life imprisonment."[63] In fact, the Model Sentencing Act provides that only murder in the first degree is punishable by a life term (subject to parole); a commitment for any other crime is limited to a maximum of five years or less, as fixed by the judge, or, for dangerous offenders, a maximum of thirty years or less.

When we discuss the Model Sentencing Act in some detail, the considerations (including public protection) entering into this limitation of terms will be discussed. But at this point we are talking only of punitiveness, which for most practical purposes is length of term. It is precisely the civil, the "treatment" commitment, that is without limit; it is indefinite, and may be for life. Dr. Winfred Oversholser, superintendent of St. Elizabeths Hospital in the District of Columbia, to which defendants acquitted under the Durham rule are committed, wrote:

> In a substantial number of cases the period of confinement resulting has been far greater than if an ordinary sentence had been imposed. Several persons have been committed to Saint Elizabeths Hospital after acquittal of such charges as threats, disorderly conduct, unauthorized use of automobile, or even drunkenness. . . . The odds are in favor of a period of sequestration in the hospital that is longer than if a sentence were being served.[64]

A justification must be sought. Dr. Overholser continues:

> In spite of the trivial nature of the charge, some of these persons have been found to be seriously ill mentally and potentially dangerous. After all, if an individual is mentally ill and dangerous, it would seem to be to society's advantage at least to keep him in custody until he can be released safely.

---

[63] Hall, Studies in Jurisprudence and Criminal Theory, ch. 15, p. 273 (1958).
[64] Overholser. Criminal Responsibility: A Psychiatrist's Viewpoint, 48 A.B.A.J. 527 (1962).

Perhaps so; but these people have not been found to be dangerous in any proceeding.

Similarly another defender of the Durham rule, Professor John Reid, writes:

> M'Naghten and related tests will insure to a greater degree that the wrongdoer will be punished while the *Durham* rule and the New Hampshire doctrine, by making more persons liable to indefinite commitment, will offer greater protection to the public by isolating the mentally ill.[65]

What an interesting transition—the appellation "punishment" given to the limited penal commitment, which is then contrasted *not* with superior treatment under Durham, but rather a more prolonged commitment as a protection to the public.

A study of the commitments to Fairview State Hospital, Pennsylvania, and the New Jersey State Hospital found that "the median commitment of persons who had been acquitted by reason of insanity and subsequently committed was extremely long when compared to that of the total institutional population—thirty-one years and nine months as against six years and four months at Fairview, and two years and two months as against five months at Trenton."[66]

Is any more evidence or argument needed to reach the judgment that the idea of Durham-commitment=treatment is a fiction (or, worse: as we shall say later—a myth)? Jerome Hall said:

> What looms large in the current penological horizon are proposals to incarcerate many so-called "anti-social" persons alleged to be recognizable before they commit any crime and to institutionalize many other thousands of convicted persons until psychiatrists certify that they have been "cured." The fact is that such penology rests upon an ideology, not upon diagnosis or knowledge of rehabilitation.[67]

---

[65] Reid, *op. cit. supra* n. 44, at 100.

[66] Note, Hospitalization of Mentally Ill Criminals in Pennsylvania and New Jersey, 110 U. of Pa. L. Rev. 78, 98 (1961).

[67] Hall, The Scientific and Humane Study of Criminal Law, 42 Boston U.L. Rev. 267 (1962).

Finally, the procedure on release must be considered in connection with the commitment. The law establishes a statutory pattern of eligibility for parole, the penal system of release. In some jurisdictions a prisoner is eligible at any time; in others, after serving some minimum term. In the federal system both rules apply according to the sentence imposed. In all cases, the maximum term has an effect on the release decision. If the maximum is a long one, the parole date is likely to come later than a term with a short maximum. A sentence to a life term usually carries a practical (if not a legal) minimum time of fifteen years or more, although it is sometimes not more than five years or so.[68]

In the District of Columbia, Sheldon Glueck notes, "Release from the hospital depends upon the patient's ability to prove, *beyond a reasonable doubt,* that he will not in the foreseeable future be dangerous to himself or others."

> In habeas corpus proceedings . . . the patient must establish beyond a reasonable doubt that the hospital superintendent has acted arbitrarily and capriciously in refusing to certify him to the District Court for discharge.
>
> Judicial control of the release of persons acquitted on the ground of insanity and thereupon committed to a mental hospital can be more strict than is administrative control of release of ordinary prisoners on parole. In this connection, several questions are presented: Is the burden of proof beyond a reasonable doubt, especially under habeas corpus, a fair one to place on the committed, but previously acquitted, hospital patient? The District of Columbia District Court has shown a tendency to be rather cautious in ordering releases, this owing partly perhaps to public feeling that the Durham test is looser than its predecessors. The court also relies heavily on expert testimony; so that a patient, to have any realistic chance of release, is required to secure outside psychiatric witnesses. Since the burden on the patient to establish the fact of sufficient recovery or remission of his illness is unduly heavy, it would seem advisable to provide for the rendering of periodic re-

---

[68] Federal Bureau of Prisons, Prisoners Released from State and Federal Institutions 1960, tables 58-106.

ports to the court on the progress of committed patients.[69]

Examination of the statistics demonstrates the unlikelihood of early release:

> Since the adoption of the Durham rule, and through April 30, 1960, 160 persons acquitted by reason of insanity have been automatically committed to St. Elizabeths. Sixty-five of these acquittals occurred prior to December 12, 1958. In that period, 20 of those 65 patients were discharged. But by April 30, 1960, of the 160 persons committed after acquittal, a total of only 24 had been granted unconditional releases.[70]

The great fear of the mentally ill offender instilled by the Durham decision is reflected also in the criteria for release from the mental hospital. For unconditional release the court must be convinced that the inmate has recovered his sanity, that he will not be dangerous to himself or others.[71] And what is the test of dangerousness in the District of Columbia? "The danger to the public need not be possible physical violence or a crime of violence. It is enough if there is competent evidence that he may commit *any criminal act*, for any such act will injure others and will expose the person to arrest, trial and conviction."[72]

Elsewhere the criteria of release are more relaxed. As Henry Weihofen points out:

> Some of the better drawn statutes do not require commitment "until cured." The New Jersey law, for example, permits parole when the person is believed capable of making a satisfactory social adjustment; most committed sex offenders are paroled under this provision, with a surprisingly low violation rate. Some of these patients, such as certain sex offenders, may be relatively poor prospects for intensive therapy; there is little the hospital can do with them under custodial care.[73]

---

[69] Glueck, *op. cit. supra* n. 6 at 124. Glueck cites Hough v. United States, 271 F.2d 458 (D.C. Cir. 1959), and Overholser v. Leach, 257 F.2d 667 (D.C. Cir. 1958) as illustrations.

[70] Halleck, *op. cit. supra* n. 15 at 314.

[71] D.C. Code § 24-301 (e).

[72] Overholser v. Russell, 283 F.2d 195, at 198 (1960).

[73] Weihofen, *op. cit. supra* n. 26, at 849.

Denial of a parole to a criminally committed prisoner is not subject to court review;[74] perhaps this is a situation that is subject to criticism. But, on the other hand, a court may not veto, a court does not pass upon, the decision to grant parole; while in the District of Columbia the court does have this power of reviewing the superintendent's decision to release the civilly committed offender, and does apply it, as Sheldon Glueck points out, "cautiously"—that is, restrictively. The court has become a parole authority.[75] Furthermore, the limit on the prison term is an inducement to the board to grant parole, or at least to consider it, whereas the civil commitment is indeterminate—potentially a life term. The Durham rule, then, has resulted in a release procedure more restrictive than parole from penal institutions.

---

[74] People v. Norwitt, 69 N.E.2d 285, 394 Ill. 553 (1946); People ex rel. Von Moser v. Parole Board, 266 App. Div. 896, 42 N.Y.S. 2d 728 (1943).

[75] "In about half the states, the power to discharge such persons [persons acquitted of crime by reason of insanity and ordered confined in the hospital until restored to sanity] is vested in the court that ordered the commitment, or in some other court."—Weihofen, *op. cit. supra* n. 26 at 863.

Chapter 3

The Durham Decision and Crime Causation

Durham and *Mens Rea*

Combining a theory of crime causation with a moral judgment, the Durham decision arrives at a new concept of legal responsibility. It first states old law: "The legal and moral traditions of the western world require that those who, of their own free will and with evil intent (sometimes called *mens rea*), commit acts which violate the law, shall be criminally responsible for those acts."

But the statement then continues: "Our traditions also require that where such acts stem from and are the product of a mental disease or defect as those terms are used herein, moral blame shall not attach, and hence there will not be criminal responsibility." The opinion contains no citations for such a proposition, which is, in fact, if intended as a legal proposition, a doubtful one. Whereas the sentence quoted in the paragraph above rightly refers to "legal and moral" tradition, this statement refers only to "tradition," for it has no legal precedents, other than the New Hampshire cases.

The law excuses certain persons, but always because of their lack of understanding—for example, young children. A child under seven is conclusively presumed not to understand the nature of his behavior and cannot be convicted of crime. Except for the precedent of the New Hampshire rule, from which Durham is derived, no line of thought suggests that the offender is excused, legally, where he is mentally ill.

Durham takes the leap from this moral posture to the legal proposition. It is troublesome on many counts. It does not progress toward a therapeutic goal any more effectively than the older rule, and perhaps it does less well. In outlook and effect it is punitive; and it has still other difficulties.

Let us examine the moral principle which holds that where violations of law "stem from and are the product of a mental disorder or defect . . . , moral blame shall not attach, and hence there will be no criminal responsibility." The Durham case has been debated by various writers, without, so far as I know, any discussion of this moral issue, which was so briefly stated, and not discussed, in the Durham decision. The only explanation I can think of is that the writers are thrown off the track in the same way that Durham jumped the track, as follows:

(a) While M'Naghten states a rule regarding *mens rea,* it uses the term "insanity," which touches the realm of mental illness. (b) The modern psychiatrists and others condemn "insanity" as an archaic term, and want a more modern one. It *is* a poor word in the psychiatric world. The point is that "insanity" is used in M'Naghten *not* for the psychiatric world, but for the legal and lay world, the world of judges and juries. M'Naghten is not really involved in the problem of mental illness, but only in *mens rea,* or criminal intent.

(c) In going from "insanity" to the more modern "mental illness," Durham loses *mens rea.* Mental illness may support the defense of insanity, but it is not a defense standing alone. It is as though we suddenly adopted a whole lay world of meaning of the legal term "negligence" and discarded the legal technicalities of the word. Similarly, when we jump from *insanity* to *mental illness,* we are dealing with a *different thing,* particularly when we have discarded *mens rea.* (d) Thus the end product, in the Durham decision, is that mental illness has been substituted for *mens rea,* not merely for insanity.

Substituting mental illness for *mens rea* may be a good thing, or it may not be. This we shall now examine; but let us be clear that this is what Durham does, with very slim legal precedent.[1]

The Moral Issue

Mens rea is intent to commit a crime. The requirement of intent is not the same as *motivation*. *Mens rea* involves capacity, not the moral issue of motivation.

A mental illness may drive a person to commit a particular act, an act which is a crime. That is, the mental illness drives him to intend to commit an act, which intention he carries out. The *intent* is essential in the law today in all jurisdictions, including the District of Columbia, where Durham governs. In the District of Columbia a person who does not have criminal intent cannot be held responsible. If his mental illness is of such a kind that he did not have the mental capacity to intend (or, did not realize the criminality or badness of the act), he is excused.

But, the Durham decision adds, we will also excuse the crime if *mens rea* was present but mental illness caused it. In short, mental illness is held to supersede intent.

What does this lead to? For one thing, it leads to a moral inconsistency. The field of criminology is filled with studies which demonstrate convincingly that criminality is associated with certain social conditions—culture conflict, social deprivation, slums, poverty, bad associations, and others. These studies make clear that the social conditions can sensibly be spoken of as the cause of this criminality, operating through the persons

---

[1] This is not accidental, but conscious, at least in the thinking of some. Dr. Diamond writes: "*Mens rea*, as an essential requisite of criminality, is rejected in the name of psychological enlightenment. This approach is typified by *The Guilty Mind*, by Judge John Biggs, Jr. If I sense his thesis correctly, Biggs regards *mens rea* as a relic of the past and as an obstacle to the application of modern psychological and psychiatric principles to criminal law and penology. He States: 'We must stop laying so much emphasis on guilt—on the "guilty mind" of the criminal. We must reappraise our concept of guilty. We look *now* only to the events in connection with the commission of the crime. . . . We must look *now* and in the *future* beneath the surface of the events immediately surrounding the commission of the crime and analyze the social and psychological background of the criminal. . . . We must look to the causes of the criminal's state of mind rather than to the fact that he possessed a guilty mind, as a guide to the disposing of him. The fact that he is guilty and possessed *mens rea* is a superficial fact when it comes to the determination of the kind and nature of the sanction to be imposed upon him.' "—Criminal Responsibility of the Mentally Ill, 14 Stan. L. Rev. 59, at 69-70 (1961); the quotation from The Guilty Mind (1955) is at 192-3.

caught in the particular social conditions. We may well speak of these conditions as "social ills."

On this point we may quote from one of Judge Bazelon's articles on the Durham rule:

> Though no conclusive scientific proof exists, the indications are strong that a good deal of criminal behavior should be viewed as a pathological function of marginal socio-economic status. Some 90 per cent of the criminal cases which come before our United States Court of Appeals involving the insanity plea concern indigent defendants.[2]

The mentally ill person, presumably, does not have totally free will; neither does the socially conditioned person. No one believes in a totally free will. (Indeed, probably the only person with totally free will is the one everybody acknowledges to be not responsible legally—the true "wild beast," the completely psychotic.)

Then is not a socially ill person who commits a crime in about the same moral position as a mentally ill person who commits a crime? Some people may have more sympathy with persons suffering from mental illness than from social illness. Presumably the Durham opinion represents such a point of view. But if excusing the mentally ill offender depends on free will, there is *no difference* in this regard between the crime mentally caused and the crime socially caused.

We can look at it another way. Let us oversimplify (yet staying within the reach of much current psychiatric theory) and say that neurosis comes from within the family setting, and crime-without-neurosis stems from community conditions. If we excuse the neurotic who commits a neurotic-crime, we have placed the blame on the parent rather than on the neurotic criminal. Correspondingly, *not* excusing the criminal-from-social-conditions is a refusal to blame the community (poverty, housing, poor education, minimal or no jobs, etc.). If we are putting our rule on an ethical base (as the Durham decision puts it, "the moral tradition of the western world"), it is, indeed, a very weak

---

[2] Bazelon, The Awesome Decision, Saturday Evening Post, January 23, 1960, p. 56.

position morally and probably not at all a part of the moral tradition of the western world.

Physical deformities have sometimes caused persons to commit crime (and the cure, in at least some instances, has come about dramatically when the physical deformity was detected as the cause and was remedied). Does the Durham decision suggest, then, that persons suffering from physical defect that led them to commit crime be excused? No one has maintained that Durham legally leads to this, but it is morally implied from the decision.

If we were thus to apply the logic of the Durham principle, as we seem entitled to, we would have to excuse practically all criminals—those who were led to their crime by mental illness, physical illness, or social illness. Is any criminal left out?

The fact is that *every* crime is caused by a multiplicity of conditions. There is anything but a sharp dividing line between mental illness and mental health. Quoting Dr. Halleck again:

> Although many factors have been invoked as the "cause" of delinquency, it is impossible to isolate a specific etiological agent. How, then, can one say that a delinquent individual is "sick" in the same sense as "being ill." Delinquents can be regarded as sick only by following the thinking of modern medicine and looking toward causative factors in the individual. Just as perhaps only 30 of a group of 100 people exposed to Asiatic flu will come down with the disease, so might only 30 of a group of 100 adolescent boys exposed to the influences of poverty and lower-class values behave in a delinquent way. Delinquency is not caused by factor A or factor B, but rather by a whole series of events that have occurred in a child's life and have left him with certain intellectual and emotional deficiencies. . . .
>
> The concept of bad *vs.* sick ignores the most important issue—that of causality or determinism. There are reasons why a person commits a delinquent act, and unless these are ascertained any quest toward effective treatment is fruitless. It is naïve to state that delinquents behave as they do simply because they are bad—this is no explanation at all. It is also senseless to say they are delinquent because they are sick, unless there is a clear implication that it is a visitation from some devil for which the individual holds no responsibility.[3]

Some of the writers on the problem are disturbed by exactly this point. Jerome Hall writes:

> Certainly no lawyer can view with equanimity the disintegration of the moral foundations of the criminal law by the propaganda of irresponsibility and the irresponsible expansion of the concept of "mental disease." Nor is there much comfort to be derived from the business of trying to persuade Americans that they are mentally disordered and that, no matter how wise they are, they may be impotent to control themselves even with regard to commiting the most serious crimes of violence.[4]

The Durham decision, if applied as logic and morality require, is socially impossible—unless we are up to the utopian point of saying that all criminals are sick (one way or another) and are all to be excused.

What the Jury Passes On

The Durham treatment of causation not only causes a moral crisis, but also presents difficult technical problems which have not been satisfactorily resolved. Durham says that "an accused is not criminally responsible if his unlawful act was *the product of* mental disease or mental defect." Establishing causation on the trial, required under this rule, is confusing and of uncertain result. (Let us remind ourselves that M'Naghten does not involve causation.)

Is the demand of cause a worthwhile contribution? Does it work? It does not for the very reason we have suggested—every act is caused by a multiplicity of factors, psychological, social accidental. The numerous cases that have come up since 1954 in the District of Columbia offer ample evidence that the new legal demand of establishing causation cannot be met; it can only be

---

3 Juvenile Delinquents: "Sick" or "Bad"?, Social Work, April 1962, p. 58 at 60. And Dr. Thomas S. Szasz—"The causes range from the way the patient's parents treated him when he was a child to his experiences five minutes before shooting."—Psychiatry, Ethics, and the Criminal Law, 58 Columbia Law Rev. 183, at 191 (1958).

4 Hall, The Scientific and Humane Study of Criminal Law, 42 Boston U. L. Rev. 267 (1962).

evaded, by dumping a package of uncertain psychiatric issues into the lap of the jury (or trial judge sitting without jury).

In a M'Naghten jurisdiction, the jury passes on the question of *mens rea*, a simple idea and, furthermore, one that is within the province of a layman: Did the defendant have the minimum mental capacity to know that he was doing wrong? On the other hand, under Durham a jury must pass on very complicated propositions: (a) Is the defendant suffering from a mental disease or defect, and (b) was the unlawful act the product of the mental disease or mental defect? In contrast to the jury in a M'Naghten state, these call not for lay decisions but for highly technical, and often highly debatable, professional judgments.

In *Campbell v. United States of America* the charge was robbery. Two government psychiatrists who saw the the defendant at St. Elizabeths, the government hospital, testified that the defendant was suffering from an "emotionally unstable personality," but a third (who had not examined the defendant before the trial) testified that in his opinion emotional instability was not a mental disease. The two psychiatrists who said the defendant had an emotionally unstable personality did not agree in their observations of the men, for example, regarding his memory. One psychiatrist made the following three statements: "[Defendant], in all probability, could not refrain from committing the alleged offenses." "We have no opinion as to the alleged offenses being a product of his mental condition or mental disease." "I don't know why he committed [the offenses]."[5] The

---

[5] Referring to the attempt of the Court of Appeals in Carter v. United States, 252 F.2d 608 (D.C. Cir. 1957) to clarify the meaning of "product" (at 616-617), the California Commission said: "The word 'product' has probably caused the most concern. . . . It is difficult to tell from the above definition whether the court meant that the mental illness must be merely *a* cause, the *principal* cause, or the *exclusive* cause of the defendant's having committed the act. The court's definition seems confusing and inconsistent. It really does not tell us what measure of casuality is required."—Calif. Special Commissions on Insanity and Criminal Offenses, First Report, 79 (1962). But is anything more definite possible? A century ago William Kingdon Clifford observed to the British Association for the Advancement of Science: "In asking what we mean by [cause] we have entered upon an appalling task. The word represented by 'cause' has 64 meanings in Plato and 48 in Aristotle. These were men who liked to know as near as might be what they meant; but how many meanings it has had in the writings of the myriads of people who have not tried to know what they mean by it will, I hope, never be counted."

jury must have an extremely difficult task with this testimony. An impossible one, in fact.

The question of psychopathy became as notorious in the District of Columbia as that of "emotionally unstable personality." The St. Elizabeths psychiatrists first considered psychopathy not a mental illness; but, in midstream, as it were (the famous week-end reversal),[6] it was decided that psychopathy *might* be a mental illness. Since the psychiatrists were up in the air about it, it was decided to leave it to the jury! The most difficult questions in psychiatric diagnosis—indeed, questions in psychiatric theory—are to be left to the obviously least competent—not the psychiatrists (the experts) or the judge (the trained arbiter), but the lay jury, the body so lauded for its democracy, so denigrated for its intellect.[7]

What this means is that the jury can decide in any case whether the defendant is suffering from a mental illness, but no one will know whether it decided that question because when it brings in its verdict it is also answering the equally mystifying

---

[6] Blocker v. U.S. 288 F. 2d 853 (1961), Burger concurring in result: "In [In re Rosenfield, 157 F. Supp. 18 (D.D.C. 1957)] a psychiatrist made it known to the District Court that between the court session on Friday and Monday morning, St. Elizabeths Hospital, by some process not then disclosed, altered its 'official' view that sociopathic or psychopathic personality disorder was *not* a mental disease. It had been decided that commencing Monday, St. Elizabeths Hospital and its staff would thereafter call and classify the condition known to them as 'psychopathic personality' as a 'mental disease' or 'mental disorder.'" To which Judge Burger adds this footnote comment: "This is reminiscent of Lewis Carroll's classic utterance: 'When *I* use a word,' Humpty Dumpty said, in rather a scornful tone, 'it means just what *I* choose it to mean—neither more nor less.'" Judge Bazelon said, "We have wrestled, for example, with whether we should permit psychopathy to be found by the jury to be a mental disease. And we have concluded that, problematic as the category is, this was one area where it was essential to leave to the jury the resolution of the conflicts between experts."—Equal Justice for the Unequal, Isaac Ray Lectureship Award Series of the American Psychiatric Assn., U. of Chic., lec. 1, p. 6 (1961). Campbell v. U. S., 307 F. 2d 597 (1962) involved a factual dispute between "alienists" as to whether "emotionally unstable personality" was a mental disease. The court noted that since November, 1957, St. Elizabeths Hospital has been regarding "emotionally unstable personality" as a "mental disease." "What seemed to be emerging under the Durham rule was that neither legal principles nor medical concepts determined the defendant's fate so much as did 'administrative label changing' by the hospital's staff."—Reid, The Bell Tolls for Durham, 6 J. of Offender Therapy 58 (1962).

[7] See the review by Bishop of Nizer, My Life in Court, in 72 Yale L. J. 618 (1963).

question of causation, to say nothing about the basic issue of facts regarding the commission of the crime. I can think of no better support for the proposition of Dr. Thomas S. Szasz that mental illness is a myth[8] than just such operation of the jury. With all due respect to an ancient institution, the jury should be left with fairly simple, clean cut problems, for its secret, esoteric process of decision making is, by common consensus, individualistic and not without a considerable element of irrationality.

Actually the jury is not being asked whether the defendant has a mental illness, although this assignment is given to it; and it is not being asked whether the mental illness (if any) was a cause of the commission of the crime, although this too is assigned to it. Since all of this, including the act itself, is being thrown into one package upon which the jury is to give a simple yes or no answer, the jury is really being asked whether the defendant should be *blamed* for the crime. We have given up the rule of law.[9]

The Durham court was influenced by the recommendation of

---

[8] Szasz, The Myth of Mental Illness (1961).

[9] Jerome Hall writes: "Much of the criticism [of M'Naghten] seems simply to ignore the importance of the rule of law—very likely because the principal effort of the critics has been to widen the definition of incapacity, to enlarge the area of exculpation. Even granting the validity of the purpose, the question remains how to achieve it without sacrificing the values of law. If no definition of 'insanity' is provided, may not a jury, instead of taking a wider view of psychosis, take a very narrow view? May not a vengeful prosecuting witness employ a psychiatrist who would testify, in effect, that only the most extreme psychotic is 'insane.' More likely, no doubt, the principal result of failure to provide a definition of serious mental disease would be to hospitalize many offenders who should be imprisoned. And this would tend to undermine the value of the rule of law, with its dual function of protecting society while it also protects individuals from abuse by the state. If people were convinced that the criminal law did not even try to cope with ordinary criminal conduct, they would act in ways that damaged both society and the legal safeguards of innocent people, defying the law or else taking it into their own hands."—Studies in Jurisprudence and Criminal Theory 275 (1958). And John Reid points out that the New Hampshire rule does not set inner limits as well as outer limits; under it a jury is not even bound to exculpate a defendant who does not know right from wrong. "And jurors being what they are the most valid criticism of the New Hampshire doctrine might be, not that it gives juries too great a license to exculpate, but that it gives them too great a license for holding mentally ill defendants responsible for their acts. It is significant that no prosecutor has been found in New Hampshire who criticizes the doctrine."—The Working of the New Hampshire Doctrine of Criminal Responsibility, 15 U. of Miami L. Rev. 14, 26 (1960).

the Royal Commission on Capital Punishment to abrogate the M'Naghten Rules and "to leave the jury to determine whether at the time of the act the accused was suffering from disease of the mind (or mental deficiency) to such a degree that he ought not to be held responsible."[10] Jerome Hall writes that it allows the psychiatrists to testify as they please:

> But what use would the testimony be to the jury, groping their way through a blizzard of scientific terminology and conflicting theories, without any guide to their objective? And how could there be any assurance at all of their reaching any sound, just objective?[11]

Lord Justice Devlin said:

> If a general question is to be left to them, why restrict it to sanity or insanity? Why not ask them in a general way whether the accused was responsible at all? Under our system the prosecution must allege and prove a definite crime. No one would suggest that the jury should be left with a general question whether the law has been broken or whether the prisoner should be punished or not. I believe that a general question on insanity would be just as objectionable. I think there is great force in the observation of the minority of the [Royal] Commission on this point at p. 286 where they say: "It is the traditional duty of our criminal law to lay down by definition, as clearly as possible, the essential elements of liability to conviction and punishment."[12]

As Jerome Hall says, the law should not change with every change in expert opinion; there is a need for stability, certainty, and predictability in the law. He cites this observation:

> Nor can we go to the other extreme and completely abandon all idea of legal formulation for this would result in a chaos of unpredictability and complete lack of stability. Each succeeding issue of the psychiatric journals that brought forth a new theory or a varied concept would then become the law. And the law would vary from journal to journal and from article to article.[13]

---

[10] Royal Commission on Capital Punishment 116 (1953), cited Hall, *op. cit. supra* n. 9, at 287.

[11] Hall, *op. cit. supra* n. 9 at 287-8.

[2] Criminal Responsibility and Punishment: Functions of Judge and Jury, I Crim. L. Rev. 661, at 683; cited Hall, *op cit. supra* n. 9 at 276, n. 28.

Such, in fact, is the reasoning of the state courts that have rejected Durham. The Indiana Supreme Court, for example, remained with M'Naghten because, it said, the Durham standard was too indefinite to lend itself to a clear jury instruction and would leave a juror to make a decision "according to his personal sense of justice." Under the Durham test, the court declared, "an accused could know the nature and quality of his act, and yet by reason of his mental disease, develop egocentric and sadistic tendencies which could produce homicide with criminal impunity."[14]

The huge effort to make the Durham decision "work"[15] is thought to have reached a milestone in *McDonald v. United States*,[16] in which the confusion of psychiatric theories presented to the lay jury is "resolved" by the decision that the jury is no longer bound by expert testimony, but "must determine for itself, from all the testimony, lay and expert, whether the nature and degree of disability are sufficient to establish a mental disease or defect." But this is hardly a rescue of Durham; rather, it would appear to be its wreckage. The Durham rule was thought to bring the psychiatric expert into his own, but now he is downgraded, made the equal of lay testimony. The jury becomes the expert, to decide not that expert views as applied to a set of facts have a certain effect, but to *be* the expert and decide whether a set of facts equals a mental illness or defect under the court's rules![17]

Other Related Rules[18]

Having examined the Durham rule and compared its operation with M'Naghten, we can deal briefly with several other related rules, in use or proposed—irresistible impulse, the rule in

---

[13] From Polsky, Application and Limits of Diminished Responsibility as a Legal and Medical Concept, in Hock & Zubin (eds.), Psychiatry and the Law 196, 198 (1955); Hall, *op. cit. supra* n. 9 at 276.

[14] Flowers v. Indiana, 139 N.E. 2d 185 (1956).

[15] "The Court of Appeals has issued more than eighty opinions since July 1954 relating to judicial administration of the insanity defense—an astonishing volume, unmatched by any other federal or state court." —Krash, The Durham Rule and Judicial Administration of the Insanity Defense in the District of Columbia, 70 Yale L.J. 905, at 906 (1961).

[16] McDonald v. United States, 312 F. 2d 847 (1962).

[17] See *supra* n. 6.

the *Currens* case in the Third Circuit federal Court of Appeals, and the rule in the American Law Institute Model Penal Code.

IRRESISTIBLE IMPULSE

"Irresistible impulse" has long been an exculpatory defense, usually added to M'Naghten, in many states and in the federal courts. It provides that even if the defendant has the understanding required by M'Naghten, he will be relieved of the consequences of his criminal act if he suffered from such a "diseased mental condition" as to create in his mind an uncontrollable impulse to commit the offense charged. In the federal statement, a defendant is not criminally responsible if "his reasoning powers were so far dethroned by his diseased mental condition as to deprive him of the will power to resist the insane impulse to perpetrate the deed, though knowing it to be wrong."[19]

The questions one would ask, as we have asked of Durham, are these: Is "irresistible impulse" a therapeutically sound rule? How may it be valued ethically? Does it provide a practical test that can be given a jury?

Is it helpful for a man who has committed a criminal act to be morally excused?[20] On this point criticism of the irresistible impulse test is not different from the criticism of mental disease in exculpation, for it is similar to mental illness. Perhaps "irresistible impulse" can be said to be a product of an unidentified mental process, if not illness. Similarly, in practical terms the civil commitment of a defendant excused for irresistible impulse is far more akin to a defendant excused under Durham than a defendant excused under M'Naghten.

---

[18] Other formulations are also brought forth. *E.g.*, The Committee on Psychiatry and Law of the Group for the Advancement of Psychiatry proposes this draft for incorporation in a statute: "No person may be convicted of any criminal charge when at the time he committed the act with which he is charged he was suffering with mental illness as defined by this Act, and in consequence thereof, he committed the act."—Criminal Responsibility and Psychiatric Expert Testimony, Report No. 26 (1954). Glueck, Law and Psychiatry: Cold War or Entente Cordiale (1962) has another proposal.

[19] Smith v. United States, 36 F. 2d 548 (App. D.C. 1930), 70 A.L.R. 659; Pollard v. United States, 282 F. 2d 450 (6 Cir. 1960); Keedy, Irresistible Impulse as a Defense in the Criminal Law, 100 U. Pa. L. Rev. 956 (1952).

[20] *Supra*, ch. 1.

The same is readily recognized for the answer to the moral judgment.

And as for the problem given to the jury, although irresistible impulse is somewhat simpler than Durham (it presents a general idea of ability to act in a certain fashion, rather than the difficult question of whether a defendant is suffering from a mental illness or defect) it is still involved in the problem of causation (not present in M'Naghten).[21]

It has also been said that the rule lacks clarity:

> The rule does not clearly distinguish between that conduct which it is the very purpose of the criminal law to deter—the flash of smouldering rage, the shocked desire to gain revenge—and that which the criminal law cannot deter because the particular offender is not responsible to the threats of punishment. The word "impulse" suggests that no one, no matter what his state of mental health, could resist the tendency to do the criminal act.
>
> Beyond this, the formula implies that the offender's mental condition underwent some sort of sudden change just before he committed the offense, whereas accepted medical opinion is that mental disorder making the defendant incapable of controlling his conduct is ordinarily a long-developing condition of his whole personality system.
>
> Furthermore, sound application of the concept has been confused by the trial tactic that is sometimes used, in which it is asked whether the defendant would have done the act if a policeman had been standing at his side. This is completely irrelevant, for the question with respect to criminal accountability is whether the person is capable of *self*-control in stress situations.
>
> Finally, the traditional formula, because of its ambiguities, is an invitation to the jury to avoid applying the criminal law, thereby tolerating the defendant's taking the law into his own hands.[22]

This is especially so in homicide cases, where "it is a standard ideally suited for use in acquitting the killer who has the jurors' sympathies, whether he is the mercy killer, the outraged spouse

---

[21] Hall, *op. cit. supra* n. 9, 283-7.
[22] California Commissions, *op. cit. supra* n. 5 at 25.

who kills on finding his mate *flagrante delicto*, or the justifiably aggrieved defendant who kills in the blindness of a righteous vengeance."[23] Perhaps these are, in fact, sympathetic cases, but sympathy would not ordinarily go so far as to excuse the killer. Again, this issue of capital punishment has entered, and in this regard irresistible impulse may be ameliorative,[24] but otherwise it has evident defects.

UNITED STATES V. CURRENS

Chief Judge Biggs wrote the opinion of the United States Court of Appeals for the Third Circuit in the *Currens* case, which, rejecting both M'Naghten and Durham, held that "the jury must be satisfied that at the time of committing the prohibited act the defendant, as a result of mental disease or defect, lacked substantial capacity to conform his conduct to the requirements of the law which he is alleged to have violated." This formula is drawn, as Judge Biggs said in a footnote, from the test proposed to the American Law Institute in its Model Penal Code, but it eliminates the Model Code's other test that the defendant lacked substantial capacity "to appreciate the criminality of his conduct." Judge Biggs noted also that his test is similar to the one proposed in England by the Royal Commission on Capital Punishment, which, he said, borrowed it from the British Medical Association.[25]

One commentator points out that *Currens* omits one of the faults of *Durham*: "*Currens* is superior to *Durham*, if for no other reason, because it omits the troublesome 'product' clause of both the *Durham* and the New Hampshire rules."[26] But it seems also to drop out *mens rea*,[27] as *Durham* does, with the

---

[23] Kuh, The Insanity Defense—An Effort to Combine Law and Reason, 110 U. of Pa. L. Rev. 771 (1962).

[24] *Supra*, ch. 1, p. 18 et seq.

[25] United States v. Currens, 290 F. 2d 751 (1961).

[26] Diamond, From M'Naghten to Currens and Beyond, 50 Calif. L. Rev. 189 (1962).

[27] California Commissions, *op. cit. supra* n. 5, minority report of Leo R. Friedman: "An inspection of the *Currens* rule as adopted by the majority of the [California] commissioners raises grave doubts that the rule as promulgated bears any resemblance to the law that a crime must consist of both an act and a criminal intent. In fact, the rule as adopted will in many cases eliminate criminal intent as part of the commission of a crime. The rule as adopted reads as follows: 'A person is not criminally responsible

consequences already discussed. In its place, it constructs a mental illness test that is different from *Durham* in appearance, and perhaps in effect, though that would remain to be seen.[28] Still it is, like *Durham*, a mental illness test, occasioning another critic to say:

> It is all a question of fact to be decided by the jury as to what constitutes insanity. This is tantamount to telling the jury or the general public to make up their own definition of what an elephant is. A zoologist may testify before the jury as to what he thinks an elephant is, but in the final analysis it is the jury that decides what the definition should be. By comparison, the District of Columbia phrases its elephant definition in terms of the great big tracks in the mud, by which a beast may be identified; and now the Third Circuit, perhaps, simply identifies elephants by their trunks.[29]

THE AMERICAN LAW INSTITUTE'S MODEL PENAL CODE

The American Law Institute's Model Penal Code is a restatement, sometimes a reformulation, of many common crimes. It

---

for an act if, at the time of the commission of such act, as a substantial consequence of mental disorder, he did not have adequate capacity to conform his conduct to the requirements of the law which he is alleged to have violated.' There is nothing in the proposed rule that makes it mandatory that the actor entertain a criminal intent. An inspection of the rule demonstrates that it contains no such provision."—*Id.* at 63. And see the statement of Judge Biggs (author of the *Currens* opinion) quoted *supra* n. 1.

[28] "The further provision in the proposed rule that 'he did not have adequate capacity to conform his conduct to the requirements of the law,' likewise is vague, indefinite and uncertain. What is meant by ability to conform one's conduct to the requirements of the law? Does this mean the person must have the knowledge that there is a criminal statute he is about to violate? Does this phrase incorporate the doctrine of irresistible impulse which time after time has been rejected by our State Supreme Court? It certainly is susceptible to such a construction. Where is there any standard by which to judge whether one's conduct conforms to the requirements of a law? The proposed rule contains no such standard. In other words, the proposed rule, if adopted, will merely open the door to uncertainty and confusion in its application. Every judge, every court and every lawyer will be able to give a different interpretation to the provisions of the rule. Instead of simplifying the matter, it will require dozens of decisions by our Appellate and Supreme Court before anyone can know just what constitutes a mental disorder that renders one irresponsible for an otherwise criminal act."—Friedman, *op. cit. supra* n. 27 at 64.

[29] Mueller, M'Naghten Remains Irreplaceable: Recent Events in the Law of Incapacity, 50 Georgetown L.J. 105 (1961).

also includes a proposed system of sentencing and correctional services.[30] In its sections on criminal responsibility it proposes a statute in place of the existing common law rules, the main part of which reads as follows:

> 1. A person is not responsible for criminal conduct if at the time of such conduct as a result of mental disease or defect he lacks substantial capacity either to appreciate the criminality [wrongfulness] of his conduct or to conform his conduct to the requirements of law.
> 2. As used in this Article, the terms "mental disease or defect" do not include an abnormality manifested only by repeated criminal or otherwise anti-social conduct.

The bracketed word "wrongfulness" is so put in the Model Code, offering an alternative word to the legislature.[31]

Most of the definition is similar to *Currens* and was influential with the Third Circuit Court. It also includes language in the alternative allowing the M'Naghten defense—"lacks substantial capacity either to appreciate the criminality [wrongfulness] of his conduct or . . ." With respect to the *Currens*-like language, it is subject to the same comment made above. With respect to the inclusion of a M'Naghten-type alternative, it is questionable whether the language is an improvement. Sheldon Glueck, for example, asks, "How substantial is 'substantial'?"[32] And Dr. Overholser comments, "I am not sure that a psychiatrist is competent to pass on whether or not the accused has 'adequate capacity' to appreciate the criminality or to conform his conduct."[33]

---

30 Wechsler, The American Law Institute: Some Observations on its Model Penal Code, 42 A.B.A. J. 321 (1956). An adverse comment—Rubin, Sentencing and Correctional Treatment Under the Law Institute's Model Penal Code, 46 A.B.A.J. 994 (1960).

31 Model Penal Code, Proposed Official Draft § 4.01 (1962).

32 Gueck, *op. cit. supra* n. 18 at 22.

33 Overholser, Criminal Responsibility: A Psychiatrist's Viewpoint, 48 A.B.A.J. 527 at 530 (1962). He notes: "I have some reservations, to put it mildly, concerning the American Law Institute formulation of criminal irresponsibility. The formulation appears to me to be a combination of the M'Naghten rule ('capacity to appreciate the criminality') and the irresistible impulse test ('conform his conduct to the requirements of law'). This formulation met the approval of the majority of the committee and has been adopted by the Institute; it is a fact, however, that all three of the psychiatric consultants on the committee take exception to it. I am not

The Model Penal Code proposal to exclude from the term "mental disease or defect" any "abnormality manifested only by repeated criminal or otherwise anti-social conduct" has come in for strong criticism. Dr. Overholser said:

> The notion that there is a "mental abnormality manifested only by repeated criminal or otherwise anti-social conduct" is, however, unpsychiatric. There is no such entity, even though the proposed Model Penal Code of the American Law Institute purports to exclude persons with a diagnosis of sociopathic personality. There are many criminals who are not sociopaths, but the sociopath who comes into conflict with the law has numerous symptoms in addition to his anti-social behavior, and is decidedly a mentally sick man. . . . Subsection (2) of 4.01, which purports to exclude sociopathic personality from the definition of mental disease or defect, fails to do so because the sociopath has many other symptoms than the mere anti-social behavior.[34]

Dr. Diamond wrote:

> Such special restrictive clauses aimed at excluding certain specified categories of individuals from exculpation simply do not make any psychiatric sense. They are as arbitrary and capricious as excluding defendants with red hair or blue eyes or Negro blood from the benefits of the law of criminal responsibility. They define by legislative fiat what is and what is not a psychiatric condition. Further, they grossly discriminate against the poor. In practically every case where the crime itself, or alcoholism or drug addiction, is supposedly the only evidence of mental disease, a skilled, competent, and interested psychiatrist who spends sufficient time could discover other manifestations of mental abnormality sufficient to exculpate under the ALI or Maine rules. But the routine case, superficially examined by court-appointed psychiatrists devoting a wholly inadequate time to the study of the defendant, would seldom end in acquittal.[35]

---

sure that a psychiatrist is competent to pass on whether or not the accused has 'adequate capacity' to appreciate the criminality or to conform his conduct."

[34] *Ibid.*

[35] Diamond, *op. cit. supra* n. 26, at 194.

Richard H. Kuh wrote:

> This provision may be the source of great difficulties. Not only is it unlikely that any psychiatrist would base his diagnosis of the criminal psychopath—the intended object of the ALI proviso—solely on criminal or anti-social conduct, but, even in the face of such diagnosis, the proviso might be ineffective both because it would be impossible for the defense of insanity, supported largely by evidence of prior crimes, to be denied as a matter of law, and because the prosecutor's invocation of the proviso with an offer to prove a history of similar prior crimes would be met with a probably effective objection that the evidence was inadmissible because of its prejudicial effect.[36]

The contention over the rule or rules of criminal responsibility has been and is being fought in the courts rather than in the legislatures. That is, the process of common law evolution has been permitted to occur, without the intervention of legislative prescription. Probably those who consider the existing rules more or less adequate, especially if they do not see a legislative substitute that is definitely superior, wish the evolutionary course to remain in the courts. Although penal codes do contain definitions of responsibility, they are restatements of M'Naghten and they have been thus interpreted.

To interpose different legislative rules runs the risk of enacting faulty rules—*vide*, the criticism of the Model Code proposal—and, in a rule of this kind, invites chaos. If a legislature can define mental illness in dogmatic terms (as the Model Code proposes with respect to sociopaths), it thus utterly defeats the very purpose of the reformers of the rules of responsibility: it rejects rather than embraces psychiatry. It is legislative rather than scientific psychiatry. And what if a legislature likes the general pattern of the model but changes a few words?[37] Is the model still model?

---

[36] Kuh, *op. cit. supra* n. 23 at 799.

[37] The Vermont legislature working from the Model Penal Code draft, adds that "the terms 'mental disease or defect' shall include congenital and traumatic conditions as well as disease" and it substitutes "adequate" capacity for "substantial" capacity.—Vermont Public Acts, 1957, Act 228. The Maine legislature in 1961 enunciated this rule: "An accused is not

criminally responsible if his unlawful act was the product of mental disease or mental defect. *The terms 'mental disease' or 'mental defect' do not include an abnormality manifested only by repeated criminal conduct or excessive use of drugs or alcohol"* (our ital.); Rev. Stats. ch. 149 § 17-B. Illinois had adopted the ALI form with slight changes—Ill. Crim. Code, Rev. Stat. (1961) ch. 38 § 6.2; as did Missouri in 1963—Rev. Stats. of Missouri § 552.010 et seq. (Laws of 1963, S.B. 143).

Chapter 4

Why the Durham Rule

Dr. Winfred Overholser, superintendent of Saint Elizabeths Hospital in the District of Columbia, said: "An interesting study could be made, perhaps, of the psychology of the reasons why the M'Naghten rule has appeared to be almost immortal in spite of all the psychiatric progress that has been made in the last 117 years."[1] The study would not be difficult, since so many courts rejecting Durham have spoken out clearly on the question (and writers have also, although more writers than courts lean to Durham).

What we have suggested in the foregoing chapters is that M'Naghten survives because it works. Dr. Overholser implies that M'Naghten is outmoded and that only irrational or unconscious reasons sustain it (aside from the inertial force exerted by any existing social institution). There is no doubt that his suggested study would be a useful one and should be made.

Perhaps a study of equal interest could be made of the psychology of the reasons why the Durham rule has appealed to certain groups. Let us explore it.

---

[1] Overholser, Criminal Responsibility: A Psychiatrist's Viewpoint, 48 A.B.A.J. 527 (1962).

What Is underneath Durham?

The Durham position is basically a highly ethical one: we do not wish to blame or punish sick people for their behavior. Unfortunately, in the context in which Durham has been raised it is inconsistent and impractical; but it is moral (or is it moralistic?) in orientation. Also, by embracing psychiatry in relation to criminal behavior and treatment of sick offenders, the position is modern and scientific in style. (Although we say it is modern in style, the formulation of the Durham rule is actually no more modern than M'Naghten. Both drew on the same climate of behavioral knowledge; both specifically related to the same work of Isaac Ray, whose influential *Medical Jurisprudence of Insanity* was published in 1838. The M'Naghten decision was handed down in 1843).[2]

Geoffrey Gorer[3] has pointed out that in most European countries psychoanalysis retains many of the features of a "cult" movement, in contrast to the United States, where acceptance of psychoanalysis is widespread. He conjectures that a partial explanation for this difference might lie in the extent to which Americans have made good health a moral imperative. It is our belief, he says, that "any white baby born in the United States is born good" and that psychoanalysis can explain the failure of any person to achieve his potential goodness, health, and happiness.

---

[2] "It is stated frequently that the rules of M'Naghten's case reflected the status of psychiatric knowledge of that day, but in fact such is not the case. When Cockburn defended Daniel M'Naghten, he frequently referred to a treatise on criminal insanity written by the eminent American psychiatrist, Isaac Ray. . . . To a very considerable extent Ray's views reflected concepts of mental function essentially dynamic in character. . . . Isaac Ray influenced another important opinion through his close correspondence with Justice Doe of the New Hampshire Supreme Court, which handed down State v. Pike in 1870 (49 N.H. 399). Also State v. Jones, 50 N.H. 369 [1871]). . . . This early precursor of *Durham* used similar language to its modern counterpart. Merely on the face of this fact, it can hardly be contended that *Durham* exceeds the status of current psychiatric knowledge. It merely catches up with knowledge well known at the time of the *M'Naghten* and *Pike* opinions."—Watson, Durham Plus Five Years: Development of the Law of Criminal Responsibility in the District of Columbia, Am. J. of Psych., October 1959.

[3] Gorer, Are We "By Freud Obsessed"? New York Times Magazine, July 30, 1961.

> It would seem [says Gorer] that very many Americans welcome the notion that individuals are not to blame for their own misfortunes: the unsuccessful, the neurotic, the delinquent, the battle-fatigued are that way because the breaks went against them, because they weren't treated right, because they were underprivileged. The popular versions of psychoanalysis made rationalizations of this notion available, and thus give people "scientific" explanations for aberrant behavior. Dr. Sheldon pointed out more than a decade ago that most young criminals in Boston could reel off their own diagnosis in psychoanalytic jargon—jargon they had learned from well-meaning social workers. The song in *West Side Story*, "Gee, Officer Krupke," suggests that this ability is still believed to be common.

Gorer was not writing about the Durham rule, and I suppose it was not in his mind at all. Yet is not the foregoing—removal of the blame from people because of causative factors they did not control, and the popularization of psychoanalytic concepts— quite applicable to an understanding of the sources of Durham? (Perhaps Durham is also an application of the Jacksonian concept that any citizen is equal to any responsibility, here attributing to the jury the powers of judgment regarding mental illness and theories of mental illness about which the psychiatrists do not agree.) The Durham decision makers may have been misled by sympathy for sick people and affinity for the field of psychiatry.

Is There a Propaganda Drive for Forensic Psychiatry?

Assuming that the culture of the United States is more receptive to psychiatry than is the culture of Europe, is this perhaps not a good thing? Whether it is or not depends on the answer to this question: Are the *claims* of forensic psychiatry in advance of psychiatric *knowledge?* Professor Jerome Hall, with full awareness of its relationship to the advocacy of the Durham rule, makes this statement:

> It is a curious and thought-provoking fact that in no other country in the world has psychiatry assumed the gargantuan proportions attained in the United States.

Nor is the propaganda of rich psychiatric institutions carried on elsewhere to any degree remotely approaching that in this country.[4]

So far as I know, the best brief documentation on this subject is an article entitled "A Critique of the Psychiatric Approach to Crime and Correction," by Professor of Sociology Michael Hakeem.[5]

Psychiatrists [charges Hakeem] have been engaged for a long time in a relentless and extensive campaign to extend the scope and power of their influence in the administration of justice, in the disposition of offenders, and in the policies and practices of correctional institutions and agencies. This campaign has now reached reckless and irresponsible proportions, and there has been resort to questionable tactics. Unseemly as it may appear, the profession of psychiatry has even gone so far as to bestow prizes, honors, and unabashed flattery upon judges who have handed down decisions that it views as favorable to its cause. And, in the service of this campaign, psychiatrists have produced a prodigious literature, much of which is propagandistic in nature. It is characterized by incautious and immodest effusions, misrepresentation, extraordinary contributions, flagrant illogicalities, grossly-exaggerated claims, biased selection of data, serious errors of fact and interpretation, ignorance of the distinction between scientific questions and value judgments, lack of sophistication in research methodology, tautological trivialities presented in the guise of technical profundities, and language, subject matter, and procedures not bearing the slightest resemblance to anything medical.[6]

---

[4] Hall, The Scientific and Humane Study of Criminal Law, 42 Boston U. L. Rev. 267 (1962).

[5] Symposium on Crime and Correction, Law and Contemporary Problems (Autumn 1958).

[6] Almost all of the recipients of the Isaac Ray Awards, given annually by the American Psychiatric Association, have been outspoken opponents of M'Naghten. Judge Bazelon, one of the Isaac Ray Award winners, in 1957 received a certificate of commendation reading in part: "In this achievement [Durham decision] he has removed massive barriers between the psychiatric and legal professions and opened pathways wherein together they may search for better ways of reconciling human values with social safety."

The sweeping language of this statement is supported by numerous psychiatric statements quoted by Hakeem. He continues:

Some psychiatrists have insisted that they are still greatly hampered in their forensic work by certain traditional concepts, procedures, and laws governing the prosecution and disposition of offenders, and they have furiously assailed these restraining formalities. They hold that many of the basic tenets of American jurisprudence, which are designed to protect the rights of offenders, and many of the limitations on administrative discretion in the handling of offenders are "stupid" and should yield to make way for psychiatric knowledge. They argue that the law frustrates their desire to deal with offenders in ways they deem best. Menninger puts the general idea as follows: "The scientific attitude as shown in psychiatry must sooner or later totally displace existing legal methods."[7] And he hurls this further challenge: "Must the lawyers still continue solemnly to apply medieval stupidities in the name of 'established precedent,' 'public policy,' and other mouthy archaisms?"[8]

Psychiatrists are quoted urging that the presumption of sanity should be discarded. Dr. Overholser called it that "hoary old legal dogma."[9] Poindexter proposed that the law should replace the presumption of sanity with the presumption of insanity.[10] (The Durham decision goes far along this path.)[11]

Hakeem points out that much of the propaganda has been directed toward the identification of criminality and delinquency as an illness. "The medical journals," he says, "have been carrying an increasing number of articles on delinquency and crime" as medical problems. He cites such an article, "Medical Responsibility for Juvenile Delinquency," by Dr. Blackman.[12] "It contained the usual rebuke of the law for not implementing

---

[7] Menninger, The Human Mind 448-9 (1945).

[8] *Id.* at 449.

[9] Overholser, The Place of Psychiatry in the Criminal Law, 16 B.U.L. Rev. 322, 329 (1936).

[10] Poindexter, Mental Illness in a State Penitentiary, 45 J. Crim. L., C. & P.S. 559, 562 (1955).

[11] *Supra*, p. 38 et. seq.

[12] Blackman, Medical Responsibility for Juvenile Delinquency, 10 Postgrad. Med. 499 (1951).

psychiatric preachments about delinquency, along with an admonition to all who deal with this problem to accept medical concepts regarding it." He cites Eugene Davidoff and Elinor S. Noetzel's *The Child Guidance Approach to Juvenile Delinquency* to the same effect,[13] and other sources could be added to his list.[14]

Does this material seem extreme? We shall presently refer to and quote from an opinion of Judge Burger, a member of the United States Court of Appeals for the District of Columbia circuit, in much the same vein.[15]

Here are other references Hakeem has gathered:

Seliger: "The whole problem of criminality or criminology is in the field of human behavior psychopathology, the understanding of which requires medical and psychiatric training."[16] Dr. Karl A. Menninger: "The modern surgical operating amphitheater developed out of dirty public barber-shops. The physicians took surgery away from the barbers a century ago; now they are taking criminology away from jailers and politicians."[17] Gregory Zilboorg and George W. Henry: "Criminology today, like demonology of yesterday, is a battlefield for the rightful possession of which the psychiatrist is still fighting."[18] Eveoleen N. Rexford: delinquents are "seriously sick children."[19] Ruth S. Eissler: "knowledge of psychopathology" is the "only means of preventing crime."[20] George J. Mohr and Marian A. Despres, listing delinquency along with "neurosis, psychosis, and psychosomatic illness" as mental illness.[21] A report of the House of Representatives, reflecting the testimony given by psychiatrists, subsuming delinquency under mental illness.[22] Glueck, in an article "Changing Concepts in Forensic Psychiatry," that some

[13] Davidoff & Noetzel, The Child Guidance Approach to Juvenile Delinquency 150 (1951).

[14] *E.g.*, Bovet, Psychiatric Aspects of Juvenile Delinquency (1951); Peck & Bellsmith, Treatment of the Delinquent Adolescent (1954).

[15] Blocker v. United States, 288 F.2d 853 (1961), *infra* p. 85.

[16] Seliger, Federal Probation, January 1946, p. 16, 19.

[17] *Op. cit. supra* n. 7, at 451.

[18] Zilboorg & Henry, A History of Medical Psychology 419 (1941).

[19] Eveoleen N. Rexford, in Douglas A. Thom Clinic for Children, Inc., Ann. Rep. 17 (1956).

[20] Ruth S. Eissler, Scapegoats of Society, in Eissler (ed.), Searchlights on Delinquency 304 (1949).

[21] Mohr & Despres, The Stormy Decade: Adolescence 210 (1958).

[22] Health Inquiry, H.R. Rep. No. 1338, 83d Cong., 2d Sess. 123 (1954).

of the knotty legal issues in criminal responsibility would be eased if crime were viewed as a sickness and not as a moral transgression.[23] Karpman: "The *Archives* [*of Criminal Psychodynamics*] will fight vigorously for the recognition of criminal psychiatry. It will fight for the recognition of the criminal as a very sick person, much sicker than either psychosis or neurosis."[24] Balint: "Using medical terms delinquency can be described as a very widespread illness, affecting mainly young people and causing gross symptoms [in certain proportions of this population].... Mild cases usually are treated at home. ... The illness, on the whole, is benign. Unfortunately [after recovery, in certain proportions of cases] it is followed by relapses. The illness then takes a prolonged course but even then in most cases heals off."[25] Bowlby: "Theft, like rheumatic fever, is a disease of childhood and adolescence, and, as in rheumatic fever, attacks in later life are frequently in the nature of recurrences."[26] Tarrasch: "When a patient goes to the hospital with a physical illness, he receives medication and therapy directed specifically to his ailment. ... We send our children to correctional institutions to be treated for an illness."[27]

Sometimes the theme is not only that crime is a medical problem, with the law standing in the way of psychiatrists dealing with it as such, but also that crime itself, without anything else, is sufficient evidence of illness. Hakeem cites: Dr. Ralph S. Banay: "Just as symptoms of physical illness are danger signals that call for remedial measures, a criminal act, in a high percentage of cases, is a signal of psychological distress and a natural appeal for remedy."[28] Louis Linn: "It is becoming increasingly apparent that chronic incorrigible criminal behavior is symptomatic of mental diseases."[29] Menninger: "The time will

---

[23] Dr. Bernard C. Glueck, Changing Concepts in Forensic Psychiatry, 45 J. Crim. L., C. & P.S. 123, 127 (1954).

[24] Karpman, Criminal Psychodynamics: A Platform, 3 Arch. Crim. Psychodyn. 96 (1955).

[25] Balint, On Punishing Offenders, in Wilbur & Muensterberger (eds.), Psychoanalysis and Culture 254, 266 (1951).

[26] Bowlby, Forty-Four Juvenile Thieves: Their Characters and Home-Life, 25 Intl. J. Psycho-Anal. 19 (1944).

[27] Tarrasch, Delinquency Is Normal Behavior, 29 Focus 97, 101 (1950).

[28] Banay, We Call Them Criminals 6 (1957).

[29] Linn, A Handbook of Hospital Psychiatry 331 (1955).

come when stealing or murder will be thought of as a symptom, indicating the presence of a disease, a personality disease, if you will."[30] Benjamin Karpman: "One may hope that a day will come when the very fact of having committed a crime will be regarded as evidence of a mental disease."[31] The American Medical Association went on record in support of the view that a diagnosis of mental disease is permissible "even when the criminal has shown no evidence of mental disease other than his criminal behavior."[32]

Hakeem cites other psychiatrists who assert that *all* criminals are mentally ill, or that crime is a sign of mental illness. One psychiatrist thinks that all offenders show traits differentiating them from nonoffenders;[33] Karpman maintains that all criminals are mentally ill or abnormal;[34] Abrahamsen says that "the 'normal' offender is a myth";[35] another doctor says that "One does not expect anti-social conduct from normally constituted individuals."[36] Dr. Banay says that "every criminal has a defective personality."[37]

How much of such thinking entered into the Durham decision?

An actual examination [Hakeem writes] item by item, of the citations in the *Durham* decision will show the complete absence of any reference to "technical medical literature" and will show that practically all the psychiatric citations are to the propagandistic literature whose defects have already been noted. Most of this literatue contains nothing medical and practically nothing psychiatric. It contains mainly pleas and proposals,

[30] Menninger, Medicolegal Proposals of the American Psychiatric Association, 19 J. Crim. L. & Criminology 367, 373 (1928).

[31] Karpman, The Sexual Offender and His Offenses 218 (1954).

[32] Psychiatry in Relation to Crime, 95 A.M.A.J. 346 (1930).

[33] Henderson, Psychopathic Constitution and Criminal Behaviour, in Radzinowicz & Turner (eds.), Mental Abnormality and Crime 106 (English Studies in Criminal Science No. 2, 1944).

[34] *Op. cit. supra* n. 31, at 562.

[35] Abrahamsen, Who Are the Guilty? 125 (1952).

[36] Peskin, The Modern Approach to Legal Responsibility, The Psychopath and the M'Naghten Rules, 1 Forensic Med. 189, 191 (1954).

[37] Banay, Crime and Aftermath: Results of a Research on the Individual Offender, National Probation and Parole Association, 1948 Yearbook 35 (1949).

based in no small measure on the value judgments of psychiatrists, for changes in the laws, in criminal trial procedures, and in correctional policies.

Propaganda—or education on behalf of a sound position? Hakeem says the Durham decision is biased—that is, one-sided in its use of sources. In fact, the views set forth by which Hakeem calls the propagandists are not accepted by all the profession of psychiatry; far from it. For example: although a statement of Karl A. Menninger was cited among the propagandistic remarks, he also has said that it is "an open professional secret" that psychiatrists do not know how to treat offenders. He also concedes that they cannot predict the possible dangerousness of offenders, and he points out that psychiatrists are not available for such work or for doing research on the problem.[38] Hakeem cites a number of authorities, leading to the judgment that "one arrives at the unmistakable conclusion that psychiatric diagnosis is grossly unreliable, is beset by numerous unsolved complexities, and is, in fact, in a state of chaos."[39] "Ironically enough," he notes, "on the very eve of the *Durham* decision, no less a source than the *American Journal of Psychiatry* editorially took

---

[38] Menninger, Book Review, 38 Iowa L. Rev. 697, 701-2 (1953).

[39] And other sources: Report of the 1951 annual meeting of the American Psychopathological Assn., from Hoch & Zubin (eds.), Current Problems in Psychiatric Diagnosis, various authors making such statements as—the concept of psychosis is not "definable" and is fallacious; schizophrenia means many different things to different people; extensive confusion exists in diagnosis; there is no agreement on psychodynamics among the different schools of thought, resulting in complete confusion in diagnosis; the personality and biases of the psychiatrist may influence his choice of a diagnostic label; looseness and ambiguity in the terms used; in military situations, psychiatrists may deliberately make invalid diagnoses in order to comply with administrative exigencies rather than medical dictates; etc. He cites Thorne, Psychiatric Responsibilities in the Administration of Criminal Justice, 2 Arch. Crim. Psychodyn. 226, 236 (1957), "Diagnostic judgments are currently so invalid and unrealiable that little weight should be attached to them." Ginsburg, The Neuroses, 286 Annals 55 (1953), that in contrast to the physical diseases, the existence of which can be determined on the basis of "a recognizable syndrome" and by the use of certain devices and tests, "in emotional and mental illnesses this is almost never the case; even in the so-called major mental and emotional illnesses, such guides to detection and diagnosis are almost entirely lacking." And Hoch, The Etiology and Epidemiology of Schizophrenia, 47 Am. J. Pub. Health 1071 (1957), "While other fields of medicine can augment or even verify clinical diagnoses by other methods—by tests that are independent of the clinical appraisal of the patient—this is generally not true in psychiatry."

to task those psychiatrists who were attacking the existing rules and laws of criminal responsibility and urging their abrogation. The editorial took the position that these psychiatrists had not presented convincing evidence that psychiatry had made the advances claimed by them and on the basis of which they were demanding changes in the laws."[40]

But it is not at all surprising that the propagandists carry their message with more vim than the skeptics. The latter must tend to soft-pedal what in effect is a position that undercuts acceptance of their own profession. As for the audiences that might hear them, it is equally not surprising that they are far readier to accept the idea of success, of psychiatry as science, than the opposite.

Hakeem's article, which brings together discordant opinions of psychiatrists, comments that psychiatry is a field of inadequately developed knowledge, a judgment which would be true, more or less, for all the professions dealing with people. Consider the following statement from the field of social work:

> Obviously, most practitioners would feel reassured if they knew that the knowledge base of their practice was sufficient to guarantee that well-trained professional persons would likely make the same kind of decision when confronted with a choice-point in the practice situation. This, however, is hardly a realistic expectation, considering the lack of research-based knowledge in many of the areas in which these reliability studies are taking place. Why should uniformity in decision-making be expected when the knowledge base has not been subjected to systematic research procedures?[41]

This appears to be the situation, in psychiatry as well as in social work. It is wish fulfillment to shape the law in relation to psychiatry as though psychiatry were the science it is not. Psychiatry can be used sensibly in penal law, and we shall discuss such use of it in later chapters. But it does appear that Durham is the product of a propaganda drive by forensic psychiatry and that Durham gave them what they wanted[42] with the results we have previously pointed out.

---

[40] Criminal Irresponsibility, 110 Am. J. Psych. 627, 628 (1954).

[41] Fanshel, Research in Child Welfare: A Critical Analysis, Child Welfare, December 1962, 484, at 496.

[42] Fortas, Implications of Durham's Case, 113 Am. J. Psych. 577 (1957).

Durham—An Authoritarian Rule?

We have said that Durham and related rules break away from the law to give a new reliance to a particular group of experts. The expertness of the psychiatrist, in the application of his special concept of causation, takes the place of the former requirement of the law, *mens rea*. With the psychiatrist placed in this position, the entire problem of criminal responsibility is taken out of the law and placed in the hands of the psychiatrist and the jury. It is not surprising to see the psychiatrist dominate the jury; it is the concept of the Durham rule that he should.

Are Durham advocates authority-minded? And what if they are? Do we not rely on experts for many things? And should we not rely on experts more and more? Must we not, as our society becomes more complex? Certainly recent decades have seen an emergence of new thinking about human behavior. Must we not turn to the practitioners in this new art?[43]

Dr. Thomas S. Szasz discusses the decision that held Ezra Pound incompetent to be tried for treason:

> It may be asked, "What can be the objections against showing kindness to Mr. Pound?" as was allegedly done by not bringing him to trial. Is this not a "fair"way to treat the so-called mentally ill criminal? The basic objection . . . is that the social sanctions which *are* employed in such cases violate the principles of the Open Society[44] by substituting for the Rule of Law the Rule of Men. If this violation of the Rule of Law is engendered by the humanistic wish to act kindly toward those who break the laws, then it is committed unnecessarily, for trial and, in case of guilt, conviction of offenders in no way prevents us from dealing with them in a manner consistent with our ideas of decency and kindness.[45]

It is not the insanity defense that substitutes the authoritarian psychiatrist for the rule of law. M'Naghten does not; it is the Durham rule that does. It does it by substituting the vagueness of mental illness and causation, all to be determined by the psychiatrist, for *mens rea,* the criminal intent that can be detected by the average man sitting on a jury.

---

43 "Art"; although the Durham decision calls it "science."

44 Popper, The Open Society and Its Enemies (1945).

45 Szasz, Politics and Mental Health, 115 Am. J. Psych. 508 (1958).

Are Durham advocates authority-minded? The operation of the Durham decision substitutes authority for law. Dr. Diamond reports that psychiatrists have testified, under oath, that a defendant was sane and mentally normal when they had absolute medical evidence to the contrary, because they believed "the defendant was too dangerous to be allowed to escape execution."[46] And he himself claimed that he had saved the life of a woman by "perjuring" himself in the other direction, testifying to her insanity.[47] "But perjury can be committed by any witness." The difference is that law governs other legal situations; under Durham, authority takes the place of law, and law no longer governs. It extends the power of psychiatrists to testify according to their conclusion that a man ought to be condemned or ought not to be.

Pragmatism and Humanitarianism

Pragmatism comes as naturally to Americans as Freudianism. It is probably typical that the argument on behalf of M'Naghten is that "it works." But the argument that I have made throughout is not merely that it works, but that it works in a particular fashion. It works better on behalf of an ameliorative penology. I am less interested in exculpation than in rehabilitation. Responsibility is a part of rehabilitation; it affords human recognition to all—the mentally ill and the mentally healthy. Aside from its failure as a rule of law, the Durham rule does not work on behalf of the well-being of the people it affects.

We call on pragmatism now because all that we have said thus far implies that the Durham rule embraces a body of illusions. What else is the function of propaganda if not the instilling of illusions? The main illusions are psychiatric—that mental illness is substantially identified with criminality; that psychiatry is able to identify offenders in whom this concurrence exists, causally; and that psychiatry—or, should we say, the mental hospital—is curative of such illness.

Even if the victim of propaganda does not start with a receptivity toward its particular message, sooner or later he assists the propagandist by helping to structure the illusions, by

---

[46] Diamond, Criminal Responsibility of the Mentally Ill, 14 Stan. L. Rev. 59, 63 (1961).
[47] *Id.* See *supra* p. 21.

finding his own means of supporting them. The main mechanism by which the Durham court has done this is the idealization of the civil commitment. Judge Bazelon does not contend that the mental hospitals to which acquitted offenders are committed are therapeutically more effective than prisons.[48] Rather, he contends that they *ought* to be. But the Durham case is a decision that goes as though they were.

Sometimes the illusion that the victim embraces presents no difficulty to the bystander. So the editorial writer of the Washington, D.C., *Post-Times-Herald*, commenting on the Court of Appeals reversal of the conviction of Jenkins, did not see the mandatory commitment as treatment, but as confinement.[49] The trial judge was Judge Curran. Said the editorial:

> Judge Curran sentenced Jenkins to 15 years in prison. With time off for good behavior he would have been eligible for parole in less than four years. This means, since he is now only 28 years old, that he might have been released at 32 at least as sick and at least as dangerous to the community as he is today. But if, after another trial, he is acquitted by reason of insanity, he will be committed automatically to St. Elizabeths Hospital and kept there, indefinitely, under treatment, until the Superintendent certifies that he will no longer be dangerous to himself or to others. Which way is more likely to promote the safety of the community?

Although the word "treatment" is used, the editorial dwells with satisfaction on the fact that the insanity acquittal will keep the man in custody longer than the penal commitment. "Treatment" is illusion; custody is fact. Indeed, *fear* of the mentally ill seems a more controlling impulse than a wish to help them. That is the meaning of the mandatory commitment of the mentally ill defendant ruled to be incompetent or acquitted after trial for his illness; of the indeterminacy (life term) of the commitment, compared with the definite limits on penal commitments; and of the difficulty of release, compared with the routine considerations of parole of the criminally committed.

Mentally ill offenders are feared as "both crazed and criminal."

---

[48] *Supra* pp. 25, 33.
[49] October 29, 1961.

Largely unconscious feelings of apprehension, awe, and anger toward the "sick," particularly if associated with "criminality," are hidden behind the more acceptable conscious desire to protect the "sick from criminal liability." What must be recognized is the enormous ambivalence toward the "sick" reflected in conflicting wishes to exculpate and to blame; to sanction and not to sanction; to degrade and elevate; to stigmatize and not to stigmatize; to care and to reject; to treat and to mistreat; to protect and to destroy.[50]

This is well put; and especially as applied to Durham.

The *Post-Times-Herald* editorial assumes that the worst aspects of penal treatment will operate and compares it with the best in the mental hospital administration. That is, the parole board will *automatically* release at the time of first eligibility, but the hospital administration will not; it will act with the wisdom called for and release only at the appropriate time, presumably later. The possibility is, of course, reversible—the hospital might release the man the day after he is received.[51]

In a 1961 interpretation of the Durham rule, the Court divided, Judge Burger bringing together the substantial criticism of the Durham rule and its consequences.[52] He quotes the following statement of Dr. Szasz:

> To believe that one's own theories are facts is considered by many contemporary psychiatrists as a "symptom" of schizophrenia. Yet this is what the language of the *Durham* decision does. It reifies some of the shakiest and most controversial aspects of contemporary psychiatry (*i.e.*, those pertaining to what is "mental disease" and the classification of such alleged diseases) and by legal fiat seeks to transform inadequate theory into "judicial fact."[53]

---

[50] Goldstein & Katz, Abolish the "Insanity Defense"—Why Not?, 72 Yale L.J. 853 (1963).

[51] Robert Irwin, one of the murderers studied by Dr. Fredric Wertham, was committed to the state hospital three times and each time discharged; The Show of Violence (1949).

[52] Blocker v. United States, 288 F.2d 853 (1961), Judge Burger concurring in result.

[53] Szasz, Psychiatry, Ethics, and the Criminal Law, 58 Colum. L. Rev. 183, 190 (1958).

Two others of Judge Burger's quotations sound quite reminiscent of the anti-propagandist authorities quoted by Professor Hakeem. The first is from Dr. Philip Q. Roche; the second is from Dr. Charles Savage:

> I will say there is neither such a thing as "insanity" nor such a thing as "mental disease." These terms do not identify entities having separate existence in themselves. . . . "Mental illness," a medical term, borrowed from the mechanistic concepts of classical physical disease, refers to an altered internal status of the individual vis-a-vis his external world as interpreted by others. In a way the term is a misnomer, since the "mental illness" is not actually something limited to a place called the "mind," but rather it is a changed interrelationship of the individual with his fellow creatures.[54]
>
> Though widely heralded as bringing legal psychiatry more in line with modern psychology, it [the *Durham* rule] actually does no such thing. It is a peculiar mixture of Aristotelean faculty psychology, metaphysics, mysticism, and medieval theology. . . . It is indeed vague particularly in the matter of the first test of responsibility: that of mental illness. There are very few people who could not qualify under this test.[55]

And there are others, dealing similarly with the Durham causation concept, in Judge Burger's opinion.

The Durham rule forgets one guiding ethical concept: the humanitarian. In its concern with the interests of psychiatry, it lost the prior concern with the people and the effect of rules upon them. So under the Durham rule an alcoholic woman can be put away for what is potentially a life term without any court determination that she is socially dangerous, violent, or even in need of treatment at the time the trial was held. This is true of any offender, petty or serious. Once he is committed, the burden of obtaining release rests on the discredited defendant, who must initiate the action and sustain the burden of

---

[54] Roche, Symposium on Criminal Responsibility and Mental Diseases, 19th Annual Law Institute, Univ. of Tenn. 1958, in 26 Tenn. L. Rev. 221, 240-1 (1959).

[55] Savage, Discussion, 116 Am. J. of Psych. 295, 296 (1959).

proof. This is what the Durham rule comes to, because it addressed itself to what psychiatry needs, or what the court thought it needs, and not to what people need.

It appears that Judge Bazelon is now disillusioned. Ten years after the Durham decision was handed down he found that its rule was not working. It is fascinating that at this point his grievance was not that the rule was in error, but that *the psychiatrists* are at fault, for not living up to expectations. He wrote:

> Psychiatrists testifying in the courts of the District of Columbia have generally failed to live up to the challenge presented by Durham. The hundreds of transcripts of trial proceedings I have read over the last 10 years force me to the conclusion that they have been unwilling, or unable, to convey to the layman an understanding of why the accused acted as he did. Their testimony is frequently phrased in technical, stereotyped language which is not only unintelligible to the jury, but a substitute for hard thinking about the dynamics of the defendant's personality and his life history. Doctors often explain to me in private that they simply did not have the time to do an adequate study of the defendant, even in the case of patients who have been committed for 90 days to a mental hospital for examination before trial. . . . I fear that the problem of interesting psychiatrists in offenders has deeper roots than the hostility they may encounter in the courtroom. The behavioral scientist is subject to the same prejudices as the rest of us. . . . And it takes more than the ability to pin an appropriate diagnostic label on an offender to understand him and wish to help him.[56]

The French poet Paul Valéry said, "Beware of your desires . . . for they will be fulfilled." At least their fulfillment brings realization, even if it is sometimes disillusionment.

---

[56] Bazelon, The Interface of Law and the Behavioral Sciences, The Lowell Institute lecture, February 26, 1964.

PART II

Sentencing

Chapter 5

Sex Offenders

The establishment of criminal responsibility or of competence to act at any stage of the proceedings is not the only area of contact between psychiatry and the law. As was pointed out in Part 1, psychiatry has a specific role at the sentencing stage, as specific as in establishing irresponsibility for mental illness.

If one were to consider the entire body of criminal definitions, there are many places where psychiatry might reasonably enter. Indeed, if a first criterion of a crime is the destructive impact of the deed upon both society and its members—including the criminal—it is possible to find in all or almost all definitions of crime, and in their penalty classifications, a role for a psychiatric contribution. That is, a sound understanding of the behavioral dynamics of acts and the inner as well as the outer impact of violations would seem a significant element in the definitions of crimes and the degree or kind of punishment authorized.[1]

Certain conclusions were drawn from the chapters on the criminal responsibility problem, and it is not surprising that they illuminate such a "psychiatric" subject as sex offenses. Aside from all other points made, I have suggested that, in effect, the Durham rule appealed to some liberal-minded people

---

[1] *Infra* p. 191 et seq.

because it appeared to be (1) technically modern, in its attempt to facilitate the use of psychiatric expertise on the trial; (2) intellectually and morally compatible with the liberal stance, simply because it spoke of treatment rather than punishment for the mentally ill. But we found that application of the Durham rule has more drawbacks than advantages—that is, the anticipated advantages are illusions. In brief, (1) the rule does not really facilitate the use of psychiatric expertise, which, we found, is better used after conviction; and (2) although the rule speaks of treatment, the treatment turns out to be nontherapeutic, and, in fact, excessively punitive, whereas the "punishment" of a criminal conviction need not be antitherapeutic at all and may be more supportive of the person's liberty than the civil disposition is. Finally, we found (3) the illusions were compounded of propaganda (self-serving to a particular group) and self-delusion.

The chief legal ingredient in the self-delusion is the civil commitment, a legal fiction by which persons charged with criminal acts are dealt with "noncriminally." When "civil commitment" is joined to "for treatment," we have a legal fiction regarded as a reality; that is, it has become an illusion.

We should be alert to discover whether these patterns are present in the sex offender legislation. Is that legislation realistic, or does it embody these illusions? Does a "liberal treatment" approach turn out to be nontherapeutic, destructive of liberal correctional services, and punitive? Here again it may be instructive to observe the way in which these laws came into being (as it was to examine the sources of the Durham decision).

"Sexual Psychopath" Laws

In view of the great emphasis on sex in the birth of Freudian psychiatry, it would not be surprising to find that a special kind of legislation has developed around sex offenders, with special psychiatric attributes (or attributes resembling the psychiatric) attached to it. But the field of psychiatry was probably not the originator of these laws. Their origin seems to have been the interest of legislators in a type of crime that occasioned special outcries. In other words, the legislation is not the result of a sympathetic understanding of the distortions in the mind of the sex offender, comparable to the "sympathetic understanding" of the mentally ill offender in general; rather, it stems from a specially punitive approach toward crimes that aroused special anger, an approach in which psychiatric elements were incorporated to support the mechanism adopted.

Half the states and the District of Columbia have enacted statutes which deal with the commitment of "psychopathic" sex offenders. They are not in agreement as to what a "psychopathic" sex offender is, and in recent statutes the word is avoided; but usually he is defined as one lacking the power to control his sexual impulses or having criminal propensities toward the commission of sex offenses. Some of the statutes set up civil proceedings, some criminal. The civil statutes permit a state's attorney to initiate proceedings to determine whether a person charged with a sex crime or suspected of having propensities toward dangerous sexual behavior is a sexual psychopath within the meaning of the statute. If, after examination by court-appointed psychiatrists and a hearing, a condition of sexual psycopathy is found, the criminal proceedings may be suspended and the defendant civilly committed to a mental hospital or other state institution for an indefinite period, release depending on recovery. In some states[2] the civil proceedings may be commenced without any crime being proved. Recent statutes usually authorize proceedings only after a conviction of crime. Upon a conviction, a hearing is held on the question of sexual abnormality, and, if the finding is affirmative, special provisions for commitment and release are invoked. Some of the old civil laws have been revised closer to this form.[3]

Half of the statutes do not provide for a jury hearing. In some states the examining physician need not be a psychiatrist. In several the psychiatrist is not subject to cross-examination and the defendant may not introduce expert witnesses. Where

---

[2] E.g., Minnesota, Minn. Stats. Annot. § 526.09 to 11. For a history and analysis of the laws, see Swanson, Sexual Psychopath Statutes: Summary and Analysis, 51 J. Crim. L., C. & P.S. 215 (1960); Bowman, Review of Sex Legislation and the Control of Sex Offenders in the United States of America, 4 Internat. Rev. of Crim. Policy No. 4, p. 20 (July 1953).

[3] California, 1952, which extended its law to make conviction of any offense, sex crime or not, a possible basis for mental examination; Michigan in 1952, Wisconsin in 1951. Of special legislation passed before 1950, only five laws remain unamended; Bowman, op. cit. supra n. 2.

the commitment is for sexual psychopathy and not for a criminal offense the commitment is not a bar to a later prosecution for the crime.[4] Under many of the statutes the prisoner-patient may be discharged only upon complete recovery, generally meaning that he is believed to be unlikely to commit any more sex offenses. In some jurisdictions, the commitment is for life, although subject to parole.[5]

How did these laws come about? Probably the best historical analysis is the study of the sexual psychopath laws by the late Professor Edwin H. Sutherland.[6] Sutherland points out that in general the sexual phychopath laws did not stem from either an increase of sex crimes or a sudden advance in knowledge of how to deal with sex offenders. They were the outcome of community panic based on a few serious sex crimes given wide publicity, with committees of inquiry turning to procedures for supposed control. The newspapers did their share in whipping up hysteria. When it reached the legislature, it usually established an investigatory commission and the law was well on its way. Psychiatrists were usually in the studies as experts. It takes an unusually independent and exceptionally well-informed commission to reject the established statutory pattern and expose the fallacies on which it is based. Few commissions rejected the pattern.

Psychiatry contributed to the pattern of the statutes with approval and support. The statutes usually came into being after a study by a specially appointed commission. Some of the studies dwelt on the psychologically deviant aspects of deviant sexual behaviour, thus directly supporting special legislation. Others, somewhat more skeptical about the "deviancy" of both the behavior and the mental pattern, nevertheless liked the plan of diagnostic clinics and a treatment approach in institutions. In effect, the psychiatrists made themselves the partners of the legislators. Dr. Wilfred Overholser writes of the sexual psychopath group as dealt with in the legislation:

[4] Swanson, *op. cit. supra* n. 1 at 219.

[5] Bowman, *op. cit. supra* n. 2. Life terms (one day to life)—Colo. Rev. Stats. § 39-19.1; Mass. Gen. Laws c. 123A § 6; New York, Sess. Laws 1950, c. 525; Barr-Walker Act, Pa. Stat. Ann. tit. 19, §§ 1167-74.

[6] Sutherland, The Diffusion of Sexual Psychopath Laws, Am. J. of Sociol., September 1950.

Although this group is not at all well-defined psychiatrically, the demand for such legislation arose as a
result of public recognition of the fact that many persistent sexual offenders show themselves to be entirely
unamenable to routine correctional treatment, that
although they are not "insane" in the eyes of the law
they are by reason of mental deviation not readily
deterrable. Some of these offenders are sociopaths,
more of them in my opinion are neurotic, but in any
event the principle has been established that there is a
group of something other than frankly "insane" persons
who should be dealt with by an indeterminate period of
detention and, where possible, treatment; actually a fair
proportion of these offenders are amenable to psychiatric treatment.[7]

How Well Do the Sex Offender Statutes Work?

A number of misconceptions about sex-law violations and
sex offenders underlie the sexual psychopath and other penal
sex legislation. Probably the commonest misconception is the
seriousness of the offenses. Dr. Manfred S. Guttmacher compares the vast majority of sex offenders with the shoplifting
woman or the man who indulges in petty pilferage. These
offenses, he says, "have little social significance and the offenders
are not really antisocial individuals."[8]

The comparable and common sexual offenses fall into such
categories as voyeurism, exhibitionism, touching. "The tempta-
tion felt by a male to caress momentarily an attractive female
by touching her body is very frequent and is often given in
to. . . . [Then] there are some individuals who commit isolated
or very infrequent sexual offenses who are not real sex devi-
ates. They often have poorly organized egos and under noxious
circumstances their defenses are momentarily broken down—
alcohol or some acutely disorganizing episode can do this. . . .
There is the group of confused adolescents, whose egos are not
fully structured, who engage in paraphilias—that is, sex devia-
tions—as a kind of instinctual groping. . . . An isolated para-
philiac act may represent the impulsive, almost panicky, attempt

---

[7] Overholser, Criminal Responsibility: A Psychiatrist's Viewpoint, 48
Am. Bar Asso. J. 527, 530 (1962).
[8] Sex Offenses: The Problem, Causes and Prevention 17 (1951).

of an individual who has great difficulty in relating to others to form some kind of basic intimacy."[9]

Most aggressive sex offenders are not psychiatrically disturbed:

> The sex statutes were passed largely to control the violent acts of rape and sexual assault. Yet, available evidence suggests that as a group, such offenders are less likely to exhibit clear-cut pathological symptoms and may have more in common with non-sexual offenders than with the passive sex deviants. . . . The aggressive offenders are more likely to be judged normal by psychiatric diagnoses. They are less inhibited sexually and tend to give fewer indications of severe emotional disturbance. Fewer of them are judged to have been exposed to severe emotional deprivation during childhood. Significantly, their prior arrest histories show few sexual offenses, but many nonsexual offenses. . . .
>
> Evidence from the California studies of sexual deviation supports the pattern noted above. . . . Of the thirty-seven serious offenders studied, half had previous records for non-sexual offenses, only three had previous sex arrests.[10]

Weihofen notes:

> A report by the Group for the Advancement of Psychiatry points out that most of the persons committing sex offenses punishable by the law "are not involved in behavior fundamentally different from that commonplace in the population; such persons are not necessarily to be regarded as suffering with psychiatric disorders or as socially dangerous." In California, one of the few states that makes much use of special sex offender legislation, most of the persons committed are not vicious criminals who have committed brutal crimes. They are more likely to be passively dependent and passively hostile characters. The crimes with which they are most commonly charged involve no more than sex fondling, etc. Coitus was not usually even intended.[11]

---

[9] *Id.* at 17-18.

[10] Stanton & Wheeler, Sex Offenders: A Sociological Critique, 25 Law & Contemp. Problems 272, 274 (1960).

[11] Institutional Treatment of Persons Acquitted by Reason of Insanity, 38 Tex. L. Rev. 849 (1960).

It is equally erroneous to describe six offenders as recidivists. Of all types of criminals, sex offenders have one of the lowest repeater rates; and of those who are repeaters, a majority commit some crime other than a sex crime. The studies just noted find such to be the case. In a study of the 206 offenders committed under the New Jersey sex offender law to the state's three mental hospitals between June 1949 and April 1953, fifty-seven had been released by the end of April 1953, some on parole and others without parole. A study of the subsequent records of these fifty-seven showed that none had been returned or violated his parole.[12]

The sexual psychopath statutes also imply that treatment methods to cure deviated sex offenders are known and are used. But Dr. Henry A. Davidson wrote:

The thread that runs through popular thinking on sex offenders is this: sexual psychopathy is an illness, not a crime; the offender needs treatment, not punishment. Most psychiatrists promptly say "amen" to that noble sentiment. The difficulty is that we have no way of successfully treating the sexual psychopath. Cures, if any, must be extremely rare. The demand, therefore, that these offenders be "treated" is still a sterile one. Why do we want jurisdiction in those cases transferred from the courts to the psychiatrists? It looks as if we have talked ourselves into the privilege of holding the bear by the tail. . . . When we do discover an effective method for treating the aggressive sex offender, we should insist on his transfer from the prison to the hospital. Today, we have nothing to offer but custody—a field in which penal authorities are far more efficient than we are. Perhaps it is time to confess this is an era in which we may have been overselling psychiatry. It is, of course, a good thing that popular and legal thinking about the sex offender is veering away from the purely punitive. But it is not yet at the point where the psychiatrist can appear before the public as the man who has the answer.[13]

The foregoing conclusions are amply supported by other

---

[12] A Follow-Up Study of 206 Sex Offenders Committed to State Mental Hospitals in New Jersey, Dept. Inst. and Agencies (1953).

[13] Legislation Dealing with Sex Offenders, Am. J. of Psych., November 1949 at 390.

studies of results under one or another of the sexual psychopath laws. In Pennsylvania the Barr-Walker Act provides for a sentence of one day to life for sex offenders convicted of indecent assault, sodomy, assault with intent to ravish (rape), or rape, if the judge is "of the opinion that any such person, if at large, constitutes a threat of bodily harm to members of the public, or is a habitual offender and mentally ill." Before such a sentence is imposed, a psychiatric examination must be had, either through the welfare department or by a psychiatrist appointed by the court. The commitment may be to any state institution or county jail.[14]

Such an act produces a great disparity of sentences. The judge may choose to sentence under the usual penal code provision, and most judges do. Thus, to the variety of sentences under the penal code, another—one day to life—is added. Does this provide greater flexibility rather than disparity? Unfortunately not. Flexibility is achieved under a sentence form that allows wide or complete discretion to a parole board, not by a choice of sentence forms each of which is dogmatic in its own way, particularly in the use of a minimum term of parole eligibility. No; the choice is made according to the personality and attitude of the judge, not the defendant.[15] Fifteen counties used the act, fifty-two did not. Three counties committed 37 per cent of the B-W's; the two most populous counties hardly used the act.[16]

Were the defendants sentenced to life terms dangerous men?

---

[14] Cited *op. cit. supra* n. 5.

[15] Yeager, Characteristics of "Barr-Walker" Cases in the Bureau of Correction, Dept. of Justice, Bur. of Correction (1957) mimeo, covering the cases from June 15, 1962 to June 30, 1957. P. 9: "The intent of the Act is not clear to the judges. Some have interpreted the Act to be an effective segregating one; others are apparently under the impression that the Act is designed to give an extensive treatment program to sex offenders." "The Hennepin County Attorney's office does not seek commitment of a person as a 'psychopathic personality' unless the person has made actual physical contact with his victim. It is their belief that the framers of the law intended the law to provide treatment for the repeater and did not intend the law to be used to commit a first or minor offender. Contrasting with this view is the commitment of a person on the basis of the person's masturbation, with no evidence of harm to any other person. Such a commitment was upheld by the Minnesota Supreme Court in Dittrich v. Brown County, 1943, 215 Minn. 243, 9 N. W. 2d 510."—Report of the Minnesota Legislative Interim Commission on Public Welfare Laws, Sexual Psychopath Laws, January 1959.

[16] Yeager, *op. cit. supra* n. 15 at 4.

Sixty-six per cent were committed for sodomy. "Most of the sodomy 'victims' were actually accomplices in homosexual gangs. . . . Sixty-one per cent of the 'victims' participated in the offense with the offenders." Some of the commitments have represented "drives" by individual counties against homosexual rings of long standing. Reports the Bureau of Correction: "The Bureau receives many serious assault cases every year, many of a compulsive repetitive nature; this latter group alone, whose sentences are averaging 1½ to 5 years, are far more dangerous potentially to society than the far majority of Barr-Walkers received to date."[17]

The Bureau concludes:

> While it can be said that the B-W's have been subjected to more "correctional treatment" than other offenders in the Bureau of Correction, such treatment administered to date may be said to be at a minimum. . . . Psychological and psychiatric counseling plus organized group therapy sessions conducted by clinical psychologists are the only feasible methods of individualized treatment possible for B-W's in the Bureau of Correction. Due to the necessity of periodic reviews and to the emphases placed in the Barr-Walker Act, B-W's in turn cut into the potentiality and availability of these techniques for individuals of other groups of offenders who may be more seriously in need of and more amenable to the minimum amount of professional individualized treatment possible to date in the Bureau of Correction. . . .

> The importance of probation as a modern correctional tool is not recognized by the Act. Correctional and mental institutionalization are not the only effective correctional devices for sex offenders. It does not seem possible to have a fully effective indeterminate sex offender law as long as probation cannot be accepted, applied, and as long as adult probation remains in its present rudimentary conditions at the county level in Pennsylvania.[18]

---

[17] *Id.* at 12.

[18] *Id.* at 10, 11. Wisconsin has also found that: "Our attempt at individual therapy for this group has decreased our ability to provide for the

The California Department of Mental Hygiene published a more comprehensive study, more clinically oriented, and based on a broader view. In it Dr. Karl M. Bowman arrives at conclusions along the same lines as those already cited:

> Psychiatry has been oversold in legal efforts to define the term sexual psychopath; to predict potentially dangerous sex offenders; and to obtain permanent cures through effective methods of treatment.[19]

Referring to an article derived from the study:

> First of all, we found the concept of sexual psychopathy far too vaguely defined for effective judicial or administrative use. . . . Neither the type of mental disorder nor the conduct fits easily into standard diagnoses of mental disorder or deficiency. . . . The result is confusion in diagnosis and commitment, as many observers have noted. For example, according to psychiatric diagnoses the proportion of psychopaths among criminals in similar penal institutions has varied from 5 to 90 per cent. . . . We therefore expressed the opinion that psychiatry cannot furnish the precise, easily applied definitions and diagnostic criteria "needed for the type of sex offender law now being written." . . .
>
> A girl of 15 was walking one evening along a Queens street in New York City; she told police a strange man whom she only glimpsed walked up behind her and said, "Hi, honey," and then she felt a sharp pain in her back. She had been stabbed by a sharp tool, probably a file, and was in critical condition in a hospital. In New York and many of the other 19 jurisdictions such a criminal, if apprehended and convicted, could not be committed on indeterminate sentence [under the sex offender legislation].

---

general run of prisoners. Today we have one half-time and two full-time psychiatrists with each having a caseload of 40 plus their initial studies of new admissions. Eighty percent of their time is devoted to this group, with the remaining twenty percent devoted to new admissions, emergencies, and rquests for help from individual prisoners."—Coogan, Wisconsin's Experience in Treating Psychiatrically-Deviated Sexual Offenders, 1 J. of Soc. Therapy 3, at 6 (1955).

[19] Bowman, *op. cit. supra* n. 2, at 20.

Dr. Guttmacher wrote:

> An analysis I carried out some time ago of one
> hundred consecutive sexual offenders examined in the
> Baltimore Supreme Bench Clinic showed that thirty-
> six were convicted of crimes involving the use of force
> or threats of force. Of this group of aggressive sex of-
> fenders, only one had previously been convicted of a
> sexual offense, exhibitionism; on the other hand, eight
> had been previously convicted of burglary. Our research
> clearly indicated that the basic personality structure of
> the burglar resembled that of the rapist far more closely
> than that of the exhibitionist. In fact, the legal term,
> "breaking and entering," bears such a connotation.[20]

The sexual psychopath statutes rely in the main on institutional
treatment; in contrast, the usual penal code provisions authorize
probation and fine as well as commitment. Bowman writes:

> In general, . . . individuals committed under special
> sex offense legislation are assigned to prison sections or
> to overcrowded mental hospital wards where treatment
> is almost wholly lacking and the prisoner-patient waits
> out his indefinite term in idleness. The problem of homo-
> sexual offenses, which comprise a large proportion of
> total sex crimes, is especially difficult. As I pointed out
> in "The Problem of the Sex Offender" and in "The
> Problem of Homosexuality," prison and hospital con-
> finement offer little chance to help the offender establish
> a more normal sex life. "Segregating a male homosexual
> for months or years in a prison where he will see only
> other men and where he will often be isolated with a
> group of other homosexuals can hardly result in anything
> but reinforcement of the homosexual tendencies." In
> such cases treatment is even less efficient than usual.
> Since few sex psychopath laws provide for conditional
> release under parole or probation it is all the more
> difficult to judge the offender's capacity for heterosexual
> adjustment.
> For example, a psychiatrist dealing with Illinois sex
> criminals points out as a defect in the present act the
> lack of probationary or parole arrangements. No ex-

---

[20] Guttmacher, Dangerous Offenders, 9 Crime and Del. 381, at 382
(1963).

perienced psychiatrist can evaluate recovery until the individual has had a chance "to face problems and temptations of community adjustment," since in penal conditions there are "no women whom the aggressive rapist may have an opportunity to assault; there are no female relatives (with whom to have) incestuous relationships . . . and there are no little boys or girls under the age of 14" with whom to commit indecent liberties. For that reason the present Illinois legislature is being requested to provide a parole period in the community "prior to the formal jury procedures alleging full recovery."[21]

---

[21] Bowman, *op. cit. supra* n. 2, at 20-3. Guttmacher concluded: "It is my belief that these new measures to regulate sexual behavior are ill-conceived and fail in their highly commendable purposes for the following reasons:

"1. First, they are designed primarily to control serious sex crimes—the rapes and the forced sex relations with children. In the series which I have reported only one of the 36 offenders falling into these categories had ever been previously arrested for an adult sex crime. If this dramatically negative incidence in this small group of 36 cases is confirmed by other studies, are we not forced to conclude that we are locking the stable after the horse is gone?

"2. The popular conception which, it seems to me, must be a basic postulate of these laws, that serious criminal sexual behavior evolves progressively from less serious sexual offenses, is false. Evidence points to the contrary. The individual who has found a method of releasing his neurotic tension, as for example in exhibitionism, has adopted this way of acting out his unconscious needs. He is conditioned to it and he is very unlikely to seek other methods to accomplish this end.

"3. I contend that burglary, the offense of breaking and entering at night—the very words themselves suggest the possible symbolism—is far more likely to be a forerunner of rape than homosexuality, voyeurism, exhibitionism or any other type of sexual offense. Six of the eighteen rapists in my series had been previously involved in burglaries. Perhaps we need to readjust our focus in our attempt to prevent serious sex crimes, and give indeterminate sentences to burglars rather than to exhibitionists.

"4. A certain number of pedophiles are recidivists, and surely this is a type of offense with potentially serious consequences. But in our experiences the older offenders adjust easily with relatively little supervision and the younger offenders often offer promising material for extramural psychotherapy.

"5. Exhibitionism, voyeurism, transvestism, fetishism and homosexuality—paraphilias with really high rates of recidivism—are pathetic instances of individual maladjustment; but from society's point of view they are seldom seriously harmful. Surely we do not need this specially drastic legislation merely to curb these activities."—Guttmacher, *op. cit. supra* n. 8 at 131-2.

Illusions and Self Delusion

There is very little disagreement with these studies, and where there is, it is of special interest in relation to our assertion of illusions and self-delusion in the Durham problem.[22]

We have observed that the recidivism rate is not the product of therapeutic success, for the rate is low even where no treatment resources are used and where the civilly committed sexual psychopath is in the same prison, subject to the same program (or absence of program), as other offenders. Yet it is possible for one to say: "We have a sex offender law that works very well, as can be readily seen from the low recidivism rate of those released after being processed under the law."[23] A determined

---

[22] Ch. 4 *supra.*

[23] "One thing is definite—we are providing protection to the community against acts of aggression of this kind. This is one of our objectives; the other is treatment. . . . These people are treatable more often than not, and our three years of experience with them in this respect amply proves such a contention in that their demonstrated ability to adjust sexually in free society is proof of such." From July 27, 1951 to June 30, 1954, 520 men were studied under the law. Of these 199 were returned to the court with a recommendation for treatment, 303 for handling under the criminal code and 14 for commitment to Central State Hospital as insane or feeble-minded.

"The majority of those found to be sexually deviated were committed to the treatment facility at the Wisconsin State Prison, where both treatment and custody are available. Subsequently, 86 persons under treatment were released to parole supervision on a trial basis. Eight of the 86 were returned to the institution for further treatment because of parole violations. Of the eight returned, four were returned for new offenses and four committed various violations of the parole agreement which did not involve aberrant sexual behavior.

"During this same period 31 individuals were discharged with maximum benefits. Those discharges were granted upon the recommendation of the department psychiatric staff. It is interesting to note that in not a single instance has any person so discharged been convicted of further aberrant sexual behavior. Treatment has not always been effective with this particular group, as may be noted from the fact that twelve men have been returned to court for judicial review of the department's order continuing them under its control beyond the legal limits imposed by the criminal law for their particular offense."—Coogan, *op. cit. supra* n. 18 at 4, 6. This "success" reminds one of the patient who, constantly snapping his fingers, came to the psychiatrist. The psychiatrist asked him why he did it: "To keep away the elephants." "But," said the psychiatrist, "there are no elephants within a thousand miles." "Well," said the patient, "see how well it works!" In addition to other sources cited, we may add Ploscowe's conclusion: "The basic task of the sex-psychopath laws is to differentiate dangerous sex offenders from minor criminals who commit sex crimes and who

legislator or psychiatrist can perhaps get some comfort from such a view. To me (and, I trust, to those who review the totality of the legislation and its effects) it is, rather, another aspect of the way in which the illusions connected with the sex offender are fostered. Taking credit for this appearance of success is reminiscent of the case, cited by Guttmacher, of the arsonist whose behavior had a pathological sexual basis. Sometimes after setting a fire and thus relieving his tension, he would put it out. Accordingly, he was made fire warden of the shop in which he worked because it was observed that he was quick to discover fires and put them out before they had spread.[24]

A second kind of delusory mechanism is illustrated by two major studies of sex offenders conducted in New York. The first, by Dr. David Abrahamsen, was a study of 102 prisoners in Sing Sing, either convicted of sex offenses or exhibiting sexual perversion in prison. Anyone who has read Dr. Abrahamsen would not be surprised that he found these prisoners, or any other criminals, to be disturbed and hence proper psychiatric subjects. His book *Who Are the Guilty?*, filled with Freudian clichés, includes the proposition that *all* criminals are mentally abnormal. Their crimes, he says, fill emotional needs; the emotions they respond to are deeply repressed; and these repressed emotions, rather than any rational influences, are the prime movers of criminal behavior. But this is not very surprising or very revealing, since Dr. Abrahamsen finds that the same irrational motivations are present in almost all of us: "Antisocial tendencies are present in all of us; it follows that the large majority of criminals are not so very different from the average law-abiding citizen."

His study was the basis of the one-day-to-life law enacted in New York in 1950.[25] The legislature acted on the Abrahamsen proposition that sex criminals are mentally abnormal, rather than on the Abrahamsen view that *all* criminals are mentally abnormal—in fact, that all people are mentally abnormal and hence

---

should be handled by the ordinary procedures of the criminal law, either because they are not mentally abnormal or because they are not inherently dangerous to the community. *The sex-psychopath laws fail miserably in this vital task.*"—Sex and the Law 212 (1962).

24 Guttmacher, *op. cit. supra* n. 8 at 40-1.

25 Session Laws 1950, ch. 525.

sex offenders are, by and large, not different from other persons.
Thereafter a second study was made, by Dr. Bernard C. Glueck,
Jr.[26] It says little about the first report, except that it was pre-
liminary, "empirical rather than experimental," and laid "the
groundwork for a more percise method of investigation which
was needed in order to meet recognized criteria for validity and
reliability." (But it resulted in the legislation authorizing a life
term.)

Albert Ellis and Dr. Ralph Brancale studied the first 300 offenders referred under the New Jersey law requiring diagnostic
study of sex offenders.[27] Their report is critical of the Abrahamsen study. They point out that almost one-fifth of the 102 "sex
offenders" were not originally sentenced for a sex offense. "It is
quite doubtful whether individuals who are convicted of a sex
crime may be legitimately mixed, for research purposes, with
those who are not convicted of such a crime, but who show
deviant sex patterns of behavior after their imprisonment." They
also question the validity of any study of "sex offenders" as such,
calling it an impossibility, since there was "such a sharp difference in the personality patterns, motivations, and general behavior of the men studied."

The second New York study (by Glueck) concluded that the
person who commits a sexual offense is emotionally disturbed,
frequently seriously so, but "that psychiatric treatment techniques can be effective in helping the sexual offender to a
socially more acceptable pattern of behavior still remains to be
conclusively demonstrated."[28] It evidently relied greatly on a
high recidivism rate among the men studied, 46.5 per cent of
them having been convicted of at least one previous sex offense.

How meaningful was this rate? Ellis and Brancale point out
that a large proportion of convicted sex offenders, usually from
one-fourth to one-third, are placed on probation, and these pro-
bationers may be different from incarcerated sex offenders.
About 10 to 20 per cent of convicted sex offenders are committed
to a local workhouse or reformatory rather than a state prison,

---

[26] Final Report, Research Project for the Study and Treatment of Persons
Convicted of Crimes Involving Sexual Aberrations, June 1952 to June 1955
(1956).

[27] Ellis & Brancale, The Psychology of Sex Offenders (1956).

[28] Op. cit. supra n. 26 at vi.

and their personality structure is likely not to be identical with those sent to prison. Also excluded are sex offenders sent to state hospitals or other specialized institutions; those sent to state prisons have not committed the gamut of sex offenses but, almost exclusively, rape, sodomy, and carnal abuse.

There is a possibility that sex offenders who are intensively examined after they have already been incarcerated in prison for varying lengths of time may show emotional characteristics which are partly a function of their incarceration, and which have only an indirect relationship to their original sex offense. . . .

In deciding whether or not an individual is to be committed to a state prison for a sex offense, the court will normally consider his past criminal history; with the natural result that individuals who have committed previous sex and/or non-sexual crimes are more likely to be sent to prison than are those who have had no previous criminal records. This means that imprisoned sex offenders may include an unusually high percentage of sexual and other recidivists, and on that count may again not be representative of sex offenders in general. Indeed, they may be more representative of non-sexual than of sexual offenders.

The Glueck study recognized this, too. It notes:

An additional sampling error in our material was created by the inclusion of a large number of men who were sentenced for a term of one day to natural life. Thirty-five of the original group of fifty men, and 82 of the total group of 170 sexual offenders were "day-to-life" offenders. Since this sentence is discretionary with the court, and is supposedly used in the more serious offenses, or with men who have a history of repeated offenses, the inclusion of so many "day-to-lifers," almost half of the total group, weights our results in the direction of severity of criminal record, and intensity of personality disorganization. It may also explain the high percentage of recidivism found, although this appears open to question, since many of our non-day-to-life offenders were involved in several offenses, for which they may or may not have been arrested.[29]

---
[29] *Id.* at 84.

The study included a statement of other potential sources of error, including agreement with the Ellis-Brancale observation that the sampling technique might be a source of bias; "this distortion, if it exists, is in the direction of increased phychopathology." Another source of error, says the report, "lies in the personal biases of the individual examiners. . . . An even more important potential error lies in the basic orientation of the entire research group, which was, as has been described, primarily a psychodynamic orientation. A final, and very important, source of error stems from the interviewing procedures and techniques. . . . The fact that the research group was inevitably involved in disposition plans, through reports to the Parole Board, and the Administration of the Prison, added to this difficulty."

Thus more than one study revealed that reliance on a low recidivism rate as a measure of success in dealing with sex offenders is a delusion, and that the fact that a group of sex offenders shows personality deviation is no proof of a general pattern of deviation among the body of sex offenders. But, alas, the Brancale-Ellis study, so firm on these points, itself concluded: "Should there be a Sex Offender Act such as the New Jersey Acts of 1949 and 1950? The writers believe that the answer to this question is a resounding 'Yes.' "[30]

Why? Evidently because the New Jersey law avoided some of the errors of the other acts. It did not provide for either an illusory civil commitment or a reliance on a supposed therapy for sex offenders; it provided only for a presentence clinical workup of sex offenders. But this too falls into error, the errors we have already pointed out—that sexual deviation in offenders may come out in violent crimes other than sexual; that sex offense does not correlate with dangerousness or even personality deviation; that clinical workups are needed for other offenders as well as sex offenders, with as much (or little) presumption arising from the category of the crime.

The sentencing of sex offenders requires a different approach.

Sex Offenders and the Model Sentencing Act

If the civil commitment and the other versions of the sexual psychopath statutes provide no solution to the problem of the

---

[30] *Op. cit. supra* n. 27, at 75.

sex offender, is the only alternative the ordinary penal statute? The ordinary penal statute is not a bad product, at least compared with the newer versions we have been discussing. But it has two defects. First, the statutes make criminal certain sexual behavior that most studies declare to be normal.[31] Second, the penalties are chaotic, overly punitive, and inadequate to protect the public. Where then do we turn?

The experience and research findings in the reports, with respect to both sexual behavior and statutory and administrative attempts at control, lead to fairly obvious conclusions. *First*: to the extent that psychiatric services and facilities are provided under the sexual psychopath statutes (where anything at all exists), either in diagnosis or treatment, they are at worst a total waste and at best a poor use of scarce psychiatric talent in correctional treatment. Certainly diagnostic resources are needed both in sentencing and in treatment, but it is obvious that to channel the bulk, or all of such services into dealing with sex offenders is to deal with a generally nondangerous group for whom psychiatric treatment is at best unpromising and, in the lean measure given in correctional services, entirely unproductive.

Second: if treatment of petty sex offenders is neither justified nor practical, then the only sensible justification for attention to this group is protection of the public. Certainly horrendous crimes, originating in sexual aberrations, occur. People who commit them are dangerous, and measures to protect against them are needed. The current sex offender statutes do not give protection—because, in part at least, they neglect the defendants who are dangerous sex offenders but whose crimes are not violations of sex laws. A statute that dwells only on sex offenders, rather than dangerous offenders, may appear to offer protection to the community. The existence of such a statute not only is a sad deception to those who do not understand what actually happens, but also is a barrier to going ahead with truly practical legislation.

In brief, these statutes should be repealed. But what should take their place that would improve on the ordinary penal statutes? If the legislation is "sold" to legislatures in the first instance on the ground of public fear of violent crime, does this

---

[31] *Infra* pp. 107-11.

not represent a sound requirement in legislation? It would seem so; and this suggests, therefore, that the thing to stress, the thing to obtain, is whatever resources are needed at the point of sentencing—psychiatric assistance or other assistance to the sentencing court.

But we have to be clear as to how to use the resources. The experience with the sex offender laws teaches us that sex offense is not a way of detecting the dangerous offender. Sometimes the more seriously deviated sex offender will behave dangerously in other than sexual patterns. For example, we know that frequently an arsonist is a person whose underlying motivation may be sexual. Earlier we cited Dr. Bowman's illustration of a man who stabbed a girl—not a sexual crime, under the statutes, but in all likelihood sexually motivated and committed by a mentally disturbed man. The important lesson is that the dangerous offender—the offender dangerous to the person—is most often not a sex offender in any sense.

Sentencing resources are needed to assist the court in detecting dangerous offenders at the point of sentencing, no matter what their offense. There is nothing wrong in a provision for referral to a diagnostic clinic at the point of sentencing, if it is done with more reason than under the sex offender laws. In fact, if there is one useful suggestion that remains in these laws, it is the concept, and occasionally the services, of the diagnostic referral.

We come then to the point at which we had arrived in the discussion of the M'Naghten-Durham controversy: that what is needed is a modernization of our penology, particularly our sentencing system. The Model Sentencing Act, discussed in chapter 9, has no special provision for sex offenders. Indeed, it lists the sexual psychopath statutes for repeal, yet it purports to be a sounder approach to public protection. The Act provides for a referral to a state diagnostic clinic before sentencing but after conviction, in *any case of a crime that inflicted or threatened serious bodily harm.* We have noted instances of sexually disturbed persons who commit serious crimes that are not sexual in legal definition but are in terms of the aberration behind the act. Other crimes against the person are committed by disturbed persons without relation to sexual aberration. If the report and other materal before the judge establishes that the defendant is suffering from a severe personality disorder that may lead him to commit further crime—that is, if he is a dangerous person and appears likely to remain so for some time—he may be committed, under the Model Sentencing Act, for a long term. The judge fixes the term and may fix it to as high as thirty years, but not to life.[32] The defendant is eligible for parole. The diagnostic center is thus available for all serious cases and is not wasted on other cases.

Statutes Defining Sex Offenses

Much quite common sexual behavior is declared to be criminal in many jurisdictions. There is nothing unique in this. The history of legislation is replete with examples of everyday behavior prohibited on moral grounds. Probably the most extensive of the "blue" laws were those of our Puritan days, but there is no lack of recent or current examples. Prohibition failed, and by the time it was repealed it had caused great damage. Gambling today is illegal in some states, legal in others (and debated in both).

So it is with sex offenses. Dr. Manfred Guttmacher writes:

> One need only refer to the epochal studies of Professor Alfred Kinsey. He has estimated that in the United States six million homosexual acts take place every year per twenty convictions and that nearly 100 per cent of the adult male population has, at some time, committed voyeuristic or exhibitionistic acts. Then, what is it that we are talking about when we talk of sex offenses and sex offenders?[33]

The Kinsey report on male behavior states:

> At least 85 per cent of the younger male population could be convicted as sex offenders if law enforcement officials were as efficient as most people expect them to be.[34]

For our present discussion, the first point that should be made about this is that it is illogical and unsound to consider violation of such laws by most persons as an indication of psychopathy.

---

[32] *Infra.* pp. 182-189, for discussion of the abolition of life terms.

[33] *Op. cit. supra* n. 8, at 14-5.

[34] Kinsey, Sexual Behavior in the Human Male 224 (1948).

Yet these and other laws prohibiting similarly common behavior are the basis of adjudications of psychopathy. It is as illogical as calling a drinker during prohibition or a gambler today a psychopath.

Second: we are concerned with sentencing of sex offenders. Disparity (inequality) in the sentencing of sex offenders is probably as great as for any group of offenses; it is matched only by the disparity in enforcement of these laws. Dr. Karl Bowman points out that several years ago when New York reduced ordinary homosexual acts from a felony to a misdemeanor, California raised the penalty from a maximum of ten years to a maximum of twenty years, later fixing a minimum of one year and a maximum of life imprisonment for anyone "guilty of the infamous crime against nature, committed with mankind or with any animal."[35]

But he points out, "Scientific observations show that many of the higher mammals indulged in various sexual practices such as masturbation, fellatio, cunnilingus and sodomy. To many investigators of human behavior, it seems that man inherits from his mammalian ancestry some or all of these tendencies."

It was ancient Hebrew law that made sodomy a capital offense, Dr. Bowman writes:

> The Mosaic law . . . included only thirty-six capital crimes; half of them involved illegal sex relations. Three of these described unnatural sex relations: (1) between man and animal; (2) between woman and animal; and (3) between one man and another. The Christian religion largely took over the Jewish laws concerning sexual behavior. Sodomy came to be the crime "peccatum illud horrible inter Christianos"—that abominable sin, not fit to be named among Christians. The medieval ecclesiastic courts made it a serious crime, even when committed in secret.[36]

Disparity of enforcement seems built into our sex laws. Third: our inconsistency is enormous. Under the law, rape may be

---

[35] Bowman, Too Many Sex Laws, The Nation, Oct. 25, 1958.

[36] "The statutes of Henry VIII's time (25 Henry VIII C. 6), which are the basis of our law in this matter, prohibited buggery with mankind or beast under penalty of death. But buggery includes only genital-anal contact between man and man or between man and woman and what is now termed bestiality—genital contact with animals. It did not include fellatio

committed only by men; evidently we do not disapprove seduction, or, indeed "rape," by women, even of young boys. The worst crime—sodomy—is probably as common among women as among men, but women are not prosecuted for it, even when they sexually seduce young girls.[37]

This writer agrees with Bowman and would say that only sexual acts that do violence to others, acts upon children, or those that come within the realm of disorderly behavior, should be illegal. The horror and harm done by our unnatural sex laws, the heartbreak, victimization, and death, are inestimable.[38] The prac-

---

(oral-genital contact) or cunnilingus (oral-vaginal contact). . . . Because of the omissions of the statute of the 1500's, a defendant convicted of sodomy by an English court in 1817 for an act of fellatio with a child, was directed to apply for a pardon. The judges of England had met and decided that these facts did not constitute the crime of sodomy. Even into the twentieth century, many American courts recognized the authority of this case and felt compelled to follow it despite their reluctance to do so. . . . The Indiana and Wyoming statutes . . . declare an individual guilty of sodomy if he entices, allures, instigates, or aids any person under twenty-one to commit masturbation or self-pollution."—Ploscowe, op. cit. n. 23, at 185, 187.

[37] Ploscowe writes that female homosexuality is far more widespread than is generally realized: "Katherine B. Davis studied twelve hundred unmarried college graduates who averaged thirty-seven years of age. Of this number half had experienced intense emotional relations with other women and over three hundred or one-fourth of the total, reported sexual activities with other women. Of one hundred married women studied by Hamilton, one-fourth admitted homosexual physical episodes." He points out that much of the female homosexual activity (like that of males) violates sodomy and crime-against-nature statutes.—*Id.* at 190, 193. It is an everyday matter for women to share a bed, but not so for men. See, for homosexual seduction among women, Caprio, Female Homosexuality 139-48, and ch. 14 (1962). The role of the female in aggressive sexual assaults on males or in enticing or provoking assaults by males has been noted by many.

Under one of the most recently revised penal codes, that of Illinois of 1961, father-daughter incest is considered "aggravated" incest, punishable by up to 20 years, but mother-son incest is "ordinary," punishable by up to ten years.—Noted in Masters, Patterns of Incest 69 (1963), which also observes: "That a man committing sodomy or fellatio with his son offends less grievously than a man copulating with his adopted daughter is in keeping with the strong pro-homosexual bias of the Code. The Code has, it may be noted, moved strongly against prostitution while eliminating all penalties for adult homosexual intercourse."

[38] The victimization (including blackmail) of homosexuals; the million illegal abortions a year resulting in an unknown number of deaths, illness, humiliation and fear; venereal disease; anxiety, frigidity, and unhappy marriages. "If the sexual difficulties of later life can to a considerable extent

tices are not abolished; they are driven underground, thereby increasing suffering.[39] To use the language of Madison Avenue: more doctors have given up smoking than sodomy,[40] despite the fact that smoking is legal and sodomy is not. Very few readers of this book have not committed a sex crime. (That makes our legislation hypocrisy rather than prudery or morality, does it not?)

Only sexual acts that do violence to others, or are committed by adults upon children, or come within the realm of disorderly behavior should be illegal. What reason is there to take any other view? This may do violence to some religious tenets, but violation of church law should be left to the church.

Perhaps some of the behavior is thought not respectable.

> The Parlor Maid: "But do you think it would ever be thought respectable, sir?"
>
> Conrad: "My good girl, all biological necessities have to be made respectable whether we like it or not; so you needn't worry yourself about that."[41]

—George Bernard Shaw, "The Gospel of the Brothers Barnabas"

---

be prevented by proper upbringing, it is reasonable to assume that measures of psychological understanding would produce better results than the moral opprobrium and punishment inflicted on sexual offenders under present laws. A person is forced into a deviant form of sexual adaptation by the injection of fear into the normal sexual function. Hence, the law itself unwittingly encourages the commission of sexual offenses by inflicting drastic penalties and paying too much attention to them. Much in the manner of Victorian taboos, penal clauses more often than not aggravate the problem instead of resolving it."—Slovenko & Richards, Psychosexuality and the Criminal Law, 15 Vanderbilt L. Rev. 797 at 827 (1962).

[39] Dr. Louis Hellman, director of the Obstetrics and Gynecology Department at Kings County Hospital, Brooklyn, N.Y.—"Criminal abortion has always been a severe problem. But in the last few years the law has really cracked down on the professional abortionist and put many of them out of business. By professional I mean well-trained but unethical physicians. Also, since the Castro revolution closed down Cuba, which used to be wide open for abortions, women can't go there either. *So where do they go? To the amateur*"—that is, to those not qualified to perform the abortion. Quoted in Davidson, The Deadly Favor, Ladies' Home Journal, November 1963; our ital.

[40] In a 1954 survey of the smoking habits of Massachusetts physicians, 34 per cent stated they were not smoking. In a resurvey in 1959, the percentage had risen to 45. Among those smoking one pack a day or more, the rate changed from 30.5 per cent to 18, a reduction of over 40 per cent.—261 New Engl. J. Med. 603 (1959).

[41] Indeed, some forms of sodomy are certainly becoming respectable, and

are presented as indicated practices in marriage manuals readily available to all. Ploscowe writes: "Much of the sexual activity of husbands and wives also falls under the ban of sodomy and crime-against-nature statutes. Anyone familiar with problems of marriage is aware of the fact that the sexual behavior of married couples is not limited to that which is conventional in character. For example, anal coition has long been used as a form of birth control by certain classes of society. Fellatio and cunnilingus are frequently indulged in by husbands and wives either as part of the forepleasure to a normal act of sexual intercourse or as a means of inducing orgasm. So common have these practices become between husbands and wives that the modern marriage counselor apparently no longer looks upon them as perversions. For example, Stanley Jones writes: 'Many of the variants of conventional sexual technique which were formerly regarded as perversions are now acknowledged as playing a legitimate part in the forepleasure that leads up to happily consummated intercourse. . . . It is now recognized that any form of bodily manipulation which can be used as an adjunct to mutual sex orgasm may in no way be regarded as a perverse or unnatural addiction.' "—Ploscowe, *op. cit. supra* n. 23 at 189.

"Hannah and Abraham Stone's authoritative and widely sold book, *A Marriage Manual*, states: 'I do not think that we can consider any particular method of sexual union as normal or abnormal. . . . Variety in the sexual approach is much to be desired for marital sexual satisfaction. . . . There is nothing perverse or degrading, I would say, in any sex practice which is undertaken for the purpose of promoting a more harmonious sexual adjustment between a husband and a wife in marriage.' And one of the most conservative marriage manuals of the 1960's, Dr. Rebecca Liswood's *A Marriage Doctor Speaks Her Mind About Sex*, notes that 'when a couple is showing affection, there is nothing wrong with any sex practice that appeals to them.' Presumably, for recommendations like this, the Stones, Liswood, and many other writers of modern sex manuals should be arrested and jailed for inciting to the commission of a felony in most of the states of the Union."—Ellis, The American Sexual Tragedy 96 (1962).

"Certain acts . . . are employed by many couples as sexually stimulating practices before intercourse. These practices are so common and, from the moral standpoint, so acceptable that one cannot find fault with them. These include such sexual play as oral stimulation of the genitals, anal intromission, spanking, biting, and so forth as long as these practices are acceptable to both partners and as long as the act ends properly with the ejaculation taking place in the vagina. Legally, however, most such acts are forbidden and punishable."—Cavanagh, Sexual Anomalies and the Law, 9 The Catholic Lawyer 4 (1963).

Chapter 6

Narcotics Law Violators

In the way the law deals with drug addicts and its surrounding problems we again encounter illness and a clash between programs to treat or punish. Again we meet the issue of civil or criminal commitment, as against the alternative, in this instance (as with certain sex offenders) of avoiding any commitment, a person having the right to treatment being given voluntarily. Do we again encounter illusions? Do the illusions infect the program of civil commitment of addicts?

Narcotics Laws and Their Administration

Some medical uses of narcotics were known in antiquity. Addiction was perhaps first dealt with as an alarming public health issue in China in the eighteenth century. A trickle of narcotics was arriving in America even before the Revolution. The hypodermic needle was invented shortly before the Civil War. Patients were encouraged to use it on themselves. By 1865, many thousands of soldiers had received numerous injections to relieve their suffering from wounds and sickness. In addition, patent medicines, containing easily obtainable narcotics, spread without hindrance. Drugs, including morphine, were available at moderate prices not only from the local pharmacist, but from the grocer as well. Not until the 1890's, when there were several hundred thousand or more addicts, did doctors learn and warn about the dangers of opium addiction. When heroin was first produced in 1898, it was thought to be nonaddictive. World War I cut down sharply on the supply of narcotics at the same time that the demand for medical purposes increased. States and cities set up clinics to provide for the needs of addicts.

In 1912 the United States entered into the international Hague Opium convention, undertaking to control the domestic production and use of opium products. The Harrison Act,[1] passed in 1914, was not a criminal statute but a regulatory measure imposing an excise tax, to be evidenced by stamps on the package. The act made it unlawful for anyone to purchase, sell, or dispense any narcotic drugs, except in or from the original stamped package; and any sale or giving of such drugs had to be pursuant to a written order on Treasury Department forms. Persons involved in handling narcotics drugs (importers, doctors, others) are required to register with the Treasury Department and pay a tax. In 1937 marijuana was subjected to a similar pattern of control, except that the tax rate was prohibitory—one dollar per ounce on any transfer to a person registered under the act and one hundred dollars per ounce on transfer to an unregistered person.

Under the act physicians may prescribe or administer drugs to patients in the course of professional practice without the Treasury Department order form and without regard for the stamped package requirement; and persons possessing drugs obtained pursuant to a prescription, or received directly from a registered practitioner, are excepted from the general prohibitions against transportation and possession.

For the first ten years of the Harrison Act's operation physicians were unhampered in their prescription of narcotics to patients and a number of clinics for addicts were operating. Indeed, "the Treasury Department's 1919 report encouraged local health departments to set up clinics where addicts could receive carefully regulated amounts of drugs and be encouraged at the same time to overcome their habits. Such clinics were established in forty-odd cities. Some of them appeared to be fairly successful,

---

[1] Act of December 17, 1914, c. 1, 38 Stat. 785, as amended, 26 U.S.C. §§ 4701-36 (Internal Revenue Code).

although many took insufficient precautions to assure that addicts would not obtain drugs from more than one source or failed to ascertain that they were treating actual addicts, so that sometimes peddlers came and sold the drugs they received from the clinics."[2]

Suddently a change occurred. America was at a psychologically tragic moment in its history. For crime and its rational treatment, for civil rights, the moment was to have permanent ill effects. The entrance of the United States into World War I and the resulting climate led to repressive changes, the adoption of Prohibition, the Palmer Raids, and a wave of fear in the country.

As I have pointed out elsewhere, in penology it marked the sharp reversal of legislation to abolish the death penalty, the passage of increased penalties for various crimes, the spread of the Baumes laws for repeated offenders, and laws restricting the use of probation.[3] The narcotics control program is another instance.[4]

In 1920 the Narcotic Division of the Treasury Department was merged into the new Prohibition Unit, then launching its crusade against liquor-drinkers and bootleggers. It also launched an attack on the medical profession. In 1919 a Dr. John Webb had been prosecuted for flagrant violation of the narcotics law by indiscriminately selling prescriptions, by the thousands, for fifty cents apiece. He was found guilty and appealed to the Supreme Court, which affirmed in a 5-4 decision, writing that "to call such an order for the use of morphine a physician's prescription would be so plain a perversion of meaning that no discussion is required."[5] A second case of outrageous abuse was appealed to the Court, and the conviction was upheld.[6]

Writes Mr. Rufus King:

> Next came the case that contained the joker, *United States v. Behrman*, decided March 27, 1922.[7] Here too, the abuse was flagrant. Dr. Behrman had given a known addict, at one time and for use as the addict saw fit, prescriptions for 150 grains of heroin, 360 grams of mor-

---

[2] Murtagh & Harris, Who Live in Shadow 181 (1959). Also King, Narcotic Laws and Enforcement Policies, 22 Law and Contemp. Problems 113 at 125 (1957).

[3] The Law of Criminal Correction ch. 1 § 22 (1963).

[4] See Nyswander, The Drug Addict as a Patient ch. 1 (1956).

[5] Webb. v. United States, 249 U.S. 96, 99 (1919).

[6] Jin Fuey Moy v. United States, 254 U.S. 189 (1920).

[7] United States v. Behrman, 258 U.S. 280 (1922).

phine, and 210 grams of cocaine. But the indictment was drawn so as to omit any accusation of bad faith; it charged, in effect, that this treatment was for the purpose of curing the addict, and thus, its validity depended on a holding *that prescribing drugs for an addict was a crime, regardless of the physician's intent in the matter.* The District Court sustained a demurrer, and the Government invoked its right to appeal directly to the Supreme Court. A majority of the justices, no doubt moved by the flagrant facts, which they set forth fully in the opinion, ruled that the indictment was good. Three dissented tersely: "It seems to me wrong to construe the statute as creating a crime in this way without a word of warning. Of course the facts alleged suggest an indictment in a different form, but the Government preferred to trust to a strained interpretation of the law rather than to the finding of a jury upon the facts. I think that the judgment should be affirmed." The dissenters, besides Holmes, who wrote for them, were Justices Brandeis and McReynolds.

Armed with that came to be known as the *Behrman* indictment, the Narcotics Division launched a reign of terror. Doctors were bullied and threatened, and those who were adamant went to prison. Any prescribing for an addict, unless he had some other ailment that called for narcotization, was likely to mean trouble with the Treasury agents. The addict-patient vanished; the addict-criminal emerged in his place. Instead of policing a small domain of petty stamp-tax chisellers, the Narcotics Division expanded its activities until it was swelling our prison population with thousands of felony convictions each year. Many of those who were caught had been respected members of their communities until the T-men packed them off.[8]

---

[8] King, *op. cit. supra* n. 2. "Prosecution of a number of psysicians had made others doubly wary. Of the 8,100 physicians practicing in New York City, less than forty continued to prescribe narcotics for addicts. And the Bureau seized upon this fact further to discredit the physician's role. These physicians, besieged by addicts, were of necessity giving out a large number of prescriptions. Accused of 'trafficking in drugs,' they were all indicted. The term 'trafficking physician' carried such opprobrium that practitioners who valued their reputation could not afford to administer drugs no matter how ill the addict. The Bureau had won the day in New York, and the private physician's right to treat the ill had been abrogated."— Nyswander, *op. cit. supra* n. 4 at 6.

The Behrman ruling was challenged by Dr. Charles O. Linder, who after a lifetime of honorable practice in Spokane, Wash., was induced by one of the Division's addict-informers to write a prescription for four small tablets of cocaine and morphine. Several agents thereupon descended on his office, conducted a search, and took him off to jail. He was indicted in the *Behrman* form, convicted, sentenced, and lost on his appeal to the Circuit Court of Appeals. He carried the fight to the United States Supreme Court, where he was completely vindicated.[9] The unanimous opinion set forth what is still the Supreme Court's interpretation of the Harrison Act:

> The enactment under consideration levies a tax, upheld by this court, upon every person who imports, manufactures, produces, compounds, sells, deals in, dispenses or gives away opium or coca leaves or derivatives therefrom, and may regulate medical practice in the States only so far as is reasonably appropriate for or merely incidental to its enforcement. It says nothing of "addicts" and does not undertake to prescribe methods for their medical treatment, and we cannot possibly conclude that a physician acted improperly or unwisely or for other than medical purpose solely because he has dispensed to one of them, in the ordinary course and in good faith, four small tablets of morphine or cocaine for relief of conditions incident to conviction.

The Court warned that its opinions in the *Webb* and *Jin Fuey Moy* cases should be narrowly limited to the facts there involved, and it dismissed the *Behrman* case (and the *Behrman* indictment) in these words:

> This opinion related to definitely alleged facts and must be so understood. . . . The opinion cannot be accepted as authority for holding that a physician who acts bona fide and according to fair medical standards, may never give an addict moderate amounts of drugs for self-administration in order to relieve conditions incident to addiction. Enforcement of the tax demands no such drastic rule, and if the Act had such scope it would certainly encounter grave constitutional difficulties.

---

[9] Linder v. United States, 268 U.S. 5 (1925).

But by 1925, writes Mr. King, it was too late to change the pattern:

> The trick had worked. The doctors had withdrawn, and they never permitted the addict to reapproach them. The peddler had taken over, and his profits soared as enforcement efforts reduced his competition and drove his customers ever deeper into the underworld, where they were easy prey. It is significant that the present-day regulation of the Narcotics Bureau advising doctors of their rights in dealing with addicts blithely ignores what the Supreme Court said in the *Linder* case and still paraphrases the discredited language of *Webb v. United States.*

The policy of the Narcotics Division led to a packing of the prisons. A 1928 census of prisoners in federal institutions revealed that in that heyday of Prohibition there were two prisoners serving sentences for narcotic-drug-law offenses for every one incarcerated for a liquor-law violation. Prisoners committed for violation of the drug laws constituted one-third of the total federal prison population, 2,529 out of 7,138.[10]

World War II depleted state and federal prisons. In 1946 narcotics violators constituted 4.3 per cent of the federal prisoners, but the situation was to become worse. In 1951 the Senate committee on organized crime turned its attention to narcotics and marijuana, receiving testimony that drug addiction was on the increase and had captured school children and teen-agers.[11] The Narcotics Bureau urged harsher penal measures. Congress enacted a bill, introduced by Hale Boggs, of Louisiana, providing for mandatory minimum penalties and prohibiting the possibility of suspended sentence or probation for second offenders. In 1955 a subcommittee of the Senate Judiciary Committee was authorized to make a study of the Harrison Act. Under the chairmanship of Senator Daniel, it rendered a report calling for even more severe legislation. The result was a new law which raised mandatory minimum penalties and included the death penalty.[12]

---

[10] King, *op. cit. supra* n. 2, citing Schmeckebier, The Bureau of Prohibition, Service Monograph No. 27, p. 143, Institute for Government Research, Brookings Institute (1929).

[11] Senate Special Committee to Investigate Organized Crime in Interstate Commerce, Final Report, S. Rep. No. 725, 82nd Cong., 1st Sess., p. 27 (1951).

By 1960 15 per cent of the federal prison population was made up of narcotics law violators. The increase was accounted for by longer sentences, mandatory minimum sentences, and restrictions on parole. The federal laws designed to be "tough" on narcotics offenders are proving to be tough on the federal prison system, producing an increasingly difficult administrative problem. Said James V. Bennett, director of the Federal Bureau of Prisons:

> The provisions of this statute [the 1956 Narcotics Control Act] permitted no discrimination between defendants, the circumstances surrounding their offenses, and their relative roles in the narcotics traffic as major racketeers, small-time peddlers, or the actual victims, the addicts. The law, in its very inflexibility, produced inevitable disparities. With no demonstrable compensating advantages in terms of deterrence, this law has made a travesty of our concepts of justice as far as it concerns the defendants sentenced to life in prison for selling narcotics; he is the only lifer in the Federal Prison System who is not eligible for parole, and there are many other lifers whose crimes—including multiple murder—were much more heinous. A colored disc jocky, a first offender, was sent to prison for 50 years. A garment factory clerk, a first offender, got 50 years. A hat check girl, first offender, got 40 years. An addict, who had a prior record which did not involve narcotics, was sent to prison for 80 years.
>
> If these defendants had robbed banks at gunpoint they would have received sentences of 10 or 15 years; if they had organized themselves into a gigantic conspiracy to rig prices, they could get at most one year. As

---

12 Pub. L. 728, 84th Cong., 2d Sess., 70 Stat. 567 (1956). The mandatory minimum sentences were raised to two, five, and ten years for successive offenses in the possession, prescription, and registration categories; first sale, transfer, and smuggling offenses carry a minimum sentence of five years, ten for succeeding offenses, without possibility of suspension of sentence, probation, or parole. For sale or transfer to a person under 18, the minimum sentence is ten years; if the drug is heroin, the court may impose life imprisonment or the jury may direct the imposition of a sentence of death. Drug addiction and drug-law violation are made grounds for deportation. The act also made special provisions for police work of the Narcotics Bureau. Customs and Narcotics Bureau agents may carry arms and make arrests without a warrant.

it is, these drug victims have only the prospect of spending the rest of their lives in prison. With interminable sentences and no possibility of parole, these offenders are accumulating from year to year in the federal prisons and now compose the second largest group of prisoners, their number exceeded only by the car thieves. They have utterly no incentive to improve themselves in prison, and their very presence, bulking ever larger, is creating a formidable handicap and a discouraging atmosphere for the prison staffs who are doing their best to rehabilitate both the narcotic offenders and the many other types of prisoners in our institutions. The sentences in the narcotic cases, instead of promoting the rehabilitation of the offender and the public safety, are proving to be socially destructive in their effects.[13]

The federal government operates two hospital for addicts—at Lexington, Ky., and Forth Worth, Tex. The inmates include those who, on conviction, are sentenced to confinement in them, those who are ordered to submit to confinement there as a condition of probation, and patients who apply voluntarily for treatment. The addict is gradually withdrawn from the drug, and a program of physical rehabilitation is undertaken. The recidivism rate is high. Dr. Kenneth W. Chapman, Assistant Chief of the Public Health Service, states that only 15 per cent of the patients have been permanently cured.[14]

The state laws are in the style of the federal acts as interpreted by the Federal Bureau of Narcotics. Practically all states have enacted the Uniform Narcotic Drug Act.[15] The Uniform Act, like the federal narcotics laws, makes possession generally unlawful. A physician is allowed to administer drugs "within the scope of his employment or official duty, and then only for scientific or medicinal purposes"; he may prescribe drugs "in good faith and in the course of his professional practice only." One study reports that "though very few cases have arisen which interpret these phrases, it seems clear that the Uniform State Narcotics Acts will

---

13 Bennett, The Sentence—Its Relation to Crime and Rehabilitation, U. of Ill. L. Forum v. 1960, p. 500, at 509.

14Cantor, The Criminal Law and the Narcotics Problem, 51 J. Cr. L., Crim. and P.S. 512, at 524 (1961).

15 Id. at 516.

be so interpreted as to make unlawful prescriptions to an addict for the purpose of treating his addiction."[16] The penalty section in the Act is left blank, but typically the states provide explicitly for mandatory minimum terms, increasing in severity for repeated offenses; some include life imprisonment, or death in offenses involving minors. Some of the acts are similar to the federal law in barring probation or parole.

What Has Been Achieved

How many addicts do we have? Would we have fewer with another policy? Are we successful in treating addicts, within the framework of the present policy? Would we be likely to be more successful with another policy? Is the extent of crime associated with narcotics greater or less with the present policy than with another policy?

It is estimated that New York City has 25,000 to 50,000 drug addicts. The rest of the country, it is estimated, has an equal number of addicts; but the statistics are notoriously unreliable.[17] Although the Federal Bureau of Narcotics claims the number is less than before the federal program of control was initiated, a reduction it sees as a sign of success for the federal policy, the number of addicts appears to most observers to be increasing.

The Mayor of the City of New York, Robert F. Wagner, stated to a conference on narcotics called by the White House in 1962:

> Only a tiny percentage of these addicts are able to support their habit out of their regular income or capital. The rest have to resort to special activities to get the money. . . . Women generally turn to prostitution and men to theft. Stolen goods . . . must be sold, generally bringing no more than one-fifth of their replacement value. We estimate that it costs the average addict $10,000 a year to support his habit, or $50,000 in stolen goods. If 25,000 addicts each steal this much, the total comes to well over a billion dollars a year. If only half this many addicts steal to this extent, the total is still $625 million. Even if one adjusts conservatively further

---

[16] *Ibid.*

[17] The papers by Chein, Eddy, Eldridge, Proceedings, White House Conference on Narcotic and Drug Abuse 131-42 (1962). Cantor, *op. cit. supra* n. 14 at 519.

downward, it is hard to place the figure below a half billion dollars. . . .

Nothing that has been tried to cure addiction has really worked on a lasting basis. A relatively few addicts have undoubtedly been helped to give up their habit, but that number is not great. On the police and enforcement side, it is true that one dope ring after another has been smashed by brilliant police work; many traffickers in drugs have been put in jail. . . . Add it all up, and still the fact remains that the number of addicts is increasing, and so is the drain of addiction on our society.[18]

The reference to "dope rings" is not to isolated little teams of growers or peddlers. The little man is the one who is caught; but those behind him are big business indeed, organized crime with great power and wealth.[19] The interest of the crime syndicates in narcotics is of modern vintage; it did not exist before the Harrison Act was passed. But in the twenties and thirties it achieved great power, international ties, and influence over "police departments and mayors, judges and district attorneys and juries."[20]

What can we expect the future of the current policy to be? Again citing Wagner:

If I thought police action by itself would control the problem, I would be for that exclusively; but we have overwhelming evidence that it does not. No thinking person today would claim that any amount of money and surveillance can keep narcotics out of illicit channels. . . . We must study and learn and establish means whereby the addict, when he has returned from detoxication or from withdrawal or from confinement or shelter, can fit into society.[21]

Just as years of Prohibition contributed to the growth of gangs, the present policy of making the drug unavailable to the addict from legal sources has contributed to the prevalence of organized crime in the business of supplying the drug illegally, and at a handsome profit. The present enforcement policy is also the reason why most physicians—and, in fact, even specialists—know

---

18 Proceedings, *op. cit. supra* n. 17 at 17-8.
19 Cantor, *op. cit. supra* n. 14 at 521.
20 Anslinger & Oursler, The Murderers 4-7 (1961).
21 Proceedings, *op. cit. supra* n. 17 at 20.

so little about the cause and cure of addiction. At least, it is responsible for the barring of physicians from the practice and experience from which the knowledge might have been gained.

The enforcement policy has made criminals out of patients. And the severe penalties for violators has crowded the prisons with narcotics violators, a hopeless mass, hampering any rehabilitative program for themselves or other prisoners.[22] Senator Dodd presented to the White House Conference on Narcotics a survey of the views of federal judges, probation officers, prison officials, and district attorneys on the law requiring minimum prison sentences and denying probation and parole for federal narcotics offenders. It showed that 92 per cent of the wardens, 73 per cent of the judges, 83 per cent of the probation officers, and 50 per cent of the prosecuting attorneys opposed the mandatory minimum sentence provision. Opposition to the denial of parole and probation was even more emphatic: 97 per cent of the wardens, 86 per cent of the judges, 86 per cent of the probation officials, and 55 per cent of the prosecutors were in opposition. Senator Dodd condemned the program of long prison sentences in these terms: "This solution is so demonstrably ineffective as a deterrent to narcotic crimes, wreaks such havoc within the penal system, does such damage to the individual involved, . . . that all reasonable observers will eventually agree that the tragic and many-sided toll of blind and rigid imprisonment procedures is too great to pay for the fancied and illusory gain."[23]

The Position of Medicine

Among the victims of the present narcotics situation is the medical profession. Doctors have been prevented from treating addicts by the federal narcotics administration. In the words of the New York Academy of Medicine, the history is one of "a relentless, unceasing campaign of intimidation."[24]

---

[22] James V. Bennett, director, Federal Bureau of Prisons, Proceedings, *op. cit. supra* n. 17 at 231.

[23] *Id.* at 232-3.

[24] Report on Drug Addiction-II, 39 Bull. N.Y. Acad. of Med., 2d Series 417, at 466 (1963).

It started in 1919 and still continues. It has not been an idle threat. Hundreds of physicians imprisoned on narcotics charges—many, if not most, unjustifiably—from 1920 to 1940 provide abundant evidence. . . .[25] The means of intimidation of physicians was dictation by the Narcotics Bureau on the method of treating addicts. Its views were incorporated into its regulations, which have the effect of law. Deviation brought possible arrest, conviction, and imprisonment. True, the Supreme Court of the United States through its interpretation of the Harrison Act has denied the legality and validity of this encroachment on the practice of medicine. Nevertheless, the Narcotics Bureau has continued to disregard this ruling of the highest court and has retained the section in its regulations to this day.

Thoroughly intimidated by a nonmedical policy agency which had dictated the clinical procedure for treating addicts, physicians silently and completely withdrew from the scene. Loss of good name and professional ruin were too high a price to pay for even the most urgently needed humanitarianism. . . . As long as the Narcotics Bureau persists in its policy of dictating how addicts may be legally treated and threatens to or actually does prosecute those physicians who deviate from it—a stand it has never publicly rescinded—physicians will be wary. Despite the supposed security provided by the Supreme Court ruling, physicians do not entirely trust the Narcotics Bureau. With good reason they suspect a trap, a device that has been frequently used over the years in the punitive campaign. Furthermore, the Narcotics Bureau's defiance of the Supreme Court, apparently with impunity, is not reassuring.[26]

A memorandum issued by the Prohibition Commissioner in 1921 to narcotic agents stated: "This Bureau has never sanctioned or approved the so-called reductive ambulatory treatment of addiction. . . . This bureau cannot under any circumstances sanction the treatment of mere addiction where the drugs are placed in the addict's possession, nor can it sanction the use of

---

[25] *Id.* at 432.
[26] *Id.* at 419-20, 434.

narcotics to cover a period in excess of 30 days, when personally administered by the physician to a patient either in a proper institution or unconfined. If a physician, pursuant to the so-called reductive ambulatory treatment, places narcotic drugs in the possession of the addict who is not confined, such action will be regarded as showing lack of good faith in the treatment of the addiction and that the drugs were furnished to satisfy the cravings of the addict." In direct conflict with the Supreme Court and other rulings, the regulations of the Narcotics Bureau still provide: "An order purporting to be a prescription issued to an addict or habitual user of narcotics, not in the course of professional treatment but for the purpose of providing the user with narcotics sufficient to keep him comfortable by maintaining his customary use, is not a prescription within the meaning or intent of section 4705 (c)(2), and the person filling such an order, as well as the person issuing it, shall be subject to the penalties provided for violations of the law relating to narcotic drugs."[27] But the United States Court of Appeals has said: "There is no doubt that the [Linder] case ruled that a physician may lawfully prescribe narcotics for an addict purely because of his addiction, provided the amount is not so large as to put it within the power of the addict to sell part of the drug in violation of the Harrison Act."[28]

The intimidation consisted of not only the imposition of a medical regulation and the initiation of prosecutions, but "dictation, threats, hounding, and oppression from the narcotics force over the years, . . . still continuing."[29] In 1955-56 the American Bar Association and the American Medical Association—than which there are no organizations more respectable—appointed a Joint Committee on Narcotic Drugs to explore the problem of addiction and the enforcement and other elements related to it. The Committee Staff prepared a fairly comprehensive interim report on the subject. Before presenting it to the parent bodies, the study director sent it privately to the Commissioner of the Federal Bureau of Narcotics, inviting comments and suggestions. The commissioner replied: "My suggestion is that the person

---

[27] Code of Federal Regulations, Title 26 § 151.392, 1961 Supp. (1963).
[28] Hawkins v. United States, 90 F.2d 551 (1937); to same effect Bush v. United States, 16 F.2d 709 (1927).
[29] *Op. cit. supra* n. 24 at 433.

(unquestionably prejudiced) who prepared this report should sit down with our people to make necessary corrections." The study director asked for a bill of particulars. A few months later —nothing having yet been published by ABA-AMA—the Bureau published a 186-page document: Comments on "Narcotic Drugs, Interim Report of the Joint Committee of the American Bar Association and the American Medical Association on Narcotic Drugs" by Advisory Committee to the Federal Bureau of Narcotics.[30] The Comments were widely distributed. Lindesmith notes: "The sale of this pamphlet was discontinued after an attack upon the Supreme Court which it contained was given unfavorable newspaper publicity, but by this time the document had already been widely circulated to libraries and law enforcement officials throughout the country." The ABA-AMA Interim Report itself was not published until 1961.[31]

It is not surprising that the medical groups most outspoken in criticism of the official policy should be those in New York, where the incidence of narcotics and, hence, the frustration of doctors are greatest. At its meeting in February 1962 the Medical Society of the County of New York passed a resolution endorsing "as ethical conduct the participation of member physicians in a pilot, experimental, controlled project on narcotic addiction in which a most carefully selected group of addicts would be treated on an ambulatory basis for their addiction at a clinic center and simultaneously undergo psychiatric and other types of medical care to rehabilitate them to a normal life. This interpretation of ethical conduct by physicians is taken with the understanding that the proposed pilot project would be under the joint supervision of the medical profession, the law enforcement officials and voluntary agencies of citizens' groups to insure that abuses do not occur and that addicts are not merely maintained on drugs but instead are also given intensive medical sociological and other aid to effect their rehabilitation to a normal way of life."[32]

The New York Academy of Medicine is more outspoken, and

---

[30] 1958.

[31] Drug Addiction: Crime or Disease? Interim and Final Reports of the Joint Committee of the American Bar Association and the American Medical Association on Narcotic Drugs (1961), Introd. by Alfred R. Lindesmith, p. x.

[32] Editorial, 18 N.Y. Med. 559 (August 1962).

demands that doctors be free to operate clinics and administer maintenance doses when necessary. It clearly explains why:

> Sudden withdrawal is the only procedure recognized and sanctioned by the Narcotics Bureau. It is recommended, indeed insisted upon, by them for all addicts. It is their Procrustean bed on which they would make all addicts lie, some never to rise again. Those physicians expert in the treatment of addiction maintain that even in the most humane and effective form it should be applied to a particular group, the most easily curable. Applied to others, especially if rigorously, it may produce untoward results, even death. Cold turkey should never be permitted; it has no place in treatment.

"Cold turkey," it says, "is cruel, barbarous, inhuman, and dangerous. It undermines the addict, already burdened and handicapped by his psychological difficulties."

> It is erroneously assumed that all treatment is directed to cure. . . . Different kinds of treatment may be distinguished on the basis of their goals. Cure is one goal, the highest, of treatment. But it is not always possible to achieve complete cure by reversal of the pathological process of eradication of disease. Sometimes the clinician must strive and settle for the next best goal, amelioration. His aim is to bring about improvement by retarding or arresting the pathological process and abating the disease."[33]

Some addicts are incurable by present methods. Some are curable, but are resistant to or rebellious against treatment. Some (the Academy statement points out) have a concurrent illness that contraindicates certain modes of treatment. The medical judgment is that the preferred procedure for treating even strongly addicted patients is reduction and gradual withdrawal, not cold turkey: furthermore, "a preparative period is advisable in which the addict receives his accustomed drug until he is adjusted to the hospital environment." Withdrawal before psychological treatment is wrong because the sequence is "the reverse of what it should have been. Since the narcotic is a

---

[33] New York Academy of Medicine, *op. cit. supra* n. 24.

crutch for the addict, it should never be taken from him until it is ascertained that he has another support."

Furthermore, there are some addicts who must be maintained on drugs for an appreciable period. These include the incurables, for whom the probability of improvement or success from withdrawal is low or nil and the chance of worsened physical outcome is high. There are "confirmed addicts, well-adjusted and leading useful, productive, and otherwise exemplary lives which would probably be upset by removing their drug. They are contented with their present status, do not desire treatment, and would resist change. The wisdom of disturbing them is to be questioned; for the result, socially and economically, might be destructive and bad. Kolb cites addicts who did not benefit but rather actually suffered from enforced withdrawal. In contrast, he describes a man, age 74, who had lived 'an efficient and useful life as an addict for 41 years.'" Sometimes temporary delay in withdrawal is indicated "to gain time to overcome the addict's resistance and start under favorable circumstances. . . . The addict may be reluctant to be subjected to withdrawal; his refractory attitude may arise from one or more emotions or feelings such as apprehension, lack of familiarity, resignation, despair. . . . An addict's attitude is important to the success of treatment. If the unwilling addict is allowed a longer period of preparation and adjustment for the procedure, it may be somewhat easier for him to undergo the ordeal; it may carry enhanced chance of a lasting outcome."[34] As Marie Nyswander points out, before 1914 the drug addict, having little or no involvement with criminal activity, carried on his job and maintained his home and family life. "His illness did not inflict injury on anyone other than himself."[35]

---

[34] *Ibid.*

[35] *Ibid.* The "British plan," to which many attribute the small number of addicts in England and the absence of illegal drug syndicates, is, in effect, the freedom of the doctor to treat, including prescription of maintenance doses when needed. See Bishop, The British Approach, in Nyswander, *op. cit. supra* n. 4; Lindesmith, The British System of Narcotics Control, 22 Law and Contemp. Problems 138 (1957); Brill, Great Britain's Treatment Approach to Narcotics Addiction, Proceedings, *op. cit. supra* n. 17 at 72; Schur, Great Britain's Treatment Approach, *id.* at 110. "The guiding principle in this regard continues to be that laid down by a Departmental Committee in 1926: '. . . morphine or heroin may properly be administered to addicts in the following circumstances, namely (a) where

The medical approach says that if we treat addicts medically (and psychiatrically), with drugs administered where necessary, even in maintenance doses by doctors (as in England and generally in Europe),[36] we may discover more effective ways of treatment than are known or applied at present. In addition, since drugs will, if medically prescribed, be available to addicts at no great cost, they will no longer be customers of the peddlers, and thus the market of the racketeers will tend to dry up. If this approach is as successful here as in other countries, it will contribute to eliminating organized crime from drug peddling. "Destroying the illicit traffic by removing the profit would be carried out most sensibly, readily, and effectively by turning the authority and responsibility for application of narcotics completely over to physicians."[37] (After all, addicts *are* being maintained on the drug; what has happened, as Dr. Nyswander puts it, is that "the criminal underworld has taken over the task of treating the addict.")

But, says the New York Academy of Medicine, "the very thought of such a development is an abomination to the Bureau.

---

patients are under treatment by the gradual withdrawal method with a view to cure, (b) where it has been demonstrated, after a prolonged attempt at cure, that the use of the drug cannot be safely discontinued entirely, on account of the severity of the withdrawal symptoms produced, (c) where it has been similarly demonstrated that the patient, while capable of leading a useful and relatively normal life when a certain minimum dose is regularly administered, becomes incapable of this when the drug is entirely discontinued.' Ministry of Health, Department Committee on Morphine and Heroin Addiction Report 19 (1926). This statement is reprinted in the circular distributed by the Home Office, The Duties of Doctors and Dentists Under the Dangerous Drugs Act and Regulations, 14 (D.D. 101, 6th ed., 1956)."—Schur, British Narcotics Policies, 51 J. Cr. L., Crim. & P.S. 620 (1961). Although the official Bureau of Narcotics approach is to oppose such a plan, Lindesmith cites cases of prominent persons securing maintenance doses, including one in which Narcotics Bureau Commissioner Anslinger himself "permitted" a member of Congress to obtain his drugs by prescription in exchange for his promise not to go to underworld pushers;—Lindesmith, "Beginnings of Wisdom," in Wakefield (ed.), The Addict (1963). An experiment in providing maintenance doses to addicts was inaugurated by the Commissioner of Mental Hygiene of New York in the closing months of 1963 (*New York Times* September 14, 1963, March 9, 1964). It was said to be with "permission received orally from the Federal Bureau of Narcotics." But how can the Bureau give permission for an activity that it defines as illegal?

[36] *Op. cit. supra* n. 4.
[37] *Op. cit. supra* n. 24 at 451.

For, it really does not trust physicians. Basically, the Bureau's distrust arises from its insistence that there is only one way to treat all addicts and its deepseated commitment to one plan, abrupt abstinence." Whatever the source of the Bureau's position may be, the arguments it offers against the foregoing medical approach—one which includes discretion by the doctor to give maintenance doses—are that (1) the doctors would be creating addicts, and (2) the plan would fail to cure.

Do doctors create addicts? Perhaps they did once, before the drugs were as well understood as they are today. But in recent years, with the doctors ousted from prescribing drugs, except in connection with other illnesses, the upsurge in new addicts has come about through other sources—a particular under-privileged culture, using illegal distributors of narcotics. As for the fear that the doctors will fail to perform cures—what of it? At worst, failure means that an addict will not be cured—an outcome no worse than before—and at least he will not have supported the racket or committed crime to obtain the drugs.

One is inclined to suspect that what the Bureau fears is not failure but success. More than that, the Federal Bureau of Narcotics *does not want the program tried. It fears and opposes the program, whether it succeeds or fails.* If it were convinced that the program would fail to cure addicts, it could establish its point for all concerned simply by allowing the program to fail.

If the medical program is *tried* at all extensively, *even if it fails to cure addicts, it will have a favorable effect on the law enforcement problem.* If extensively applied, it would withdraw the addict from the illegal market, and, to some extent, would cause the racket to shrink. The addict would no longer have to turn to crime to sustain his habit. If very extensively applied, the racket would practically dry up, and an appreciable amount of crime would be prevented.

Such a complete success would be slow in coming. The Narcotics Bureau is probably right on that point. But at the same time, it is obvious that the medical program cannot really fail. If it succeeds in cures, wonderful; if it does not, the program is less wonderful but still highly desirable. It in no wise makes more difficult the remaining program of law enforcement against illegal importation and distribution of drugs. Law enforcement will have gained allies in the medical profession.

This is a far cry from free access to drugs. Like other dangerous drugs, narcotics must be controlled. As with control of other
drugs, however, administration must rely on doctors (as well as
governmental bureaus). The New York Academy of Medicine
report does, in fact, recognize the need for effective law enforcement and severe sentencing, but in a sound perspective:

> Obviously there are defects in a method that in execu-
> tion fails to catch the real criminals, the key men in the
> syndicates, but makes statutory criminals of sick persons,
> succeeds in bringing some of them to dock, places
> some in jail, fails to provide proper medical care for
> them and, instead, erects almost insuperable barriers to
> medical management. Such enforcement is harsh and
> cruel. Its basic defects are grossness, lack of discrimina-
> tion, and failure of selectivity. It does not draw a dis-
> tinction between a sick person and a criminal, between
> an addict peddler and a nonaddicted illicit dealer. That
> there may be no misunderstanding about the Academy's
> position on the law, it should be emphasized that it
> objects to the misuse of the punitive approach. Too
> often, if not mostly, in practice it has been applied to
> addicts. As for the nonaddicted illicit dealers and ped-
> dlers, the Academy condemns them in strongest terms,
> applauds all efforts to run them down, understands the
> difficulty in apprehending them, and would impose upon
> them the full weight of the law. But all addicts are sick
> persons. Those driven to peddling drugs or engaging
> in other illegal activities are no exception. They need
> medical care, not imprisonment.

The Model Sentencing Act deals specifically with racketeers
in narcotics. As with all other commitments of dangerous offenders, it has no minimum term and would allow parole. It
avoids the mandatory features of the federal law. It is the kind of
sentencing act the Academy would approve. With that approach
it was natural for the Advisory Council of Judges to take a
position consistent with the Academy's with respect to who
should be sentenced:

> The narcotic drug addict is a sick person, physically
> and psychologically, and as such is entitled to qualified

medical attention just as are other sick people. . . . The traffic in narcotic drugs is properly controlled by legislation and effective penal sanctions. Since the illegal handling of narcotic drugs today is a big business of organized crime, state and federal law enforcement efforts should concentrate on reaching the criminals at the upper administrative level. The addict should be directed to medical help and should not be criminally prosecuted. . . . In recent years the penalties for narcotics crimes have become more and more severe, the theory of the legislation evidently being that the greater the penalty, the greater the deterrence. The result in practice is to glut the penal institutions with small-fry pushers and addicts serving long terms, without any deterrent effect on the racket but with deteriorating effect on the prisoners and the correctional institutions. We oppose mandatory terms in narcotics cases and the exclusion of narcotics offenders from eligibility for probation or parole.[38]

Civil Commitments

Do we find the same approach here as we did in the examination of civil commitment of mentally ill offenders and sex offenders? The prevailing system of dealing with narcotic addicts is *against* the interest of the doctor and his former patient, and this is not true of the treatment of the mentally ill or the sexual offender. The medical profession is under no illusions regarding drug addicts. Here the claims of success are those of law enforcement; and if they are illusions, the physicians do not share them. The official position has been maintained not by illusion but by power and coercion.

Under attack, as it is, the official position may change, but not very much. Penalties for violations will probably be reduced, against Bureau opposition. The position it will give up last is likely to be control of the physician, whose freedom of practice has been defended by the New York Academy of Medicine, among others. In this "struggle for freedom" of physician and patient, a great impediment is likely to be the civil commitment,

---

[38] NCCD, Advisory Council of Judges, Narcotics Law Violations—A Policy Statement (1964).

the same device we have encountered before. In a substantial number of states[39] the law permits a drug addict to be civilly committed—that is, committed against his will (although some laws authorize "voluntary self-commitment") to an institution, but without a conviction of crime.

Civil commitment of addicts is described by some as the "medical approach" and is supported by advocates of special hospitals, especially those constructed with federal funds. Thus in 1962 the governor of New York, approving legislation for civil commitment of addicts, requested that the federal government establish a narcotics treatment hospital in the New York area.

The Federal Bureau of Narcotics embraces this approach, at least some aspects of it. It apparently supports a bill to allow addicts to be treated civilly despite an original criminal charge of crime.[40] It is not a great concession. First of all, the Supreme Court of the United States has invalidated a California statute which, like the law in some other states, made addiction a crime,[41] and it might take to frowning on statutes or procedures that condemn the addict for crimes (such as possession) that are inherent in his addiction-illness. Secondly, the civil commitment plan does not necessarily give up the criminal charge, but (as is true under the New York legislation), if the defendant fails on the civil commitment, he may then be prosecuted.

In the next chapter we shall discuss the general problem of civil commitment as used in narcotics cases, mental illness, and sex offenses and shall raise what seem to us to be serious legal and philosophical questions about the present civil commitment laws and practices. Here it is suitable to examine the wisdom of civil commitment for narcotics addicts. Two broad questions are involved: (1) Are special hospitals for drug addicts indicated, on the basis of present knowledge? (2) Whether they are the best medical approach or not, is the civil commitment to special hospitals truly a medical approach at all?

---

[39] Thirty-seven states and the District of Columbia have enacted laws that provide for civil commitment; *op. cit. supra* n. 24 at 423.

[40] Proceedings, *op. cit. supra* n. 17 at 32.

[41] Robinson v. California, 370 U.S. 660, 8 L. Ed. 2d 758, 82 S. Ct. 1417 (1962); Kolb, Drug Addiction: A Medical Problem (1962). See *infra* ch. 7.

There is no indication whatever that anything but the present "medical" position of the Bureau of Narcotics would apply in these hospitals. That is, the regimen would be total and prompt withdrawal, which the New York Academy of Medicine statement so thoroughly demolishes. Thus the latest "official" statement continues to declare that withdrawal is the regimen to be followed with drug addicts, except only for administration of "limited quantities of narcotics for a few days in a hospital or other secure setting which is reasonably certain to be drug free in order to relieve acute withdrawal symptoms." And "withdrawal on an ambulatory basis is generally medically unsound and not recommended on the basis of present knowledge."[42] It reiterates earlier statements that "the maintenance of stable dosage levels is generally inadequate and medically unsound and ambulatory clinic plans for the withdrawal of narcotics from addicts are likewise generally inadequate and medically unsound. . . . Ambulatory maintenance can be considered ethical medical practice only if . . . (a) withdrawal would be hazardous to life, or (b) continued drug administration is necessary for a chronic or terminal painful condition other than the drug addiction itself and for which no other mode of treatment is feasible."

The statement endorses civil commitment: "Certification to civil facilites is possible in a number of states and its broader application is recommended. It may supply the element of compulsion toward maintenance of treatment which most addicts require." This is no longer a medical statement, and the statement does not explain why such a legal process is necessary. The offender does not require isolation in the sense that smallpox cases do.

The experience with such a regimen in hospitals under civil commitments is not at all promising, as we have pointed out

---

42 A Statement of the American Medical Association's Council on Health and the National Academy of Sciences-National Research Council, June 1963, announced as having been made with the approval of the Federal Bureau of Narcotics. Finally the statement says that "a physician must comply with local, state and federal narcotics laws and regulations." "The present official position of the national association of doctors is, with slight liberalization, the product of the Bureau of Narcotics of the United States Treasury Department."—Dimock, review of Eldridge, Narcotics and the Law: A Critique of the American Experiment in Narcotic Drug Control, 48 Am. Bar Asso. J. 1067 (1962).

earlier. It is supported (at least by some) as a device to avert the drive toward medical freedom to reach those who suffer from this illness.

The plan, finally, is illusory in its pretense of noncriminal procedure; it is noncriminal in phraseology only. One of its most voluble advocates is Richard H. Kuh, of the New York District Attorney's office, who described the plan to the White House Conference on Narcotics. To make any sense, even from the point of view of its advocates, this program presents a logistical problem of gargantuan proportions, in the face of the alternative of medical treatment as proposed by the New York Academy of Medicine. It seems to visualize nothing less than the institutionalization of practically all drug addicts. Kuh writes:

> If a program of removing addiction "carriers" from circulation is to have any impact on the narcotics traffic, and is to terminate the contagion, such removal must be of more than a "selected sample" of the addicts. Although all the addicts in the New York City area could not be committed overnight, there is the need to "think big"—not in terms of institutions with a capacity of 25 or 55 or 140 beds. Total capacity must be measured initially in thousands—and ultimately in terms far in excess of 10,000 addicts, simultaneously removed from the community to rehabilitative institutions. Although such capacities may seem incredible, our New York State penal institutions now house some 17,000 convicted criminals.[43]

What a picture! Institutions for addicts exceeding the total capacity of all state prisons—in the state with one of the biggest prison populations in the country. These would not be cheap institutions: Apart from the expense of constructing and equipping them, their annual operating costs would run well into the millions. Expenses at Riverside Hospital in New York City have run to about $10,000 per bed per year. The per-bed expenses at the federal institutions at Lexington, Ky., and Fort Worth, Tex., also run into the thousands. It goes without saying that it would be impossible to operate such institutions for rehabilitation, certainly not as a medical plan. They would be run as prisons are

---

[43] Kuh, Dealing with Narcotic Addiction, N.Y.L.J., June 8 to 10, 1960.

run—humanely, free of drugs (except for smuggling), and with programs for athletics, vocational and academic training, etc. To call such a procedure "civil," noncriminal, is to play with words. To call it a medical program is ridiculous. Furthermore, there would be no end of newcomers for admission. The Kuh statement seems to consider that if the program is fully applied, the end of the problem would be in sight: "If there were no markets here for drugs, because substantially all prospective purchasers had been put out of circulation, drug importers would be driven out of business." With addicts out of the way, the racketeers would have no customers and go away. Since (the argument goes) the addicts are the main contagious element, no new addicts would be made. Hence, once fully applied and with the addicts held for an appreciable period of time (several years), the whole problem would be solved, and the hospitals would be closed or used for other purposes. The latter good result is my own extension, not Kuh's, but it seems as unlikely a result as the possibility that the full program will ever actually be tried.

It is hard to believe that racketeers who have not been defeated by all the efforts of government all these years would find no new addicts. Nobody claims that the civil commitment laws have made any inroads in the racket. The drug is brought in by the racketeers, not by the addicts. The self-same culture that produces addicts today would continue to produce them, to say nothing of the men released from the hospitals, whose rate of recidivism is notoriously high.

Besides, the premise of hospitalization as an effective means of dealing with addicts is by no means accepted. Dr. Ray E. Trussell, New York Commissioner of Hospitals, also spoke to the White House Conference. "Before coming to the conclusion," he said, "that 50 more hospital beds—federal built and operated—will solve the addict problem, let us examine what is accomplished by such hospitals. . . . I must voice a note of caution about over-expectation from medical services to heroin addicts and state the realities of the current situation as I see them in the light of our experience to date, an experience which is quite similar to that of the Public Health Service in operating its hospital in Lexington." Dr. Trussell referred to 247 addicts who had been admitted to New York City's Riverside Hospital for the first time in 1955:

> Eleven . . . were dead—on a falling death rate for this age group; 95 per cent had been re-hospitalized or re-arrested, or both, one or more times. Only eight had abstained from the use of drugs and all of these were people who were never truly addicted. They had been caught, committed, put in their time, and left; and never went back to the drug. . . . The hard cold fact is that in the light of today's knowledge, a hospital is useful (1) for research, (2) for humane short-term detoxification and making aftercare arrangements, or (3) for long-term care of carefully selected patients. All of these activities have been going on in New York City for years. . . . Hopefully this White House Conference will broaden the foundations on which we work and lay the groundwork for immediate federal aid to state and city. Money can be used at once. A federal hospital will take years to build and will add nothing new except numbers.[44]

Rev. Norman C. Eddy, another member of the conference, also warned against the program:

> The conclusion to be drawn from the experiences of the private groups is that there are a variety of signs of hope in the treatment of addiction, but that there is as yet no single method which is better than another. We of the New York Council on Narcotics Addiction are fearful that one approach may preempt the field. Specifically, we oppose the civil commitment and parole programs except on an experimental basis. Instead, we make three recommendations for dealing with addic-

---

[44] Proceedings, *op. cit. supra* n. 17 at 69-70. Dr. Ray E. Trussell, New York Commissioner of Hospitals, said: "Contrary to some current misconceptions, we have no waiting lists for adolescent addicts (in fact we have about 60 empty beds) or for adult female addicts. We have developed a waiting list of adult males, and several weeks ago made arrangements to open another 38 short-term treatment beds on October 1 at Manhattan General. This brings the total of city-operated or city-supported beds to 418. In addition, there are 155 beds for addicts in State hospitals as part of a research program originated by former Governor Harriman and now being expanded to 555 beds in a program just announced last week."—*Id.* at 68.

tion in the United States at the present time: (1) The development and strengthening of all medical facilities for the treatment of addiction so that addicted persons who look for help of their own free will can find it readily as private citizens, not as a stigmatized breed apart. (2) The support of many experimental and research programs. (3) The support of referral and aftercare programs in the neighborhoods where addiction is the most prevalent.[45]

Just as we examined the phychological ingredients that led to the Durham rule, someone ought to examine the unconscious and other psychological ingredients in the mind of the Narcotics Bureau, fiercely adherent to a sentencing policy that threatens to cripple the rehabilitative program of the federal correctional system. Neither medicine nor sentencing is within the province of law enforcement.

Edwin M. Schur has some comments on the point:

> In some respects, law enforcement authorities may . . . have a sort of vested interest in maintaining the status quo. Rufus King has argued that the Narcotics Division of the Treasury Department (the early enforcement arm of the narcotics laws, known since 1930 as the Federal Narcotics Bureau), "succeeded in creating a very large criminal class for itself to police (i.e., the whole doctor-patient-addict-peddler community), instead of the very small one that Congress had intended (the smuggler and the peddler)." How else can one explain the continuing support of policies which run counter to common sense and the vast bulk of available evidence—policies which cannot help but perpetuate the drug traffic? Why else would Commissioner Anslinger keep on asserting, as he did in a recent article, that the essence of the addiction problem is "hoodlumism," and that, "In a sense it may be true that every hoodlum is a psychiatric problem, but in a practical sense one must treat the bank robbers, the gambler, and the thief as criminals"?
> The American treatment of addicts may also be attributed to the addict's serving as a convenient scapegoat—one more enemy in the perpetual battle against

---

[45] *Id.* at 177.

crime and immorality of which Americans seem so fond. In his perceptive essay, "Crime as an American Way of Life," Daniel Bell stressed that, "In no other country have there been such spectacular attempts to curb human appetites and brand them as illicit, and nowhere else such glaring failures. From the start America was one and the same time a frontier community where 'everything goes,' and the fair country of the Blue Laws. . . . In America the enforcement of public morals has been a continuing feature of our history."[46]

[46] Schur, " 'The British System,' " in Wakefield, *op. cit. supra* n. 35 at 157-8.

Chapter 7

Civil Commitments —
The Biggest Illusion

The notion of civil commitment arising in contexts that basically involve criminal behavior raises more than one question of legal and social soundness. In the situations thus far examined, we have seen defendants civilly committed after discharge from a criminal charge by the defense of insanity, sex offenders civilly committed on the basis of criminal behavior, and drug law violators civilly committed upon being apprehended. Similar instances are the civil commitment of juvenile and youthful offenders.

We have suggested that illusions exist in the approaches in each of the classes of offenses discussed. Now we confront the proposition that the civil commitment as applied in these cases is a particular illusion, of questionable merit and validity.

Quasi-criminal Civil Commitments

The so-called "civil commitments" of defendants acquitted of crime for insanity, or of sex offenders, or addict violators of drug laws, have one common ingredient—they are derived from a criminal charge that is averted, although sometimes only partially or temporarily. Is this procedure legally warranted? If a person is to be punished (by commitment or otherwise) for crime, due process in criminal proceedings must be observed. If criminal due process is not observed, the charge of crime is not established and cannot serve as the basis for any sanction applied to the defendant.

How does this apply to the civil commitment of defendants acquitted on criminal charges for insanity or mental illness? Not all of the commitments are alike in their process. We have noted that some are mandatory, automatic—they have no criteria for commitment whatever except the criminal charge and the ground for its dismissal. Others are discretionary, and these may or may not have independent criteria of commitment. Assuming that such a dismissal at the same time establishes the crime, as does the English plea of guilty but insane, the court is then committing a person who has committed a criminal act but is not legally responsible for it. The otherwise criminal act for which a defense is established does not result in conviction. So if the defense is insanity and there is no conviction, some criteria of commitment other than a criminal conviction must be met if the defendant is to be committed. But the cases have upheld commitments without separate criteria.[1]

In Chapter 5, discussing sex offenses, we referred to the statutes providing for commitment of "psychopathic" sex offenders, some of them utilizing criminal and some civil procedures. Here we are interested in the civil proceeding. As already noted, the civil statutes permit a state's attorney to initiate proceedings to determine whether a person charged with a sex crime or suspected of having propensities toward dangerous sexual behavior is a sexual psychopath within the meaning of the statute and may be committed. In some states the civil proceeding may be commenced even though no crime has been proved. The cases, with some early exceptions, have upheld these civil commitments.[2]

---

[1] *Infra,* pp 34-40.

[2] People v. Sims, 382 Ill. 472, 47 N.E. 2d 703 (1943); State ex rel. Sweezer v. Green, 360 Mo. 1249, 232 S.W. 2d 897 (1950). The cases that uphold the statutes do so on little more than the fiction of non-criminality. Compare the legal reasoning in two Michigan cases, the first of which struck down a sexual psychopath statute, and the next upheld a new version: People v. Frantczak, 286 Mich. 51, 281 N.W. 534 (1938), statute

Another instance of civil commitment for quasi crime is the juvenile court process, by which a child's violation of law is deemed to be not a crime, but "delinquency," a status which is noncriminal but which, when established, may result in commitment to a quasi-penal institution (a training school, sometimes a reformatory). These civil commitments have been upheld.[3] Several youthful offender proceedings are similar.

The foregoing civil commitments are to be distinguished from other civil commitments which are well established and well based in law. Indeed, it is the concepts of these better-established civil commitments that serve as the rationale for the more recent forms, in which the term "civil" is attached to quasi-criminal situations.

The older civil commitments in use are (1) quarantine of those ill of contagious diseases and (2) commitment of those who are incompetent. For both of these, the power of the state is derived from two related, specific, and well-recognized legal doctrines. The first is the concept of *parens patriae*, the sovereign's power of guardianship over persons under disability; the second, the state's police power, the power to do those things necessary for the protection of the populace. Sometimes the two concepts are combined; for example, in the criterion generally governing commitment of the insane—that the person is a danger either to himself or others.

Neither doctrine is absolute.[4] Although the statutes set up the class of persons who are committable, a proceeding, either judicial or administrative, must determine that the condition of the particular individual meets the criteria. Thus, not every

---

held invalid; People v. Chapman, 301 Mich. 584, 4 N.W. 2d 18 (1942), statute upheld. See *infra*, n. 50.

[3] Ex parte Loving, 178 Mo. 194 (1903); Commonwealth v. Fisher, 213 Pa. 48 (1905); Mill v. Brown, 31 Utah 473 (1907); In re Sharp, 15 Idaho 120 (1908); Robison v. Wayne Circuit Judges, 151 Mich. 315 (1908); Nicholl v. Koster, 157 Cal. 416 (1910); Marlowe v. Commonwealth, 142 Ky. 106 (1911); Ex parte Januszewski, 196 Fed. 123 (1911); in re Powell, 6 Okl. Cr. Rep. 495 (1912); Lindsay v. Lindsay, 257 Ill. 328 (1913); State v. Burnett, 179 N.C. 735 (1920); State v. Buckner, 300 Mo. 359 (1923); Cinque v. Boyd, 99 Conn. 70 (1923); Ex parte Daedler, 194 Cal. 320 (1924); Hills v. Pierce, 113 Ore. 386 (1924).

[4] Every state power, including the police power, is limited by the inhibition of the Fourteenth Amendment.—Southern Railway Company v. Virginia, 290 U.S. 190, 78 L. ed. 260 (1933).

insane person is committable, and the statutes do not say they
are. The element of either dangerousness or helplessness must
(or should) be found. The protective functions must be sensibly
related to the actual needs of the person or the community. So
a vaccination is not imposable if the person is not a fit subject of
vaccination, or if it would impair his health.[5] It is not likely that
the courts would uphold the quarantine of persons suffering from
a common cold, or, correspondingly, would uphold the punishment that might be meted out to a person with a cold who
refused to quarantine himself or submit to quarantine (if that
is what the statute called for).

But these commitments are to be distinguished from what we
have called quasi-criminal commitments ("civil" commitment of
persons acquitted of crime for insanity or committed as sexual
psychopaths or drug addicts, children committed as delinquents).
The quasi-criminal commitments are called civil only to enable
the state to deal with the persons in procedures other than
criminal. Nevertheless the criterion is, usually, the criminal act,
rather than the tests of dangerousness or helplessness. Many
sexual psychopaths—for example, adult homosexuals—who are
neither helpless nor dangerous are "civilly" committed.

The quasi-criminal civil commitments are sustained, usually
in language drawing on *parens patriae* or the police power, but
they are not civil commitments in the sense of the commitment
of the insane person or the quarantine of the contagiously sick
person. The "civil" character of the quasi-criminal commitments
is, in brief, a legal fiction.

Legal Fictions, Legal Myths

Jerome Frank points out that a legal fiction is a false affirmation made with knowledge of its falsity but with no intention
of deceiving others.[6] A myth, he adds, differs from a fiction. A
myth is a false affirmation made without complete knowledge
of its falsity. Many legal fictions are valid and useful, just as
scientific "models" serve a useful purpose so long as it is kept in
mind that they are models only and are not assumed to portray

---

[5] Jacobson v. Mass., 197 U.S. 11 (1905).

[6] Frank, Law and the Modern Mind 40, and Appendix VII, "Notes on
Fictions" (1963).

reality. When a legal fiction is, in fact, a myth—a pretense of being reality—it has lost its basis for validity.

Thus Frank writes:

> It is often desirable to treat A "as if" it were B. Mathematics, for instance, finds it useful to employ the fiction that a circle is a polygon; *i.e.,* to be dealt with, for certain purposes, as if it were a polygon. Medical thinking is aided by the fiction of the completely healthy man. So in law, it is helpful at times to treat a corporation as if, for certain purposes, it were a real citizen, distinct and apart from its flesh-and-blood stockholders, directors, officers, and agents. But there are a vast number of so-called fictions which are really bastard fictions or semi-myths, where the "as if" or "let's pretend" factor has, in some measure, been submerged. It is said, not that A is to be treated *for certain purposes* "as if" it were B, but instead it is said and believed, incorrectly, that A *is* B. . . . The law has suffered much from such bastard fictions or semi-myths.

Frank gives some illustrations of such bastard fictions, semi-myths.

When civil commitment is used in relation to criminal or quasi-criminal or para-criminal behavior, is it a valid fiction or a bastard fiction, a myth or a semi-myth? If the latter, what legal validity does it have? Do we recognize the fiction for what it is, or are we under illusions about its reality?

Broadening the rule of criminal responsibility as the Durham case proposes involves the first illusion—that the civil commitment (upon exculpation of the defendant on the criminal charge) is a better setting for treatment. The opposite is true: for defendants mentally ill but with sufficient cognition not to be within M'Naghten, the criminal charge is superior as a setting for treatment. What of the assertion that the criminal commitment equates with punishment whereas the civil commitment equates with treatment? This difference does not exist in reality, and to some degree at least the *civil* commitment of the criminal is more punitive than the *criminal* commitment, in practice and in concept. The reliance on psychiatry is extended to such lengths as to be unrealistic; the impact of such reliance is a grand illusion.

A host of errors, illusions, myths, underlie the so-called civil commitment procedures for sexual offenders. The assertion that the civil commitment of narcotics law violators is a treatment process as contrasted with punishment under the criminal commitment of such violators does violence to reality. There are further myths in the civil commitment of juvenile delinquents and youthful offenders (which we shall consider presently).

The courts have upheld all of these statutes (with few exceptions), but relying on the fictions, and without examining to see whether the fictions are, in fact, myths. By and large, the difference between the tags of "criminal" and "civil" has been enough for the courts, with the fictional-mythical difference between treatment and punishment brought in without much realistic examination.

The Supreme Court of the United States recently decided, in *Robinson v. California,* that a drug addict, being sick, could not on that basis alone be deemed a criminal. To declare a sick person a criminal, it said, constitutes cruel and unusual punishment.[7] The decision is based on nothing more than the distinction between civil and criminal, and not the measure of punishment:

> We hold that a state law which imprisons a person thus afflicted as criminal, even though he has never touched any narcotic drug within the State or been guilty of any irregular behavior there, inflicts a cruel and unusual punishment in violation of the Fourteenth Amendment. To be sure, imprisonment for ninety days is not, in the abstract, a punishment which is either cruel or unusual. But the question cannot be considered in the abstract. Even one day in prison would be a cruel and unusual punishment for the "crime" of having a common cold.

Does the decision imply that a *civil* commitment of a sick person would be valid? It implies this, but its language is, of course, dicta on this point. But this is the point we are concerned with.

---

[7] Robinson v. California, 370 U.S. 660, 82 S. Ct. 1415, 8 L. ed. 758 (1962).

In the interest of discouraging the violation of such laws, or in the interest of the general health or welfare of its inhabitants, a State might establish a program of compulsory treatment for those addicted to narcotics. Such a program of treatment might require periods of involuntary confinement. And penal sanctions might be imposed for failure to comply with established compulsory procedures.

The statement is a dictum, and no precedents are cited. Justice Douglas, concurring, also says, "The addict is a sick person. He may, of course, be confined for treatment or for the protection of society." Again there is no precedent cited for commitment of the addict. Does the Court avoid the criminal commitment only to step without looking into another trap, "civil" commitment?

"Even one day in prison," says the Court, "would be a cruel and unusual punishment for the 'crime' of having a common cold." Would the Court countenance a civil commitment of a person with a common cold, perhaps for a day, or perhaps a year? Or for life? Its saying so appears to be needless, or too casual. Shall we undertake—would the court sustain—a program of committing cigarette smokers? Surely realistic criteria must exist before a person may be civilly committed, and the courts recognize this, the principal criteria being that the person *realistically* be dangerous to others or to himself and that the confinement is necessary to protect him or the public against that danger. A person with smallpox may be quarantined; a person with active tuberculosis may be confined.[8] But the drug addict is a good illustration of a sick person whose sickness is *not* contagious in the sense, shall we say, of a person with smallpox; not dangerous to others, especially if he is under treatment, with a maintenance dose when necessary. It is not necessary to confine him in order to treat him (again, particularly if a maintenance dose is allowed, as it is under the laws of the United State).[9] The decision takes no note of the fact, mentioned in passing,

---

[8] American Jurisprudence, title Health § 32 (1940).

[9] "There is no doubt that the [Linder] case ruled that a physician may lawfully prescribe narcotics for an addict purely because of his addiction, provided the amount is not so large as to put it within the power of the addict to sell part of the drug in violation of the Harrison Act."—Hawkins v. United States, 90 F. 2d 551 (1937); Linder v. United States, 268 U.S. 5 (1925); Bush v. United States, 16 F. 2d 709 (1927).

that although Robinson was called an addict, at the time he was arrested he was neither under the influence of narcotics nor suffering withdrawal symptoms. Would the Court say such a person was sick to the point that commitment would be justified?

The dissenting opinion of Justice Clark contains an extremely interesting discussion on the very question of distinguishing between a valid and an invalid commitment when the commitment is based merely on the tag of "criminal" or "civil." He offers a solid argument on the proposition that what matters is what we do with a person, not whether we call it a civil or criminal process. I do not agree with his position that would uphold the criminal commitment of the drug addict. I believe no commitment is justified, civil or criminal. I believe, with the majority, that a criminal commitment must be carefully guarded, for it does have special stigmatic and punitive consequences. But to use the word "civil" as though it magically removed these consequences is improper. The question of the nature of the proceeding has to be determined by all the elements in the statute and in its application to individuals. Clark's discussion is valuable to dispel the illusion that merely calling a commitment civil gives it a totally new character.

He writes as follows:

> Although the section is penal in appearance—perhaps a carry-over from a less sophisticated approach—its present provisions are quite similar to those for civil commitment and treatment of addicts who have lost the power of self-control. . . . The "criminal" provision applies to the incipient narcotic addict who retains self-control, requiring confinement of three months to one year and parole with frequent tests to detect renewed use of drugs. Its overriding purpose is to cure the less seriously addicted person by preventing further use. On the other hand, the "civil" commitment provision deals with addicts who have lost the power of self-control, requiring hospitalization up to two years. Each deals with a different type of addict but with a common purpose. This is most apparent when the sections overlap: if after civil commitment of an addict it is found that hospital treatment will not be helpful, the addict is confined for a minimum period of three months in the

same manner as is the volitional addict under the "criminal" provision. . . .

The fact that § 11721 might be labeled "criminal" seems irrelevant, not only to the majority's own "treatment" test but to the "concept of orderly society" to which the states must attain under the Fourteenth Amendment.

A footnote here added this comment: "Any reliance upon the 'stigma' of a misdemeanor conviction in this context is misplaced, as it would hardly be different from the stigma of a civil commitment for narcotics addiction." The point made here is in reply to the comment of the majority opinion that a "prosecution for addiction, with its resulting stigma and irreparable damage to the good name of the accused, cannot be justified as a means of protecting society, where a civil commitment would do as well." Justice Clark's comment is an appropriate answer to the point, and the wrongness of the observation of the majority is underlined when one considers the stigma of any civil commitment, such as a commitment to a mental hospital for mental illness. For the community at large, the stain on the personality of the person involved is often worse than a criminal conviction.[10]

The *Robinson* distinction was promptly used by a California Supreme Court ruling in a subsequent case. A defendant was convicted under Sec. 11721, but the criminal proceedings were suspended because of the Supreme Court holding in the Robinson case, and the defendant was certified for proceedings under Penal Code Sec. 6450, authorizing commitment to the Department of Corrections for five years. In both cases the proof required was that the defendant was a drug addict. Is a commitment of five years to the Department of Corrections a penal commitment? Certainly not, said the California court, simply quoting the U.S. Supreme Court that "a state might establish a program of compulsory treatment for those addicted to narcotics."

The magic of "civil" commitment, fully believed in by the Cali-

---

10 Special Committee to Study Commitment Procedures of the Association of the Bar of the City of New York in Cooperation with Cornell Law School, Mental Illness and Due Process; Report and Recommendations on Admission to Mental Hospitals Under New York Law 78 (1962).

fornia court, permits it to distinguish between "civil felons" and "civil misdemeanants"! Sec. 6450 permits a five-year commitment for the civil "misdemeanant" addict, and Sec. 6451 ten years for the civil "felon" addict. The contradiction in "civil felon" is obvious. Says the California court: "If a principal cause of narcotics addiction is the psychosocial maladjustment of the user, and if a person convicted of a felony tends to suffer from greater psycho-social maladjustment than one convicted of misdemeanor, then it would not seem unreasonable to expect that a longer period of readjustment and rehabilitation may be necessary for the felon addict than for the misdemeanant addict."[11] What a neat combination of legal myth and psychiatric illusion! (That "a person convicted of a felony tends to suffer from greater psycho-social maladjustment than one convicted of misdemeanor" is a new proposition for which no evidence is brought forth.)

Before the *Robinson* decision, a drug addict committed under Penal Code Sec. 6401 who escaped or attempted to escape was "deemed a prisoner committed to a state prison for the purpose of the laws punishing escape." A 1963 amendment (ch. 1706) no longer calls him a prisoner; now it reads simply that if he attempts escape he is "guilty of a crime punishable by imprisonment in the state prison for not exceeding seven years."

Some old state cases involving alcoholism illustrate the oddity of the law struggling with the concept of criminal/civil for the person it wishes to protect. An alcoholic may be civilly committed.[12] Is he like the insane person who is civilly committed? The statutes do not say. In a Nebraska case, the petitioner was adjudged by the Antelope County commissioners to be an inebriate and was committed to the hospital for the insane until cured, but for not more than three years. The Nebraska Supreme Court discarded one feature of the act—a parole provision. It

[11] In re De La O, 59 C. 2d 128 (1963), 28 Cal. Rptr. 489, 378 P. 2d 793, *cert. denied*, 374 U.S. 856, 10 L. ed. 2d 1076, 83 S. Ct. 1927. New Jersey also, in a case that came after Robinson v. California, upheld its criminal statute for one's being under the influence of a narcotic drug,—State v. Margo, 191 A. 2d 43 (1963). The Illinois Supreme Court got around the Robinson decision also,—People v. Davis, 188 N.E. 2d 225 (1963).

[12] Alcoholics may be hospitalized in thirty-six states.—Lindman & McIntyre (eds.), The Mentally Disabled and the Law 18 (1961).

was too much like criminal control, it said: the commitment was otherwise held protective and civil and was upheld.[13]

In a Wisconsin case the statute failed to say whether the proceeding was criminal or civil. The Wisconsin Supreme Court undertook to determine, from related elements in the statute and some technical features in the code, that it was civil, despite the use of the terms "charged," "offenders," "convicted," and "sentenced."[14] But in this case the Court rightly went on to consider whether the criterion of helplessness had been met. It was not, and the relator was discharged, as having been deprived of his liberty without due process. The statute sought to sustain a commitment on the mere ground that a man was a drunkard. This was not enough, said the Court: "Such habit might exist and yet the victim be kind and generous hearted, fully capable of attending to his business, gradually increasing his estate, tenderly providing for the wants of any dependent upon him, and without endangering the personal safety of himself or others." The case illustrates two points: the type of language used in the statute does not determine whether the proceeding is civil or criminal; and, if the proceeding is not criminal, whether the defendant is subject to control depends on whether his condition is serious enough to require the intervention of the state.[15] Mere addiction (to alcohol) is not enough.

Mere illness, then, does not warrant a commitment; commitment is warranted only in case of dangerousness or helplessness. It goes without saying that a statute cannot declare a class of individuals subject to commitment unless it is a class that is inherently one or the other—criminal or in need of protection;

---

[13] Ex parte Schwarting, 76 Neb. 773, 108 N.W. 125 (1906).

[14] State ex rel. Larkin v. Ryan, 70 Wis. 676, 36 N.W. 823 (1888).

[15] To determine whether a law is penal or not "inquiry must be directed to substance"; "a statute that prescribes the consequences that will befall one who fails to abide . . . is a penal law. . . . Even a clear legislative classification of a statute as 'non-penal' would not alter the fundamental nature of a plainly penal statute."—Trop v. Dulles, 356 U.S. 86, 95, 97 (1958). I use the word "helplessness" as more accurate than "dangerousness to self," but the latter, or an even weaker formulation, is usual; *op. cit.* n. 12 p. 17.

and even then a judicial finding, made in accord with the requirements of due process, would be necessary.[16]

Let us examine another application of the civil commitment plan. As we have noted, the adoption of the Durham rule for the insanity defense was quickly followed by enactment of a statute providing that upon such acquittal the defendant was automatically to be committed to a mental hospital. The U.S. Court of Appeals for the District of Columbia upheld it. On what grounds?

"The test of this statute," it said, "is not whether a particular individual engaged in the ordinary pursuits of life is committable to a mental institution under the law governing civil commitments. . . . This statute applies to an exceptional class of people —people who have committed acts forbidden by law, who have obtained verdicts of 'not guilty by reason of insanity,' and who have been committed to a mental hospital pursuant to the Code."[17] However, no criteria of commitment are stated.

A later case suggests reasons for justifying commitment, but again no criteria. In *Ragsdale v. Overholser*,[18] a defendant charged with robbery and acquitted for insanity was committed and afterward escaped. His history had evidence of dangerousness. But for ten months as an escapee he worked for several employers without showing abnormal behavior and lived at home with his wife and family. Said the Court: "No penal or punitive considerations enter into this procedure. It has two purposes: (1) to protect the public and the subject; (2) to afford a place and a procedure to rehabilitate and restore the subject as to whom the standards of our society and the rules of law do not permit punishment or accountability." It goes on: "Inherent in a verdict of not guilty by reason of insanity are two important elements: (a) that the defendant did in fact commit the criminal act charged, (b) that there exists some rational basis for belief that the defendant suffered from a mental disease or defect of which the criminal act is a product. . . . Some time gap between

---

[16] Sherry, Vagrants, Rogues and Vagabonds—Old concepts in Need of Revision, 48 Calif. L. Rev. 557 (1960); Dubin & Robinson, The Vagrancy Concept Reconsidered: Problems and Abuses of Status Criminality, 37 N.Y.U. L. Rev. 102 (1962).

[17] Overholser v. Leach, 103 U.S. App. D.C. 289, 257 F. 2d 667 (1958), *cert. denied* 359 U.S. 1013, 79 S. Ct. 1152, 3 L. ed. 2d 1038 (1959).

[18] Ragsdale v. Overholser, 281 F. 2d 943 (1960).

the verdict and the appraisal of the defendant's then existing mental condition is unavoidable under any scheme which would provide adequate safeguards."

The line of reasoning is found to skip and falter, when examined. Is it reasonable to assume that a finding of not guilty for insanity is at the same time a finding of committability for insanity? Although the term "insanity" or "mental illness" may be used for the acquittal test as well as for a commitment, the test of commitment is actually different—dangerousness or helplessness. Not all mentally ill or insane persons are dangerous, and not all mentally ill or insane persons are helpless. Again, we come back to the point that one may not be committed merely for illness.

Furthermore, the "reasonable inference" regarding continued insanity slurs too hastily over the actual process of justice. Insanity may well disappear between the time of the offense and the time of the trial. In Chapter 1 we cited one such instance—a mother who had murdered her child. Typically, not exceptionally, the time lag between the crime and the trial is months or years. This is especially true in insanity cases, since the defendant will usually have been hospitalized as incompetent to stand trial. The "reasonable inference" of continued insanity is not based on what happens; it is another fiction—or myth. Furthermore, "it is anomalous, to say the least, that a person who is deemed capable to defend his liberty in court can at the same time be 'presumed' to be so mentally ill as to require confinement in a mental hospital."[19]

More: acquittal for insanity is not a finding that the defendant is insane—it only means that the prosecution has not proved beyond a reasonable doubt that the defendant was sane, once the issue of insanity was raised. "Although not plainly stated in the majority's opinion, the court seems clearly to admit that the jury's verdict of not guilty by reason of insanity means, at most, only that there is reasonable doubt about the defendant's sanity;

---

[19] Statement by Lawrence Speiser, before the subcommittee on Constitutional Rights of the Committee of the Judiciary, U.S. Senate, May 2, 1961. "How can an insane person be informed of the nature and cause of the accusation against him, or how could he employ counsel to assist in his defense?"—State ex rel. Mackintosh v. Superior Court, 45 Wash. 248, 253, 88 Pac. 207, 209 (1907).

the verdict does *not* represent an affirmative finding of insanity."[20] There should at least be a requirement of a finding of mental condition at the time of the trial (as in some jurisdictions).[21]

Another fault: The Court said, "Some time gap between the verdict and the appraisal of the defendant's then existing mental condition is unavoidable under any scheme which would provide adequate safeguards." But the difference is great. We would say that a procedure after acquittal, even one that involved keeping the defendant in custody (if the judge considered him dangerous, *prima facie*) would be valid if the procedure was had for the purpose of determining a commitment. This would individualize the disposition, which we say is necessary; and, *it would not assume what had to be proved*. In fact, once the defendant is committed to the mental hospital, the burden of proof is on him; and with the reluctance of some hospital superintendents to go out on a limb, it is an onerous and perhaps an inherently unfair requirement.

Judge Fahy, concurring in *Ragsdale v. Overholser*, adhered to the line of thinking we have presented. He said:

Since an accused is entitled to be acquitted on the ground of insanity although the evidence may merely

---

[20] Halleck, The Insanity Defense in the District of Columbia—a Legal Lorelei, 99 Georgetown L.J. 294, at 305 (1960). For a comprehensive analysis of the mandatory statutes, critical of the decisions upholding them—Compulsory Commitment Following a Successful Insanity Defense, 56 NW. U. L. Rev. 209 (1961).

[21] In Illinois, Maryland (procedure changed in 1963), Mississippi, Missouri, Oklahoma, Texas, and Washington, if a defendant is acquitted for insanity, the jury must also find whether the defendant continues to be insane. A verdict that he has recovered gives him the unconditional right to be at liberty.—Weihofen, Institutional Treatment of Persons Acquitted by Reason of Insanity, 38 Texas L. Rev. 849, n. 3 and 4 (1960). Correspondence by the author with the attorneys general in these states elicited the general response that information on the operation of the statute is not contralized, but no untoward incidents were known by any. In Mississippi there were three such discharges in fifteen years, and none of the defendants thereafter got into trouble. Maryland in 1963 added an alternative procedure, by which on a finding of not guilty by reason of insanity the court may, in its discretion, commit the defendant to a mental hospital to determine whether or not, by reason of mental disease or defect, he is or will be a danger to himself or others; on a negative finding, he must be released;—Md. Code Art. 59 § 9(b).

have led the jury to entertain a reasonable doubt as to his sanity when the offense occurred, the validity of continued confinement under the mandatory commitment provisions of section 24-301 may require that, unless within a reasonable time he progresses toward becoming not dangerous to self or community the person committed can be held only by a separate civil adjudication of unsoundness of mind, and not solely by reason of section 24-301. It is by no means clear that society can continue to deprive a person of liberty by attributing to a jury's doubt about his mental condition, which led to his acquittal and mandatory commitment, any and all evil or criminal propensities he may be thought to have, and to keep him in confinement because of them. This would transform the hospital into a penitentiary where one could be held indefinitely for no convicted offense, and thus even though the offense of which he was previously acquitted because of doubt as to his insanity might not have been one of the more serious felonies.[22]

In summary: a statute authorizing or requiring civil commitment for illness must be realistically examined against the limits of state power and should not be sustained unless the person whose commitment is sought is, in reality, dangerous or helpless. The use of the term "civil" to describe the procedure should be deemed to create no presumption; the nature of the proceeding should be judged by the operation of the statute.

---

[22] "To reform the situation in Washington, D.C. and elsewhere, the [Civil Liberties] Union suggested adoption of a post-acquittal statute similar to one now in force in 18 states. Under this law, any person acquitted on grounds of insanity may be ordered to a mental hospital for observation for 10 days; if he is found mentally ill, a threat to himself and others and in need of institutional care, the court can refer him to a state commission on mental health for formal commitment proceedings. If, however, after hospital examination discovers no mental illness, the court may discharge the defendant. The Union also suggested federal legislation which would, among other things, declare the right of a mental patient to challenge his confinement by habeas corpus petition at least twice a year; guarantee independent psychiatric confirmation of mental illness claims, including the right to challenge judicial commitment within five days; assure frequent inspection of public mental health facilities by federal inspectors."—American Civil Liberties Union, 41st Annual Report, July 1, 1960-June 30, 1961.

Limitation of Punishment in Civil Commitments for Crime

In practice, persons accused of crimes are punished at least as severely under the so-called civil commitment as under the criminal conviction, and in most instances more severely. Thus a person civilly committed as a result of discharge in the criminal court on the defense of insanity is subject to what is, in effect, a life term. In contrast, if he were sentenced on the criminal charge the term might be a minor one; or he might be placed on probation, or fined, or the sentence might be suspended—that is, if criminally convicted, the defendant might have his freedom. The New York sex offender act and similar acts in other states authorize a "civil" indeterminate term of one day to life; whereas if the defendant were criminally sentenced, the term would be a definitely limited one.

In effect, what these statutes provide is that if less than criminal due process is given to a defendant who is being protected,[23] he may be punished *more*, because the limitations on punishment for crime do not apply. This is a fantastic notion. It is reminiscent of the song of the king in the musical play, *The King and I*, who sings of the "puzzlements" facing the monarch of a small country. He is particularly worried about alliances with presumably protective nations. But, he sings, if allies are strong, "might they not protect me out of all I own." Thus, the alcoholic lady who, if prosecuted as a criminal, might have been fined $10, was protected: she was "civilly" committed (because mentally ill) for an indeterminate term, potentially for life.[24]

One is entitled to think he is smelling a rat. In the words of Mr. Bumble in *Oliver Twist*, "If the law supposes that [state of the law], the law is a ass, a idiot." Considering the instances of civil commitment we have thus far discussed, it is worse than an ass. The constitutions give the defendant in a criminal case certain enumerated rights and other rights embraced under the heading of due process of law, without observance of which he cannot be convicted and his liberty cannot be encroached. The

---

[23] Aside from the customary procedural protections given a defendant in a criminal case, he also has recourse to consideration for executive clemency, which a civilly committed person does not.

[24] *Supra*, page 28.

law evades—evades, not avoids—these requirements by calling the procedure "civil," that is, noncriminal, hence not requiring criminal due process. How is this accomplished? Only by the magic word formula. We go after the criminal, and process him without the final declaration that he is a criminal. We skip that judgment, thus avoiding calling him criminal. Meanwhile we skip some of the procedural protections he would have if he were dealt with as a criminal, *and* we then proceed to punish him more severely than we could under the criminal law—a longer term of incarceration, lessened eligibility for probation or parole, no better treatment.

The fraud is immense. Treating the fiction (civil commitment) as though it were real (treatment, not punishment) is part of the mechanism for erecting the illusion we have talked about in Chapter 4. The civil commitment—being noncriminal—is thought to be "treatment," because, the same people say, a criminal sentence is punishment. The facts, if honestly faced, demolish this notion, as we trust we have shown in Chapter 3, regarding defendants civilly committed upon acquittal, and in Chapter 5, regarding sexual psychopaths.

If the quasi-criminal "civil" commitments are to be sustained on the ground of protection (which is the only ground, because punishment is restricted to sentences in criminal actions), the first limitation on these commitments would appear to be that deprivation of liberty under them could not exceed the deprivation of liberty under the criminal sentence for the same act. Certainly the civil commitments' deprivation of liberty, which is punishment, whether called penal or protective, would be a glaring injustice if it were to exceed the limits of the penal commitment.

Let us remember that in most instances the *sole* difference in dealing with the civilly committed defendant and the one criminally sentenced is the length of term. The special acts affecting youthful offenders are a good example. Often reformatory commitments, usually limited to youthful offenders, are for longer terms than commitments of adults to the penitentiary. A reformatory sentence of five years for a crime punishable by not more than two-and-a-half years if committed by an adult was upheld.[25] The Indiana Minor's Act, under which a minor could be sentenced to one to ten years for an offense which, if committed by an adult, would be punishable by a small fraction of that term, was upheld in these words: "The fact that a hardened criminal conceivably might receive 2 to 5 years whereas a minor might receive 1 to 10 years does not make the statute bad from the point of statutory construction, nor does it mean the court is to reform rather than punish persons who have committed crime, and the legislature in changing the law to give trial courts discretion over the sentencing of minors obviously thought it desirable to give trial judges an area of latitude in this field."[26] This is hardly classifiable as either legal or social reasoning.

Is the longer term justified on the ground of dangerousness? Not under the statute; quite the contrary, these defendants are deemed reformable, and reformation is the purpose of the act. Furthermore, if dangerousness were the motive (as it is said to be, though refuted by practice, under the sexual psychopath acts), certainly it should be dealt with in a penal statute. That is precisely what penal statutes are for. It is true that the statutes do not protect well against the dangerous offender, but that is a failure of statutory draftsmanhiup, a failure that is not at all remedied by a longer term for the youthful or other offenders. A penal statute *can* be drafted to make long terms coincide with dangerousness, as demonstrated by the Model Sentencing Act.

Is the longer term justified on the ground of treatment necessities? There is no evidence of it in the statutes or in practice. Furthermore, the cases seem to reject the idea that treatment is a necessity under the civil commitments![27]

Another important application of the "civil" commitment based on a criminal act, with resultant increase in length of com-

---

[25] People ex rel. Vivona v. Conboy, 181 N.Y.S. 2d 68, 7 A.D. 2d 810 (1958), *motion for leave to appeal denied*, 6 N.Y. 2d 706, 159 N.E. 2d 706, *cert. denied* 361 U.S. 847, 80 S. Ct. 102, 4 L. ed. 2d 85 (1959).

[26] Lee v. State, 239 Ind. 232, 156 N.E. 2d 78 (1959), interpreting Burns Ind. Ann. Stat. § 9-1815. Similarly, lengthening of terms for youthful offenders as compared with adult offenders, under the "youth authority" acts,—Cunningham v. United States, 256 F. 2d 467 (5 Cir. 1958); State v. Meyer, 228 Minn. 286, 37 N.E. 2d 3 (1949); People v. Scherbing, 93 Cal. App. 2d 735, 209 P. 2d 796 (1949).

[27] See *Infra*, pp. 159-166.

mitment, is the juvenile court laws. With few exceptions, a child within the juvenile court age (in most states, under eighteen or under seventeen) who violates a penal law is not deemed a criminal but a juvenile delinquent, a civil status, and if committed he is committed for his minority. That is, if a child of fourteen steals a small amount of money or property, an act that would be petty theft if committed by an adult and punishable by a short term, he is committed until he is twenty-one—a commitment of seven years, several times longer than the probable sentence for the adult. If the delinquency is merely truancy, a very common provision in juvenile court laws, the commitment is still for minority. A truant child of ten may be committed for eleven years! A seventeen-year-old who commits a traffic violation can be held for four years.[28]

It is true that in practice most children are released from training schools in a year, more or less; but cases of children held longer occur fairly often. For example, in 1959-1960 in the federal system, the average time served prior to release by all offenders —youths, delinquents, adults—was 16.4 months. Youth Corrections Act offenders served an average of 19.7 months; juvenile delinquents served 18 months; the average time served was smallest for adults![29] (The actual disparity is even greater than these figures show, since the higher figures for juveniles and youths are included in reaching the average for "all" offenders.)

The justification for this difference is the tiresome cliché of "treatment" in the juvenile institution, as compared with "punishment" in the correctional institution. The courts and the legislatures ought to be concerned that punishment of juveniles should at least not exceed that of adults for corresponding violations and that "treatment" in the institution should be a reality, a fact, not a fiction.[30] In a majority of states some juveniles com-

---

[28] California law (Vehicle Code § 13203) prohibits a court, other than a juvenile court, from revoking or suspending the privilege of any person to operate a motor vehicle for a period of time longer than that specified in the code.

[29] U.S. Board of Parole, Annual Report, July 1, 1959 to June 30, 1960, chart XII (p. 49).

[30] "Too often the vocabulary of therapy has been exploited to serve a public-relations function. Recently, I visited an institution devoted to the diagnosis and treatment of disturbed children. The institution had been established with high hopes and, for once, with the enthusiastic support of the state legislature. Nevertheless, fifty minutes of an hour's lecture,

mitted by juvenile courts are transferred to correctional institutions for adults committed under penal procedure, and the courts do not consistently condemn this.[31] The remedy for these patently unjust laws is plain enough, once the problem is stated. The rule should be (by statute, and if not, should be so held by the courts) that a "civil" commitment based upon a criminal act may not exceed in punishment that which could be imposed in the criminal prosecution. In fact, this is exactly what the federal juvenile delinquency law provides: a federal juvenile delinquent is committed for his minority, except when such period is longer than the maximum imprisonment imposable under the statute. In that event the commitment cannot exceed such maximum.[32] The latest edition of the Standard Juvenile Court Act moves in the same direction, limiting commitments to three years, rather than minority.[33] But the federal plan certainly seems sounder. A rule that would limit punishments in this fashion would also be consistent with those cases that hold that in a juvenile proceeding the child is entitled to more due process than in a criminal case, not less, on the ground that the civil proceeding is protective.[34]

Punishment in the other "civil" commitment cases based on criminal acts should be limited in the same way, not to exceed the allowable penalty if the offense were criminally prosecuted.[35]

---

delivered by a supervising psychiatrist before we toured the building, were devoted to custodial problems. . . . The institutional arrangements . . . include, under a properly euphemistic label, a cell for solitary confinement. Even more disturbing was the tendency of the staff to justify these custodial measures in therapeutic terms."—Allen, Criminal Justice, Legal Values and the Rehabilitative Ideal, 50 J. Crim. L, C. & P.S. 226 (1959). See Deutsch, Our Rejected Children (1950).

[31] See Sonnenberg v. Markley, 289 F. 2d 126 (1961); In re Darnell, 173 Ohio St. 335, 182 N.E. 2d 321 (1962).

[32] 18 U.S.C.A. § 5034.

[33] National Council on Crime and Delinquency, Standard Juvenile Court Act § 24 (1959). The term may be extended by further order, but not beyond majority.

[34] See Harling v. United States, 295 F. 2d 161 (1961), admissions to police made while child's case pending in juvenile court, not admissible in criminal court if the case is transferred to it.

[35] "I would not urge that a minor offender be held for life because of a psychiatric finding that his offense is rooted to a mental illness which continues. The reason is that psychiatrists do not know enough about human behavior to justify that awesome result. No one can read the divergent views commonplace in the courtroom without harboring the gravest doubt

Protective Restraint and the Necessity of Treatment

It would seem obvious that a person committed for his *condition* is committed for *treatment*. This is the very equation of the Durham rule: a mental hospital commitment is treatment (as contrasted with a criminal commitment, which is equated with punishment).[36] If treatment is not being given, would it not appear that the purpose, the justification of the commitment, has failed and that liberty should follow? Certainly it would seem so, except perhaps for the situation where a person is dangerous to the public and no treatment is known; even then, presumably, treatment should be attempted. Even sociopaths are being treated.[37]

But we have seen that "treatment" in the mental hospitals is doubtful and that the "civilly committed" sex psychopaths seldom receive treatment. At least as recently as 1956, "a startling number of those States which have legislated against drug addiction and prescribed mandatory treatment have failed to provide even the minimum facilities required for treating addicts. . . . In some states addicts may be sent to State mental hospitals, but these hospitals are not equipped to treat narcotics patients."[38] And if dangerousness is the ground of commitment, it should be established by judicial process.

An inmate of Creedmoor State Hospital in New York, civilly committed apparently without criminal act, sought his release by writ of habeas corpus on the ground that he was not being

---

about the state of their learning. In the sex-offenders statute referred to above, the legislature wisely, I think, provided that an offender consigned by psychiatric treatment may not be held beyond the maximum period of the jail term which could have been imposed. Until we know a great deal more, the post-conviction disposition must fit the offense as well as the offender."
—Weintraub, Criminal Responsibility: Psychiatry Alone Cannot Determine it, 49 A.B.A.J. 1075, at 1078 (1963). The New Jersey, Wisconsin, and Wyoming laws that authorize commitment of sex offenders to mental institutions limit the time they are to spend there to the maximum provided by law for the crime for which they have been convicted; Weihofen, Mental Disorder as a Criminal Defense 203 (1954).

[36] *Supra,* ch. 2.

[37] See Report of Commission to Study and Re-Evaluate Patuxent Institution, Legislative Council of the General Assembly of Maryland, January 25, 1961.

[38] Senate Committee on the Judiciary, Laws Controlling Illicit Narcotics Traffic, S. Doc. No. 120, 84th Cong., 2nd Sess. 45 (1956).

'reated. The court denied the writ. Its opinion offers a flat contradiction in its "reason" for the denial. It says: "It is the policy of the state to care for and protect mentally ill persons and, if possible, to cure them of disease." Presumably this justifies the commitment; there is no other ground. Then is there not an obligation to attempt to provide that treatment? "But," continued the court, "this policy does not confer on the mentally ill person a right to release in the event of claimed inadequate treatment." An inmate's attempt to have a hearing on the question of treatment or lack of treatment would appear to be reasonable. Indeed, to deny it is to deny that there is any obligation to treat whatever! But the New York court so held, and unfortunately the Supreme Court of the United States denied a review.[39]

Dr. Morton Birnbaum has argued for recognition of the right to treatment.[40] He asserts[41] that "the average inmate of a public mental institution (a) now receives inadequate medical treatment for his mental illness and (b) probably will continue to receive, in the foreseeable future, inadequate medical treatment for his mental illness." He argues that it is time the courts recognized the right to treatment "as a necessary and overdue development of our present concept of due process of law." Even an alleged criminal is granted his freedom if due process is not afforded—for example, if being indigent he is not provided with counsel.

Birnbaum urges recognition as law that "being mentally ill is not a crime; that an institution that involuntarily institutionalized the mentally ill without giving them adequate medical treatment for their mental illness is a mental prison and not a mental hospital; and, that substantive due process of law does not allow a mentally ill person who has committed no crime to be deprived of his liberty by indefinitely institutionalizing him in a mental prison. If this proposed development is to be achieved, rather than only discussed, the courts must be prepared to hold that if an inmate is being kept in a mental institution against his will, he must be given proper medical treatment or else the inmate

---

[39] State of New York ex rel. Anonymous v. La Burt, 369 U.S. 428, 8 L. ed. 2d, 7, 82 S. Ct. 880, *cert. denied* (1962), opinion below, People ex rel. Anonymous v. La Burt, 14 App. Div. 2d 560, 218 N.Y.S. 2d 738 (1961).

[40] The Right to Treatment, 46 A.B.A. J. 499 (1960).

[41] *Supra*, pp. 28-33.

can obtain his release at will in spite of the existence or severity of his mental illness."

Thinking of noncriminal mentally ill, Dr. Birnbaum finds, as we did, that illusions abound:

> The reader may have been disturbed by the use of the terms "inmate" instead of "patient," "institutionalization" or "imprisonment" instead of "hospitalization" and "mental institution" or "mental prison" instead of "mental hospital." There is an undoubted therapeutic value in mentally ill persons being told that they are patients who are being hospitalized in a mental hospital for care and treatment. . . . There is a limit, however, to the benefits of this terminology. If it allows the state to imprison the mentally ill rather than to treat them, the terminology should be analyzed in the interests of these sick people. For as long as one things about patients, doctors, mental hospitals and hospitalization, one can easily be deluded into misinterpreting reality.

Peculiarly, the right to treatment is accorded some fair measure of recognition in civil commitments in quasi-criminal cases, although it is not particularly well established.

Fahy, J.,[42] concurring, discussing the mandatory commitment to a mental hospital in the District of Columbia on acquittal for insanity, said: "This mandatory commitment provision rests upon a supposition, namely, the necessity for treatment of the mental condition which led to the acquittal by reason of insanity. And this necessity for treatment presupposes in turn that treatment will be accorded."

A commitment of a juvenile delinquent to a jail was invalidated on the ground that criminal due process may be disregarded "only if proper facilities are, in fact, furnished."[43]

A prisoner committed under the penal law in Massachusetts was transferred as a sex offender under an indeterminate term to a "treatment center" at the prison. The court rejected the "civil commitment" myth where no treatment was provided. It said: "To be sustained as a nonpenal statute, in its application to the defendant, it is necessary that the remedial aspect of the

---

[42] Concurring opinion, Ragsdale v. Overholser, 281 F. 2d 943 (1960). The case is discussed *supra*, pp. 151-153.

[43] Kautter v. Reid, 183 F. Supp. 352 (1960).

confinement thereunder have foundation in fact. It is not sufficient that the legislature announce a remedial purpose if the
consequences to the individual are penal." The only treatment
was a program of group and individual psychiatric therapy for
the total prison population. Said the court: "A confinement in a
prison which is undifferentiated from the incarceration of convicted criminals is not remedial so as to escape constitutional
requirements of due process.[44]

In a civil proceeding in Michigan the defendant was committed
as a criminal sexual psychopath to the Ionia State Hospital.
Several months after the commitment he was transferred to the
state prison. There he was under the same prison discipline and
routine as that imposed on prisoners sentenced under the criminal code except that, like other similarly committed prisoners, he
was never allowed outside the prison walls and at long intervals
was seen briefly by doctors from Ionia. Although four psychiatrists testified that incarceration sometimes helped obdurate
criminal sexual psychopaths to become more ready to accept
the treatment offered by Ionia State Hospital, to which they
might be returned, it was plain that the medical superintendent
of Ionia assumed no responsibility for the care or treatment of
defendants transferred to the prison.

Commenting on the testimony on this point, the Michigan
Supreme Court said: "In effect, the doctors' testimony really
stated that incarceration in prison under prison conditions was a
medical prescription for the type of problem which defendant
had been found to have." It referred to previous laws and
Supreme Court rulings on their constitutionality, up to the present situation in which the sexual psychopath statute is civil
rather than criminal and is deemed valid. The Court said:

> We are faced by a record which shows that a person
> committed under this remedial and corrective legislation
> for hospitalization and treatment is, in fact, serving po-

---

[44] Commonwealth v. Page, 339 Mass. 311, at 317-8, 159 N.E. 2d 82
(1959). See also, People v. Jackson, 20 A.D. 2d 170, 245 N.Y.S. 2d
534 (1963), indeterminate life term under the New York sex offender
law voided where "in the whole period of over eleven years . . . spent in
prison [the prisoner] received no psychiatric treatment. Nor is there any
proof that he would not respond to psychiatric treatment if given; or
that he would be dangerous if released. Reports of examinations made of
him in prison show entirely superficial judgments."

tentially a life sentence in our biggest state prison, treated in all respects similarly to other criminals therein confined. As far as the record before us discloses, this prisoner has never been tried and convicted of any crime. He certainly is not held in prison as a result of criminal conviction. Although the statute under which he was subjected to civil commitment required a petition charging him with criminal acts, it permits commitment where "it shall appear that such person is a criminal sexual psychopathic person." In short, it allows for commitment on medical diagnosis, without any finding of guilt or commission of any crime. We are confronted here by a record that plainly shows that a life sentence in State prison, based solely on medical diagnosis, can result from the administrative interpretations placed upon the act. And this without the person concerned ever having been found guilty of any crime.

We reject any such interpretation of the statute. We believe that incarceration in the State prison of Southern Michigan cannot constitutionally be based upon either medical diagnosis at a civil commitment proceedings, or administrative decision of the State hospital commission after civil commitment. This court holds that incarceration in a penitentiary designed and used for the confinement of convicted criminals is not a prescription available upon medical diagnosis and order to an administrative branch of government. Such confinement can only be ordered by a duly constituted court after trial conducted in accordance with the guarantees pertaining to individual liberty contained in the Constitution of this State and this nation. This prisoner has been denied the constitutional rights guaranteed Michigan citizens prior to sentence as a criminal offender. . . . This prisoner has been denied the due process of law pertaining to criminal trial to which he was entitled before penitentiary sentence or confinement. . . .

While what we have said decides the constitutional issue posed by this case, we note that the violations of defendant's constitutional rights may well have had an important practical effect upon his treatment and rehabilitation also. Defendant was committed because of a petition alleging criminal offenses and a medical diagnosis of a state or condition of sexual psychopathy. The record, however, makes clear that he was transferred from Ionia State hospital to the State prison of Southern Michigan largely because he was "adamant" in refusing to admit the sex offenses with which he had been charged. The State psychiatrist in charge of his case, who recommended against his return to Ionia, indicated clearly in his testimony that defendant's refusal to admit his guilt constituted a major part of the reason for his being held at the State prison of Southern Michigan.

After reviewing the evidence, the Court declared:

> It is obvious from the above that the practical result in this case is that defendant is now held in this State's principal prison for the confinement of criminal offenders largely because he refuses to admit that he is guilty of certain sex crimes with which he was charged before Detroit's Recorder's Court, but of which he has never been found guilty either by plea or trial. In short, defendant on this record is shown to be confined in a penitentiary largely because certain police officers and certain doctors believe that he was guilty of criminal offenses to which he has never admitted, and as to which he has been denied a jury trial. In the event that defendant were actually innocent of the offenses charged (and on this record we have no right to presume the contrary), his right to proper medical treatment would have been as badly violated by his imprisonment as his constitutional rights.

The order of assignment to the state prison was declared void.[45]

---

[45] In re Maddox, 351 Mich. 358, 88 N.W. 2d 470 (1957), our ital. "Following the Maddox decision, it was decided that all those men at the state prison serving 'one day to life' under the Criminal Sexual Psychopath Act should be transferred to the maximum security hospital for the criminally insane at Ionia which was under the jurisdiction of the Michigan Department of Mental Health. When the hospital staff learned of the proposed transfer they stated that, because of inadequate bed space, an approximately equal number of men, previously sent to the hospital from the prison because they were psychotic, would have to be returned. This exchange actually did take place and the explosive situation at the prison in the spring and early summer of 1960 could be attributed to it. The anxiety experienced by prison inmates and custodial personnel when they realized that many disturbed men were among them, was readily apparent. Other events followed adding to the difficulties at the prison. Men who

A defendant in California was committed under the civil sexual psychopath act to the Department of Mental Hygiene for placement in the Atascadero State Hospital. The procedure was essentially the same as that in the Michigan case. Seventeen months after the commitment the medical director found the defendant had not recovered and was still a menace to the health and safety of others. In accordance with the statute another hearing was held in the Superior Court, which concluded that the defendant "would not be benefited by further hospitalization," found that he was still a "menace to the health and safety of others" and that he was "predisposed to the commission of sexual offenses," and committed him "for an indeterminate period to the Department of Mental Hygiene, for placement in an institutional unit for the treatment of sexual psychopaths in a facility of the Department of Corrections; namely, the California State Prison at San Quentin."

The California appellate court upheld the transfer. It declared that there was no violation of the prohibition against double jeopardy, since the proceeding was civil. As for the fact that the defendant in a civil proceeding found himself in prison, the court said: "The place of commitment and the possibility of criminal punishment on the misdemeanor charge does not affect the validity of the objectives of the Act, which are admittedly proper. The emphasis that appellant places on the fact that he was originally convicted of a misdemeanor, and now finds himself in San Quentin, possibly for life, is misplaced. *As we have already seen, the purpose of the confinement is to protect society and to try and cure the accused.*" (Italics added.)[46] Does not an attempt to "cure the accused" require, as the Michigan Supreme Court said, something other than a penal institution placement? A person committable because he has tuberculosis in communicable form may not be placed in a jail, not

---

became psychotic could no longer be transferred to the hospital at Ionia because the previously available beds were now occupied by the criminal sexual psychopaths. The result was that severely disturbed psychotics had to be treated in the prison psychiatric clinic."—Thomas, The Dangerous Offender, 14 Syracuse L. Rev. 576, at 578 (1963).

[46] People v. Levy, 151 C.A. 2d 460, 311 P. 2d 897 (1957), our ital.; also People v. Willey, 128 Cal. App. 2d 148, 275 P. 2d 522 (1954).

even in the hospital section.[47] Logic is with the Michigan court it would appear.

In a New Jersey case the court dealt with a sex offender committed under a criminal statute. The defendant was found guilty in 1952 of several sex offenses, and when the diagnosis of severe psychiatric disturbance was given by the New Jersey Diagnostic Center he was sentenced for an indeterminate period to the state hospital at Marlboro. There he was uncooperative, hostile, and assaultive. On July 16, 1952, he was transferred to Trenton State Hospital, where he was one of seven patients who threatened a disturbance and therefore was transferred, on March 3, 1953, to the state prison at Trenton. Parole was denied to him a number of times because his condition and attitude continued to be bad. The court returned the matter for a further hearing, but in essence upheld the procedure, declaring: "If a defendant who has been committed to a hospital for treatment under the terms of the Sex Offender Act makes an affirmative showing that his transfer to the state prison was arbitrary and in conflict with the purposes underlying his sentence, he may obtain judicial relief by habeas corpus or otherwise. . . . When defendants are lawfully committed under the statute, the Department must thereafter conscientiously seek to attain fulfillment of the legislative program."

A dissent held that the state prison was not shown to be equipped with the "special treatment" facilities "needed to fulfill the legislative policy of medical and psycho-therapy." The state prison, the dissent said, is not suitable as a corrective mechanism; "here we have utter frustration of the legislative design."[48]

The *American Bar Association Journal* has said editorially: "The fact that a person has a mental ailment is not a crime. Therefore, if any one is voluntarily restrained of his liberty because of a mental ailment the state owes a duty to provide for him reasonable medical attention. If medical attention reasonably well adapted to his needs is not given, the victim is not a patient but is virtually a prisoner."[49]

---

[47] Benton v. Reid, 231 F. 2d 780 (1956).
[48] State v. Wingler, 25 N.J. 161, 135 A. 2d 468 (1957).
[49] 46 A.B.A.J. 516 (1960).

The Dangerous Offender

In our examination of the quasi-criminal civil commitments, we have suggested that several rules should be conformed to— by statute, and if not, then by the courts—in order for these commitments to be valid. First we suggested that these statutes are based on a fiction (the "civil" nature of the commitment), and that to be sustained they should be realistically related to the police power or *parens patriae*. We then said that a statute for civil commitment for illness also must be realistically examined and may not be sustained unless the tests of dangerousness or helplessness are met. In this part of our discussion we said that the mere use of the word "civil" is quite inadequate in determining whether a commitment is, in fact, civil and not criminal, and that the actual effects of the statute must be examined. Thus, commitment of an entire class of persons automatically (e.g., defendants acquitted of crime for mental illness) is a penal statute, carrying a remarkably severe punishment. That is, a defendant acquitted of crime is subject to penal punishment nevertheless! Such a statute should not be allowed to stand.

We then considered the amount of punishment imposed under quasi-criminal commitments and suggested that (assuming the statute is validly held constitutional)[50] it could not exceed that imposable under the criminal proceeding based on the same criminal law violation. Finally, we said, if a statute deprives a person of liberty on the ground of his dangerousness or helplessness because of a mental illness, it is the obligation of the state to realistically provide or do its best to provide treatment for the illness, and failing that, the person incarcerated should be entitled to his liberty.

It is not difficult to see that one element may arise in the mind of those who consider these arguments: the element of dangerousness of the offender. Surely the state has the right and the obligation to protect the community from dangerous persons.

---

[50] The constitutionality of the "civil" sexual psychopath acts requires re-examination. The United States Supreme Court case on it, Minnesota ex rel. Pearson v. Probate Court, 309 U.S. 270, 60 S. Ct. 523 (1939) upholds the Minnesota act by analogy to civil commitment of the insane in an opinion that is too facile in accepting the magic word formulae.

This has not been overlooked in our discussion. In attacking the quasi-criminal civil commitments we have not suggested that dangerousness should not be considered; quite the contrary. What we have said is that in practice, the original justification of the statutes is dangerousness, but in applicaction the test is forgotten (*vide,* the sexual psychopath statutes and the mandatory "civil" commitment of persons acquitted of crime for insanity).

But the proposition is even simpler than that. The very purpose of the penal laws is to protect society, through deterrence and incapacitation (incarceration), where necessary, as well as rehabilitation. If there is any place in our body of law where protection of the public from crime is sought through incapacitation, it is the penal law, not the protective statutes under *parens patriae.* Surely an advocate of the civil procedures would not want to argue that the penal laws are inadequate for public protection and that we therefore need the more "accomodating" framework of the civil procedure, avoiding the stringencies of criminal due process. It would not be difficult to predict that such a course would lead to prolific abuse; that, indeed, is what has happened.

Still, the penal statutes are not, in fact, adequately protective of the public. We shall discuss, in addition to the laws already mentioned, those that increase punishment for repeated offenders, and we shall find that these also do not adequately protect the public. The answer to all this is obvious: if the penal laws do not afford adequate protection, they need to be improved. Such improvement is possible without perversion of the concept of civil law. Again we refer, for a solution, to the Model Sentencing Act, a way of dealing with dangerous offenders superior to existing codes.

A Comprehensive Protective Statute

It is undoubtedly true that the stigma of a criminal conviction is significant in our culture; hence the comment above that despite the soundness of Justice Clark's point on the artificiality of the civil-criminal distinction in the California statutes, it would be unjust to sustain a criminal conviction for illness (drug addiction). But stigma is not the only attribute of a conviction;

and there is stigma to mental commitments also, as we have shown. If the stigma attaching to criminal conviction and mental commitment is socially undesirable, this negative attribute must be overcome mainly through realistic changes in treatment.

What must occur meanwhile is a clarification of the legal concepts and a lessening of the emphasis on the terms "criminal" and "civil," as well as a realistic solution of the many problems raised, such as criteria of commitment, now so vague and loose.

It should be possible to construct a statute setting forth criteria for commitment or other disposition in cases of law violation or proceedings for protection (the term that is superior to "civil" in any event)—without attaching the labels. Thus the statute could, in separate subdivisions, enumerate dispositions for violation of law (corresponding to criminal dispositions) and the commitment or other disposition for dangerousness or helplessness, giving the criteria for each, without calling the former "criminal" or the latter "civil." Meaningful criteria, not word magic, would then be operative. I suggest the term "protective" for such a statute, using the term in the two senses of protecting the public against violations of law and protecting the helpless person against harm.

It might well be that bringing the several sources of commitment together in one statute would illuminate the problems of treatment and release, leading to some consistency in these matters, not by blurring the distinctions between the commitment for law violation and for protection of a sick person but by making them matters of substance, not form. And we may note here that Durham blurs the distinction between "criminal" and "protective," whereas M'Naghten supports the distinction. Yet this is not a reversion to "criminal conviction=punishment, civil commitment=treatment."

Perhaps such a statute could provide that a commitment or disposition under any subdivision is exclusive. The result would be that a commitment for mental illness, for example, would bar a criminal proceeding on recovery. This result often obtains in practice today.[51] It would be in line with the

---

[51] Compare the discussion of the same question in connection with incompetency to stand trial, *supra* pp. 40 to 46. A District of Columbia statute provides that "on the conviction by a court . . . of any person of any crime . . . the court, if satisfied on the testimony of a physician or a

effort to unify into a single sentence the punishment of a man who has committed several crimes.[52]

---

psychologist or evidence that the person . . . is feebleminded within the meaning of this chapter, may suspend sentence . . . and direct that a petition [for involuntary commitment] be filed under this chapter"; D.C. Code Amn. §32-621.

[52] See Rubin, Weihofen, Edwards, & Rosenweig, The Law of Criminal Correction, ch. 11 §§21-25 (1963).

Chapter 8

The Repeated Offender

The concept of the recidivist or habitual offender rightly engages the attention of criminologists and psychiatrists, for it is central in the endeavor to establish criminology as a science. The recidivist pattern of behavior, not evanescent but recurrent, should be especially accessible to discovery. Recidivism is an important concept, for on it presumably will depend concepts of prevention (*i.e.*, prevention of recidivism, if not prevention prior to the individual's first crime), and treatment (*i.e.*, treatment so that the first offender will not be a recidivist). A very large percentage of prisoners are recidivists.[1] Unfortunately, no substantial body of behavioral understanding of the recidivist has been produced; at any rate, there is no evidence of its being applied in the usual statutory structure.

---

[1] Although a large percentage of prisoners, often about two-thirds of an institution's population, are recidivists (have prior records), this is decidedly not the same as the rate of repeated crime among offenders generally, or even among persons committed to prison. "The percentage of prisoners who have previously committed a crime is not a general recidivism rate. The base does not take account of persons on probation or discharged from probation, persons who have received suspended sentences or fines, persons discharged from prison, and persons on parole or discharged from parole. In fact *the recidivism rate for all offenders is always less than the percentage of recidivists among prisoners.* Why is this so? First: frequently by automatic operation of law and generally by the action of sentencing judges, recidivists receive prison terms more frequently than do first offenders. This means that the proportion of repeaters among persons who receive suspended sentence, are placed on probation, or are fined is lower than among persons imprisoned. Second: among prisoners, again

Baumes Laws

The habitual offender laws are of long standing. The American colonies had recidivism statutes, providing for increased punishment for a second, third, or further repeated offense. By now practically every state has such a law or laws. Most of them were passed in the present century, the peak of activity occurring in the 1920's. After World War I an apparent, although perhaps not real, increase in crime led to criticism of the penal laws and penal treatment and to the establishment in the 1920's of a number of permanent and temporary crime commissions. The best known at the time was the New York Crime Commission, which, under the chairmanship of State Senator Caleb Baumes, led the drive for repressive penal legislation, particularly additional punishment for repeated offenders and, best known, the life term for the fourth offender. Other states emulated the New York approach.[2] In several states the sex offender legislation initiated in the 1930's[3] resulted, as we have seen, in life terms for repeated or otherwise specially classed sex offenses, and in the 1950's and '60's several jurisdictions authorized life terms for repeated narcotics offenders (and sometimes for first offenders).

---

frequently by automatic operation of law and generally by the action of sentencing judges, recidivists generally receive longer prison terms than do first offenders. Prisoners who are first offenders are in general discharged from prison sooner than those who have more than one conviction on their record. Thus there is a faster turnover of short-term prisoners than long-term prisoners. Therefore, at any given moment the proportion of long-term prisoners, among whom are found most recidivists, will be high compared with short-termers (mainly, first offenders) or the total of all persons sentenced. That is, at any one moment the percentage of *prisoners* who have been previously convicted must be higher than the recidivism rate of all previously convicted among all persons sentenced. Since there are criminals who once discharged do not recidivate and are not among those sentenced, the percentage of recidivists among prisoners must similarly be higher than the recidivism rate of all persons discharged after conviction. . . . Probably about 20 or 25 per cent of persons convicted of felony are convicted again within a few years of freedom, and probation, imprisonment, and parole recidivism rates probably do not differ markedly from one another."—Rubin, Recidivism and Recidivism Statistics, 4 National Probation and Parole Association Journal 233 (1958).

[2] Rubin, Weihofen, Edwards, & Rosenzweig, The Law of Criminal Correction 393 (1963). The first Baumes laws in New York were passed in 1926, and additional acts in 1927, 1928, and 1929. "The designation 'the Baumes law' has become most specifically associated with the mandatory

The repeated offender laws on the books today represent the spirit of Caleb Baumes far more than any notions of scientific understanding of behavior. The psychiatrists had little share in the legislation that now exists, but they are, or ought to be, deeply involved, for the light they should shed on this problem. Meanwhile, the statutes have a disastrous effect on criminal justice, and the damage would be even worse if they were not so frequently evaded by prosecutors and judges.

Although the recidivism laws are usually mandatory, their enforcement characteristic is not mandatoriness but rather, because of their rigidity, avoidance, which occurs in legal shadows. "Quite characteristically where the habitual criminal laws are mandatory in terms, they are actually rendered discretionary by the prosecutor's powers."[4] The laws are useful in obtaining convictions—not before juries, however, but through their use by the prosecutor in bargaining for guilty pleas. This usually requires, to avoid the recidivism penalty, reduction of a felony charge to a misdemeanor charge. Contradictorily, therefore the result of these statutes is that often a sentence is reduced rather than increased,[5] although this is probably not the general effect.

In Indiana the statute was used on the average of once a year from 1907, when it was enacted, to 1931, when the Indiana

---

life imprisonment act for offenders convicted of a fourth felony. The habitual criminal act, of which this is the most noteworthy provision, also accords increasingly heavy sentences to second and third felony offenders."— Johnson (ed.), The Baumes Law, introd. and p. 3 (1929). The Model Penal Code, Tentative Draft No. 2 p. 39-40 (1954) lists these seven jurisdictions as providing for a life term on a third conviction—Calif., Idaho, Ind., Ky., Tex., Wash., and W.Va.; and seventeen jurisdictions mandating the life term on a fourth conviction—Colo., Fla., Mich., Minn., Mo., Nev., N.J., N.M., N.Y., N.D., Ohio, Ore., Pa., S.D., Tenn., Vt., and Wyo. In almost all instances the term is mandatory.

[3] Rubin et al, op. cit. supra n. 2 at 408.

[4] Tappan, "Habitual Offender Laws and Sentencing Practices in Relation to Organized Crime," in Ploscowe (ed.), Organized Crime and Law Enforcement 139 (1952). From 1940 to 1956 eleven persons subject to be sentenced to life imprisonment under West Virginia's habitual criminal law were not so sentenced to every person who was—79 sentenced to life, while 904 who could have been sentenced to life under it were not.— Brown, West Virginia Habitual Criminal Law, 59 W.Va. L. Rev. 30, at 37 (1956).

[5] Brown., op. cit. supra n. 4 at 124.

Committee on Observance and Enforcement of Law issued its report;[6] and experience elsewhere is similar. In Chicago "no judge during 1947 found any defendant guilty of the major charge of an indictment containing also an habitual criminal count!"[7] The worst part of it is that the dangerous offenders—the racketeers, for example—escape the Baumes laws, but the oft-caught petty offenders do not. A study of the 108 men who were sentenced to Sing Sing prison in New York from 1926 to 1930 under the Baumes Act showed that the great majority were not desperate criminals but persons who had committed relatively trivial offenses.[8]

The typical recidivism statutes have other defects. They usually limit the judge's discretion in the use of probation and sometimes the discretion of a parole board in granting parole[9] either by barring parole or, more commonly, by increasing the minimum term that must be served before parole eligibility. These statutes and practices are an utter repudiation of the criminological concept of individualizing treatment.

Who Needs a Long Term?

Certain implications are clearly to be taken from the experience with the repeated offender laws: they are bad because they are unjustly punitive and impair prison treatment programs, and they are not necessary for either (1) rehabilitation of the offender or (2) public protection. The long terms are not rehabilitative. Prison programs are not that constructive, and if they

---

[6] Brown, Treatment of the Recidivist in the United States, 23 Canadian Bar Rev. 640 (1945).

[7] Chicago Crime Commission, Crime—A Statistical View: Crime in Chicago, 1947.

[8] Rubin et al, op. cit. supra n. 2 at 298, n. 27. "One man was sent to our penitentiary for life for the following crimes: First felony—breaking and entering a dwelling house and stealing goods to the value of five dollars. Second felony—breaking and entering a dwelling house and stealing goods to the value of $17.65. Third felony—forging a check for five dollars. The first two convictions were for felonies committed when the convicted person was seventeen years of age. When I interviewed inmates of the penitentiary and studied their records during the course of this study, I found others serving life sentences for three relatively minor felonies." —Brown, op. cit. supra n. at 37.

[9] Sixteen states and the District of Columbia bar probation to repeated offenders, most of them barring it after the first offense; Rubin, op. cit. supra n. 2 at 399.

were, their maximum usefulness would come within not much more than a year. In that time any vocational or other training will have been given, and for those offenders—the great majority —who are not suffering from severe personality disorders, the removal from their associates and the other community ties that may have been involved in their crime will have been substantial enough for them to make a fresh start, without being so prolonged as to embitter them and warp their personalities through the process of prisonization.[10]

Although in some instances long terms are needed for public protection, the great majority of the long terms imposed through the Baumes laws are imposed for property crimes, usually petty property crimes, or relatively minor assaults. This result is not surprising, since these laws contain no criteria of dangerousness but merely increase the penalty according to the number of previous offenses.

What if one undertook to state criteria for determining which defendants require a long term? The first criterion would appear to be the dangerousness of the act—particularly, dangerousness against the person, not the property, of another. This appears to be the consensus of the critics of the repeated offender laws, and it seems a sensible judgment. A second criterion should be required—the likelihood of repetition. We have spoken of ordinary prison programs and the maximum effectiveness they have on the normal offender, who makes up the great majority of all offenders.

But if an offender has committed a dangerous crime *and* is mentally disturbed his early release is not indicated. Prolonged care might be required to deal with his mental disturbance and protect the public. The most difficult offender who comes to mind is the sociopath, whose cure is often said to be problematical. The sociopath is said to be, in general, the incorrigible, antisocial person without conscience who fails to learn from experience.

The Patuxent Institution statute defines a "defective delinquent" (convicted person who may be committed to it) as "an individual who, by the demonstration of persistent aggravated

---

[10] Clemmer, The Prison Community (1958).

antisocial or criminal activity, evidences a propensity toward criminal activity, and who is found to have either such intellectual deficiency or emotional unbalance, or both, as to clearly demonstrate an actual danger to society so as to require such confinement and treatment, when appropriate, as may make it reasonably safe for society to terminate the confinement and treatment."[11]

But the concept of sociopathy (or "psychopathy," the earlier term for exactly the same persons)—is also severely criticized. Hakeem brings together a host of observations on the subject, leading to the conclusion that the concept is not properly a clinical one ("there is no such thing as a medical [psychiatric] 'disease' called psychopathic or sociopathic personality") and that it is simply applied to a repeated offender with whom the police, courts, and institutions are not successful.[12]

Although some believe that sociopaths are untreatable, it is also generally accepted that the condition "burns itself out" after a number of years. "There are few old psychopaths. Somehow the gaudily-hued crazy quilt of their existence takes on a more somber coloration as they advance in years. Some are killed in brawls and accidents, but to those who survive, the years bring relative sobriety."[13]

But of interest to us is probably the best available clinical experience with sociopaths. The Patuxent Institution, a state institution in Maryland, was set up to receive the most difficult prisoners committed by the criminal courts. "The men committed to Patuxent as defective delinquents are often the most dangerous types of criminals. Over three-quarters have committed more than one adult offense, and the remainder averaged two and one-half conflicts with the law as juveniles in addition to the adult offenses; over one-half have committed assaultive crimes; and 30% sex crimes."[14]

---

[11] Annot. Code of the Pub. Gen. Laws of Md., Art. 31B, sec. 5.

[12] Hakeem, A Critique of the Psychiatric Approach to Crime and Correction, 23 Law and Contemp. Problems, Autumn, 1958, 650, at 674. Hakeem notes that in 1952 the American Psychiatric Association adopted the new term "sociopathic personality" in place of the old.

[13] Lindner, Stone Walls and Men 157 (1946).

[14] Commission to Study and Re-Evaluate Patuxent Institution, Report to Legislative Council of the General Assembly of Maryland, January 25, 1961, p. 24.

Under a special procedure, a person committed for any one of certain crimes, or twice convicted of any offense, may be examined by the institution to see whether he comes within the definition of "defective delinquent." If the institution report is that he is a defective delinquent, the court holds a hearing on the issue, and if he is found to be a defective delinquent, he is committed to Patuxent Institution under neither a minimum nor a maximum term.

The orientation in the institution is therapeutic. Group and individual psychotherapy are used. Punishment for rule violations, for example, is not automatic, but related to the reason for commission of the act. The treatment is evidently successful. Releases occur, often within a few years after commitment, and the violation rate of those released is no worse than that of prisoners released from other institutions.

> Since Patuxent opened in January, 1955, 287 inmates
> ... have been committed to it as defective delinquents.
> As of September 9, 1960, 42 inmates have been paroled;
> of these 16 violated their parole and were returned to the
> Institution. As of October 20, 1960, 29 men were on
> parole; three additional inmates have been approved for
> parole but have not yet left the Institution. In addition,
> 16 inmates have been given the privilege of leaving the
> Institution for short periods, nine for holidays and five
> for weekend leaves. Two inmates are on a live-in, work-
> out basis, that is, they are permitted to leave the Institu-
> tion to work at normal occupations, returning at night.
> This device seems to present no institutional problems,
> except the legal difficulty of the application of some part
> of the inmates' earnings to their upkeep. In considering
> the figures as to paroles and leaves, it must be kept in
> mind that the time required for the successful treatment
> of defective delinquents, in terms of making them rea-
> sonably safe for return to society, is necessarily a matter
> of some years. From 1955 through 1958, only 11 men
> had been paroled; in 1959 the figure was 15, and 16 were
> paroled from January 1 to September 1, 1960.[15]

Another type of offender should be mentioned in relation to length of sentence. Certainly the gravest crimes are those com-

---

[15] Ibid.

mitted in behalf of organized crime. The documentation of organized crime—racketeering—in this country shows the greatest social destructiveness. The money loss is prodigious. The methods used are cold-blooded murder and terror, where necessary, and strong-arm coercion commonly. Organized crime corrupts the police and prosecution and civil governments. We have already discussed the narcotics problem, one of the main enterprises of organized crime; others are gambling and various forms of extortion.

Existing weapons against organized crime appear to be inadequate, and one of the inadequacies is sentencing. It is often extremely difficult to apprehend the higher-ups in the rackets in the usual law violations. It could well be argued that an offender who is a part of organized crime should be subject to a long term, as a part of the massive attack against it.

Repeated Offenders under the American Law Institute Model Penal Code

The American Law Institute's Model Penal Code (whose proposal on a test of insanity we discussed earlier[16]) contains provisions on sentencing, including a plan of "extended terms" for recidivists. What does it offer, compared with the common Baumes laws and with the Model Sentencing Act?

The Model Penal Code sentencing plan would set up three grades of felony, first, second, and third, with minimum and maximum terms as follows:

Grade of Felony	Minimum Term [17]	Maximum Term*
1st degree (murder; kidnapping; rape; robbery)	1-10 years	life
2nd degree	1-3 years	10 years (+ five years of parole term)
3rd degree	1-2 years	5 years (+ five years of parole term)

(*An alternate plan is also suggested, to give the judge authority to fix the maximum at some term less than that indicated in the table.)

---

16 *Id.,* pp. 65-8.

The maximum terms indicated are not the actual maximums a prisoner may be required to serve. Every prisoner is subject to an additional parole term of five years, which, if revoked, he may be required to serve in prison. Thus the maximum for second degree is a term potentially of fifteen years; and for third degree, ten years.[18]

The Model Penal Code also provides for "extended terms" for certain repeated offenders. These terms are:

Grade of Felony	Minimum Term— Extended	Maximum Term— Extended
1st degree	5-10 years	life
2nd degree	1-5 years	10-20 years (+ five years of parole term)
3rd degree	1-3 years	5-10 years (+ five years of parole term)

The model statute (§ 7.03) provides that these extended terms may be imposed if (1) the defendant has been previously convicted of two felonies or one felony and two misdemeanors, committed at different times; or (2) the defendant is "a professional criminal"—that is, he "has knowingly devoted himself to criminal activity as a major source of livelihood"; or (3) the defendant is "a dangerous, mentally abnormal person"—in any such case the judge must make a finding that the commitment for an extended term "is necessary for protection of the public"; (4) the defendant is being sentenced for two or more felonies, or is already under sentence of imprisonment for felony, and the sentence of imprisonment will run concurrently; or (5) the defendant admits in open court the commission of one or more

---

17 The Model Sentencing Act does not authorize a minimum term. The comment on section 1 of the Act states: "The provision for a minimum term creates disparity of sentences by setting a variety of mandatory terms of incarceration. One defendant may receive a term of one to five years, another two to four, three to five, three to six, and so on, all of which disparity would not exist if there were no minimum term. In addition, the minimum term impedes the parole process, since a parole board has no discretion to consider parole of a prisoner until the minimum term has been served."

18 On the Model Penal Code supporting long terms, see Rubin, Sentencing and Correctional Treatment under the Law Institute's Model Penal Code, 46 A.B.A.J. 994 (1960).

felonies other than the one of which he has been convicted, and asks that they be taken into account.

It is solely up to the judge to determine who is an offender on whom he will impose the extended term. He has complete discretion. There is an illusion of "findings" that are required to be made; for example, the finding that the extended term "is necessary for protection of the public." A judge who has decided that he wishes to impose an extended term on a particular offender would simply recite that "he finds it to be necessary for protection of the public." The absence of data to support the finding would not serve as a ground for appeal, which is one way of demonstrating that the criterion is in no way controlling on the judge.

Although *dangerousness* is mentioned in the statute, there is no mechanism to select out those who are, in fact, dangerous. The word first occurs in the third category: "the defendant is a dangerous, mentally abnormal person." This subdivision also states: "The court shall not make such a finding unless the defendant has been subjected to a psychiatric examination resulting in the conclusion that his mental condition is gravely abnormal; that his criminal conduct has been characterized by a pattern of repetitive or compulsive behavior or by persistent aggressive behavior with heedless indifference to consequences; and that such a condition makes him a serious danger to others." The word "dangerous" is not defined. Unlike the Patuxent Institution statute and the Model Sentencing Act, the Model Penal Code does not provide for a hearing to put any allegations or findings in issue. There is nothing to deter a punitive judge from throwing the book at any of a large number of defendants, and several ways are provided for him to do it.

In brief, this section compares closely with the Baumes laws in the codes today, and in no effective way makes an extended term depend on actual dangerousness. It is worse than many in that in the last subdivision it introduces a new device allowing an extended term to be imposed on a defendant who admits that he has committed felonies other than the one of which he has been convicted. Since the admission can be extracted even at a sentence hearing, it appears to be a way of bypassing proper criminal procedure of accusing and trying a person for his crimes.

If these were easier ways of getting at the dangerous offender, there might be some argument on behalf of the plan; but
they are not. Property crimes may be the occasion for an extended term. Under the Model Penal Code, as under many Baumes
laws, a defendant guilty only of crimes against property, and
not against the person, can be sentenced to an extended term;
but this is not so under the Model Sentencing Act. The findings required under the Model Sentencing Act are significantly
different from those called for under the ALI code. The findings are specific, not general; and are findings with respect to
evidence introduced at a hearing. Hence, the findings are review-
able on appeal, a necessary attribute to overcome the complete
autonomy of the judge's decision on the sentence under present
law and under the ALI proposal.

It is a matter of congratulation that the extended term does
not go so far as to add to the list of life terms otherwise provided
in the Model Penal Code, as do half the existing statutes. But it
does increase the penalties severely. A second degree felon,
subject to a ten-year maximum (plus five years of parole term),
is subject to a twenty-year maximum if he is in any of the
extended term classes; and the third degree felon similarly has
his sentence doubled. This follows closely the typical Baumes
laws. Furthermore, the less-than-life statutes are applied in
more cases than the life cases; it is the life sentences that are particularly avoided.

Until 1937 Kansas had an act making a life sentence mandatory
in case of a third felony conviction. A new law enacted in 1939
provided for not less than fifteen years on a third conviction.
The change followed a study of the Kansas habitual criminal
law by the Kansas Legislative Council, which declared the law
too severe. It showed that while 41.3 per cent of the persons
committed to the Kansas prison over a seven-year period were
repeated offenders subject to the habitual criminal law, only
9.5 per cent were committed. Under the new, more lenient law,
about 15.7 per cent of those subject to the law were sentenced
under it (although the language of the statute continued to be
mandatory).[19]

Peculiarly, substituting wide-open discretion (as under the
Model Penal Code plan) is probably worse than the mandatory

[19] Brown, *op. cit. supra* n. 4.

provisions of the ordinary Baumes laws. The mandatory laws are narrower than the ALI plan and, as we have noted, are in practice widely avoided by various means. But the wide discretion given the judge under the Model Penal Code to impose the extended term is an invitation to its substantial use. The "mandatory" acts actually have the effect of putting "discretion" (the power to avoid) in the prosecutor's hands, and, if he does not exercise it, there is still a chance for the judge to avoid the application of the statute, despite the mandatory language. But under a discretionary act, there is less pressure on the prosecutor to avoid and there are more cases going to the judge with the potential of application of the statute. As for the judge, the problem of disparity of sentences, which enters everywhere, is worsened under a discretionary recidivism statute: "Statutory discretion under the recidivism acts enables punitive judges to be doubly punitive and thus increases the disparity between their sentences and those by other judges."[20]

Eliminating Life Terms

A characteristic of the Baumes laws, as much as an increased penalty for a second or third conviction, is the imposition of a life term of imprisonment if the offender has committed the requisite number of offenses. Half the states have such a provision. Although we have noted that the harshness and inappropriateness of such a sentence makes for a certain amount of avoidance, yet a large number of life terms are imposed. In addition, of course some crimes carry life terms without regard to the recidivism statutes. In 1960 state and federal prisons (except New Jersey and Alaska) received 2567 prisoners sentenced to life terms. Fifty-five percent were under thirty years old when sentenced. These were new commitments. On December 31, 1960, the number of prisoners serving life terms was 16,784.[21]

---

[20] Rubin et al, *op. cit. supra* n. 2 at 398. "Making the law discretionary might not do any more than make the present practice legal. It is hard to see where such a change would change the situation insofar as discrimination is concerned. As a practical matter the prosecuting attorneys get around the harshness of the law in many cases by just refusing to file the required information except in cases where the additional sentence seems merited."—Brown, *op. cit. supra* n. 4.

[21] Information received from Federal Bureau of Prisons.

Several states are credited with the lion's share of the commitments, particularly California, with 1,583. No other state committed as many as one hundred. Florida committed seventy, Georgia seventy-four, Ohio sixty-nine, Texas sixty-seven. This spread reflects the number of crimes punishable by life imprisonment, about twenty-five in California, but not more than six in most other states. All jurisdictions punish murder by life imprisonment (if not by death); but no other offense approaches universality of application of a life term. The other offense that carries a life term in a majority of the states is violent rape. In a small number of states a life term may be imposed for burglary, or sodomy, and occasionally other offenses. As we have seen, in recent years narcotics violations and sexual psychopathy have been added to this list.

True, most life-term prisoners are eligible for parole. But paroles, if granted, come after many years in most instances, and many life term prisoners are never paroled. In 1961, 106 life-term prisoners died in prison. In the same year there were forty-two executions.

Are life terms needed for either public protection or rehabilitation of any group of offenders? The offenses which in the highest number of states carry life terms are murder and sex offenses. No particular rehabilitative course of treatment is used, and it is not possible to visualize a greatly prolonged course of treatment. The "one day to life" sentence for sex offenders is *not* justified by the treatment actually practiced or visualized, as we have seen. Sex offenders after release have a low recidivism rate.[22]

As for murderers, their success rate on parole is better than for practically all other offenders. It is extremely rare for a murderer on parole to commit another homicide. One study of seventy-eight prisoners who had had their sentences reduced by clemency between 1943 and 1959 found that, of all classes of offenders in the group, "murderers are much the best risk. Only one of the twenty-three murderers on the list had a parole violation; he missed a date with a parole officer."[23]

---

22 *Supra,* p. 94.
23 New York; Harriman, Mercy Is a Lonely Business, Saturday Evening Post, March 22, 1958.

Murder in Michigan is punishable by life imprisonment without eligibility for parole unless the sentence is commuted. Between 1937 and 1961, 175 men were released by commutation of sentence. Of these, none committed another homicide, and only four were returned for committing other offenses.[24] In California 342 men were paroled from first-degree murder commitments between 1945 and 1954. Up to June 30, 1956, thirty-seven (10.8 percent) had violated their parole, but in only nine cases (2.6 per cent) did the violation consist of a new felony. The parole record was better for the convicted murderers than for almost every other category of offender.[25] The same is true of murderers adjudicated to be of unsound mind, and later released.[26]

Then is the life term needed for deterrence? There is no evidence whatsoever that a life term, or the death penalty, is a more effective deterrent than a substantial, or even a short, term of years.[27] Certainly there is no evidence that rape, sodomy, sexual psychopathy, or other sex crimes have been more effectively deterred in jurisdictions in which they carry life terms than in the several other jurisdictions with a maximum penalty of twenty years.[28] The reason is self-evident—these are crimes that, like murder, are the product of powerful psychological or circumstantial forces, irresistible to the offender. Those who are deterred by law are evidently deterred by the threat of prosecution and some punishment; but the threat of the greater punishment—life terms—adds no additional deterrence.

If the history of penology teaches us anything, it is that the concept of harsh punishment is unsound. We have abandoned torture as punishment, and to a considerable extent given up capital punishment, not only because they are inhumane, but because they are inef-

---

[24] National Council on Crime and Delinquency, The Michigan Sentencing and Penal Laws 29 (1961).

[25] Problems of the Death Penalty and Its Administration in California, Assembly Interim Committee Report, v. 20, No. 3, p. 12 (1957).

[26] Cruvant & Waldrop, The Murderer in the Mental Institution, 284 Annals 35 (1952).

[27] Rubin et al., op. cit. supra n. 2 at 349-50.

[28] Mueller, Legal Regulations of Sexual Conduct (1961) for a list of penalties for rape, state by state.

fective. Can we really believe that a person will be encouraged to commit crime because his punishment will be "only" a five-year maximum term, and perhaps more? The thought is absurd.[29]

This observation is especially true under the Model Sentencing Act, where the penalty for a dangerous act may be thirty years, not five. The five-year limit is applicable only if the defendant is not found to have a disturbed personality.[30]

If we grant that a life term is not a more effective deterrent than a term of years and is not needed for rehabilitative purposes or public protection, can we argue that we ought nevertheless not dispense with it because at least it represents society's judgment of the gravity of a particular offense, and only criminals (and their families) are hurt? Against this rationale is the bad effect of a life term, combined with other unduly long terms, on our penal system. It is the lifers and other long term prisoners who put their stamp on the correctional institutions; they accumulate, of course, while prisoners serving shorter terms are a much more transient element. The percentage of life-term and other long-term prisoners is substantially higher than the percentage of lifers among those *committed* in a single year, simply because there is a faster turnover of short-term prisoners than long-term prisoners. The long-term prisoners are almost always held in maximum security, thus determining the security for all, including short-term prisoners. They constitute the escape-risk group, and the security and disciplinary measures geared to controlling them are applied to all prisoners. "Disheartened, embittered prisoners are always a source of trouble to good prisoners, and to the administration of a penal institution."[31]

Some long-term prisoners are bad actors and escape risks; most are not or, at any rate, are not after a few years. Many

---

29 Rubin, Crime and Juvenile Delinquency 129 (1961).

30 "To the extent that sentencing also carries an element of deterrence, as it does, it derives from the *potential* punishment, the statutory potential, actually imposed in those instances in which it is warranted. . . . A penal code that authorizes a long term which is in fact imposed by the court where warranted is achieving the goal of deterrence so far as laws and courts can achieve it."—Comment on sec. 9, Model Sentencing Act.

31 Randolph, Are Long Sentences Necessary? 21 Am. J. of Correction 4 (1959).

are, in fact, not correctional problems, but geriatric problems. M. R. King, Superintendent of the California Medical Facility at Terminal Island, speaking on the subject at the 1953 Congress of Correction, pointed out that on June 30, 1953, California correctional institutions held nearly 13,000 inmates, 1,438 of them forty-five to fifty-four years old and 726 fifty-five years of age and over. He stated that older inmates often find themselves out of place and "unwanted" in institutions whose programs are geared for younger prisoners and that the great majority are no longer security risks, some indeed being so slow and infirm that they have difficulty in keeping up with the lines. At times they must be fed in their cells or admitted to the hospital for special care. In 1959 New York's prisons held 1,000 prisoners sixty-five years of age or over, housed mainly in maximum-security facilities. "This housing," said the New York Prison Association in its 1959 report to the legislature, "is costly and in some instances the physical layouts impose a hardship on the other prisoners because of conditions of health or various infirmities." The long passageways and stairways of Sing Sing and Clinton prisons were cited as examples.[32]

Crimes carrying life terms adversely affect sentencing in another way, such offenses automatically barring probation or parole. Edward G. Garrett, chief probation officer for the District of Columbia, noted that the United States and District of Columbia statutes bar offenses with potential life or death sentences:

> This bar we have found has occasionally worked an injustice on the individuals concerned. Consider for example the crime of carnal knowledge under the District of Columbia statute. It is an offense now barred to probation because it has a potential death penalty. There are many degrees of carnal knowledge, some quite serious and others relatively harmless. Notwithstanding this fact, there have been several instances where the use of probation as a treatment was thoroughly indicated but was not permissible because the offense was one barred by statute.[33]

---

[32] Rubin, op. cit. supra n. 29 at 128-9.

[33] Reply to questionnaire by Advisory Council of Judges of NCCD, November 16, 1956.

The objective examination of life terms tends toward a conclusion of their uselessness and harm. A historical view may also help. The life term has not always been with us. Rather, it is a fairly modern device, contemporaneous with and related to the extended use of capital punishment that came in with the industrial revolution.[34]

Penology for a long time used punishments other than imprisonment—corporal punishments, particularly, of which capital punishment may be said to have been the maximum application. In English law, for example, terms of imprisonment were never over a few years. Stephen points out that when penal servitude was substituted for transportation in the middle of the nineteenth century, "imprisonment had been rendered both more severe [by making the confinement in all cases separate] and shorter than it had formerly been, so that with hardly any exception the maximum punishment permissible was two years' hard labour."[35] Although it was later raised somewhat, British sentences have continued to be much shorter than ours.

In America, however, the significant change occurred immediately after the Revolution. The new state governments severely reduced the number of crimes punishable by death, but then the punishments for those crimes were fixed at life imprisonment. The first penal code in New York, for example, substituted life terms for all offenses previously punishable by death, and this was a typical pattern.[36] This "reform" of capital punishment set a tragic pattern, not yet overcome.[37]

---

[34] Rubin et al., *op. cit. supra* n. 2 at 21, 30.

[35] Stephen, 1 History of the Criminal Law of England 483 (1883).

[36] "The law of 1796 not only made two crimes alone capital, namely, treason and murder, but it also made punishable by life imprisonment, with the additional penalty of hard labor, or solitude, or both, those crimes formerly designated as capital offenses. Fourteen years was the maximum term for all first offenses above the grade of petty larceny. For a second offense in these crimes, the penalty was increased to imprisonment for life, with hard labor or solitude. Lesser offenses were visited by imprisonment not less than one year, or, for second offenses, up to three years."— Lewis, The Development of American Prisons and Prison Customs 1776-1845, 51 (1922).

[37] The life term as a substitute for the death penalty was sometimes frankly instituted on the theory that it was a more terrible penalty, hence a greater deterrent. Radzinowicz notes that Joseph II of Austria abrogated the death penalty because he considered it ineffective, his chancellor saying

Today, although the English penal law includes a significant group of offenses, even some misdemeanors, punishable by life imprisonment, in the five year period 1958-1962 the total number of life terms was 208, or an average of 42 a year. Almost all were murder (155) or manslaughter (46). Although there is an old provision authorizing life terms for habitual offenders, it has not been used for many years. The term in common use for habitual offenders is a maximum of fourteen years. The total number of terms of over ten years' imprisonment but less than life terms, for the same five year period, is 263, or an average of 53 a year—in all England and Wales, a civilian population of 46,000,000.[38]

The conclusion is clear: life terms of imprisonment are not needed, are harmful, and should be repealed, along with the Baumes laws providing for increased terms of imprisonment on second and third offenses. The Model Sentencing Act makes this simple but apparently unprecedented[39] and radical proposal (as well as providing for repeal of the special sentences for sex offenders, as we have already noted). It spells out criteria for identifying and sentencing dangerous offenders to terms up to thirty years, coinciding very closely with the common-sense criteria discussed above.

There is one exception. Under the Model Sentencing Act the penalty for murder is a life term. The explanatory comment published with the Act states as follows:

In principle, murder in the first degree should not be differentiated from other offenses, for which a life term

—"Our sovereign has only followed his own conviction that the punishment by which he proposes to replace the penalty of death is more effective owing to its duration and therefore more appropriate to inspire terror to malefactors."—Radzinowicz, A History of English Criminal Law and Its Administration from 1750: The Movement for Reform 1750-1833, 298 (1948). See Rigg, The Penalty Worse Than Death, Saturday Evening Post, August 31, 1957.

38 Information from N. Howard Avison, Institute of Criminology, University of Cambridge.

39 But an account of the English prison reformer, John Howard, notes: "In Holland—always his favorite country— . . . he first saw the maxim . . . 'Make them diligent and they will be honest.' . . . Offenders are sentenced to these houses according to their crimes, for seven, ten, fifteen, twenty and even ninety-nine years; but to prevent despair, seldom for life."—Bellows, John Howard, His Life, Character and Service (1882).

may not be imposed. Although murderers make up the great majority of life-term prisoners, the evidence is quite clear that they are good risks on parole or in minimum custody in institutions. In some states such life-term prisoners are released, sometimes shortly after sentence. In some states a term of years is authorized for murder. However, there is no doubt that murder in the first degree is generally deemed a uniquely heinous crime for which the gravest penalty under the code should be imposed. The Act does not provide for the death penalty. The entire frame of reference of the Act is that a diagnostic and treatment approach should be taken to all offenders, a stand in conflict with the death penalty.

The Model Sentencing Act authorizes parole at any time, for any offense, including murder.

Chapter 9

The Model Sentencing Act

This chapter is not an exposition of the entire Model Sentencing Act. The Act, a legislative model with broad purpose, intended to solve a series of problems in sentencing and correctional administration and treatment, is explained in its pamphlet publication, which includes interpretive comment on each statutory section. It is also discussed in a symposium in *Crime and Delinquency,* the quarterly journal of the National Council on Crime and Delinquency, and elsewhere.[1] The statutory text, not the comment, appears in the Appendix below.

The function of this chapter is not to interpret the entire Model Sentencing Act. At several points above certain problems were said to be answerable by sentencing reforms, and we referred specifically to the MSA provisions. What were these problems? (1) In the discussion of the relative merits or deficiencies of M'Naghten, Durham, and other rules of criminal resonsibility, we made the point that the issue—to take due account of the problems arising in mental illness of defendants —cannot be resolved at the point of trial but must be dealt with on the sentence, through a procedure that heretofore has

---

[1] Volume 9, no. 4, October, 1963. Rubin, The Model Sentencing Act, 39 N.Y.U. L. Rev. 251 (1964).

not been available, and we suggested that the Model Sentencing Act, with its support of a therapeutic correctional system, is such a procedure. (2) We also suggested that under existing sentencing laws M'Naghten is a superior rule to Durham and other rules, and that its merits would be increased under a sentencing system such as the one proposed by the Model Sentencing Act. (3) And we said that the function of protecting the public, carried out principally by detection and suitable sentencing of dangerous offenders, is, again, best served by a law such as that offered in the Model Sentencing Act, not by current sexual psychopath acts, current sentencing of narcotics violators, or Baumes laws. Let us start with the last problem, dangerousness.

The Dangerous Offender

We have condemned the sexual psychopath acts on various grounds, one of which is that they do not protect the public, inasmuch as the term "sex offender" or sexual psychopath or any of the other definitions does not coincide with dangerousness. It is with such a view that the Model Sentencing Act calls for repeal of the sexual psychopath acts.[2] We have condemned the Baumes laws, similarly on the ground that experience has shown they do not protect the public, because they are not applied to dangerous offenders. It is with such a view that the Model Sentencing Act calls for repeal of the Baumes laws.[3]

The MSA defines a dangerous offender—that is, the defendant on whom a long term may be pronounced—as follows: "(a) The defendant [who] is being sentenced for a felony in which he inflicted or attempted to inflict serious bodily harm, and the court finds . . . is suffering from a severe personality disorder indicating a propensity toward criminal activity. (b) The defendant [who] is being sentenced for a crime which seriously endangered the life or safety of another, has been previously convicted of one or more felonies not related to the instant crime

---

[2] Comment on sec. 23: "Specific repeals should include the . . . 'sexual psychopath' acts (since a more precise test of dangerous offenders is included in section 5)."

[3] Comment on sec. 23: "Specific repeals should include the sections governing sentencing of repeated or habitual offenders."

as a single criminal episode, and the court finds that he is suffering from a severe personality disorder indicating a propensity toward criminal activity."[4] Category (c) is the racketeer.

Involved in this definition is a value judgment with which most people agree—that the term of "dangerousness" is applicable to offenders dangerous to the person, not property offenders.[5] The thief, the check writer, or even the burglar is not subject to a long term under the MSA. The arsonist is ordinarily a property offender, but if the act of arson endangered persons, even if not so intended, then a suggestion of dangerousness is indicated. The MSA says that in such a case the defendant with a previous record may be dealt with as a dangerous offender.

The MSA sentences for the crime and according to the individual make-up of the defendant. Only for a serious (dangerous) crime can a defendant be sentenced to a long term. This, it seems to us, is morally sounder than sentencing to an indeterminate term a defendant who is mentally ill but has not committed a serious or dangerous crime—which is what the Durham rule in effect does. The same fault is committed in the sexual psychopath acts: the indeterminate sentence, potentially to life, may be imposed on a person who is not dangerous; and, we say, in practice the sentence is imposed mainly on those who are not dangerous. The same fault is committed by the Baumes laws.

Not every defendant who has committed a dangerous crime is sentenced to a long term under the MSA. The finding of personality disorder and its indications must be determined by the judge on the basis of a clinical report submitted by the state diagnostic center. If the defendant is suffering from a severe personality disorder indicating a propensity toward criminal activity, he may (not "must") be sentenced to a long term. Why should this additional factor be significant in indicating a possible long term? Because the normal offender is treatable by methods of social retraining, requiring no great period of time. What he requires is education, perhaps vocational retraining, a

---

[4] Model Sentencing Act, sec. 5.

[5] Compare Overholser v. Russell, 283 F. 2d 195 (1960), interpreting the phrase "dangerous to himself or others" in D.C. Code sec. 24-301(e): "the danger to the public need not be possible physical violence or a crime of violence. It is enough if there is competent evidence that he may commit any criminal act, for any such act will injure others and will expose the person to arrest, trial and conviction."

period of time away from an undesirable community or companions, or an attitudinal change. But for the mentally disturbed criminal who commits dangerous crimes against the person, safety of the public requires that sufficient time for a more difficult retraining, psychological treatment, be allowed.

Should the deed or the doer be our focus? The MSA is concerned with both.

The information from the diagnostic center will not always work toward establishing dangerousness. It may in many instances exculpate defendants who would have been sentenced to long terms on the basis of the offense alone if the court, lacking a diagnostic workup, were in doubt about them.

Psychiatric Evidence on the Sentence

In discussing sex offenders, we said that "to the extent that psychiatric services and facilities are provided under the sexual psychopath statutes (where anything at all exists), either in diagnosis or treatment, they are at worst a total waste and at best a poor use of scarce psychiatric talent in correctional treatment. Certainly diagnostic resources are needed both in sentencing and in treatment, but it is obvious that to channel the bulk, or all of such services into dealing with sex offenders is to deal with a generally nondangerous group for whom psychiatric treatment is at best unpromising and, in the lean measure given in correctional services, entirely unproductive. . . . Sentencing resources are needed to assist the court in detecting dangerous offenders at the point of sentencing, no matter what their offense. There is nothing wrong in a provision for referral to a diagnostic clinic at the point of sentencing, if it is done with more reason than under the sex offender laws. In fact, if there is one useful suggestion that remains in these laws, it is the concept, and occasionally the services, of the diagnostic referral."[6]

In connection with the sentencing of narcotics law violators, noting the havoc caused by the punitive, mandatory terms in the federal system and in many states, we again referred to the Model Sentencing Act, as providing a flexible correctional sentence, based on an understanding of the particular defendant— here, mainly social evidence. The Model Sentencing Act, we

---

[6] *Supra*, pp. 105, 106.

noted, requires a presentence investigation (principally a social investigation) in every felony case. We said: "As with all other commitments of dangerous offenders, it has no minimum term and would allow parole. It avoids the mandatory features of the federal law. It is the kind of sentencing act the Academy would approve. With that approach it was natural for the Advisory Council of Judges to take a position consistent with the Academy's with respect to who should be sentenced: 'The narcotic drug addict is a sick person physically and psychologically, and as such is entitled to qualified medical attention just as are other sick people.' "[7] So also the repeated offender would be treated as flexibly, and on an individual basis.

We said earlier: "The Model Sentencing Act not only provides a much more precise way of determining the dangerousness of offenders, but it also opens the way for a flexible, ample use of psychiatric evidence. . . . Under the Act the judge, if he is considering committing a defendant to a long term as a dangerous person, *must* obtain psychiatric evidence, developed at a diagnostic center, where the defendant is studied and out of which a report to the court is made. With other material in hand, particularly the presentence report of the probation department, the judge proceeds to sentence. A hearing must be held on the sentence, but it is not rigidly curtailed by the rules of evidence applicable on a trial, particularly the restrictive artificiality of the 'hypothetical question'; and, because the trial rules of evidence are not applicable, the 'battle of the experts' diminishes greatly, perhaps disappears."[8]

This is the language of the MSA: "The defendant shall not be sentenced under subdivisions (a) or (b) of section 5 [that is, sentenced to a long term as a dangerous, disturbed offender] unless he is remanded by the judge before sentence to [diagnostic facility] for study and report as to whether he is suffering from a severe personality disorder indicating a propensity toward criminal activity; and the judge, after considering the presentence investigation, the report of the diagnostic facility, and the evidence in the case or on the hearing on the sentence,

---

[7] *Supra,* pp. 130-131.
[8] *Supra,* p. 13.

finds that the defendant comes within the purview of subdivision (a) or (b) of section 5."

Although we earlier cited various cases and others to the effect that the solution to the problem of communication between psychiatry and law should be arrived at on the sentence and not through alteration of the rule of responsibility on the trial, we may cite now several sources that expressed this thought in some detail and could have been speaking of the Model Sentencing Act (although, of course, they were not; it did not exist).

Dr. Bernard L. Diamond wrote:

> For psychiatry to make a significant contribution to the law, there must be a bridge between medicine and the law which the psychiatrist may cross. And when he arrives at the other side, there must be room for him to move about—to function within the framework of his familiar values and goals.

Dr. Diamond refers to a "radically new relationship between psychiatry and the law . . . a relationship in which each profession respects the basic tenets of the other, and neither usurps the functions of the other." In such a relationship, the court will say to the psychiatrist:

> Forget about the legal definitions and the technicalities; forget about sanity and insanity; premeditation, malice, and *mens rea*—that is our concern. Tell everything that you, as a medical expert, know about this defendant. What kind of a person is he? What is wrong with him emotionally and mentally? How did he get to be the way he is now? What made him do what he is accused of? What hidden mechanisms in his mind caused him to behave in the way he did? What kind of treatment does he need to ensure his rehabilitation? Is he likely to respond to treatment? What kind of protection does society require to prevent something like this happening again? Tell us all that you know about this defendant, and we will give full consideration to what you have said; we will put it together with all the evidence from other sources: then we will

decide what is best for society to do with this defendant.[9]

Jerome Hall wrote:

It can at least be said, therefore, that psychiatric
knowledge is far from having reached the point of
unimpeachable scientific certainty. Neither in using
expert psychiatric witnesses nor in developing the legal
formulas that govern the determination of punishable
conduct need the law bow to any unassailable authority
in the bailiwick of the psychiatrists. That psychiatrists
have knowledge to offer to the law cannot be doubted;
but that knowledge must be carefully selected and fitted
into the framework in which it can be made useful.
The elements of this framework . . . [are] first, a view
of human nature that posits free choice and responsibility; second, a corresponding order of law that makes
punishment a corollary of responsibility; third, within
this order of law, stable and workable classifications
permitting consistency of treatment appropriately tem-
pered to the needs of individual cases; fourth, effective
application of these classifications through rules that
can be understood and employed by the agencies of
justice, the judge and the jury; and finally, maximum
use of available knowledge, including psychiatric testimony.[10]

Dr. Charles Savage:

When this happy event occurs [realization that reform of the penal system, not mental hospital commitment, is the answer], we can resign from the arena of
theology into which Judge Bazelon has cast us as
experts, and resume our role as physicians and scien-
tists who may be hopefully able to advise the court on
the sentencing and disposition of criminals. The jury
could stick to determining matters of fact; the judge
could return to the administration of justice.[11]

-----

[9] Diamond, Criminal Responsibility of the Mentally Ill, 14 Stan. L. Rev.
59 at 84 (1961).

[10] Hall, Studies in Jurisprudence and Criminal Theory 280 (1958).

[11] Discussion by Savage, of Watson, Durham Plus Five Years: Development of the Law of Criminal Responsibility in the District of Columbia,
Am. J. of Psych. October 1959, p. 289.

How shall the psychiatric sentencing service be organized? There are those who argue for privately retained psychiatrists. Richard H. Kuh comments:

> The pressures created by volume at public institutions, sometimes coupled with inexpertise because of poor pay, may render reports by so-called "court psychiatrists" inadequate. . . . Moreover, in view of the many divergent schools of psychiatric thought, any particular "court psychiatrist"—in expressing his own opinions, shaped by his particular discipline and prejudices— may express a view sharply at variance with the view others might entertain with equal honesty.[12]

Specialization is needed, and privately retained psychiatrists could not develop the knowledge and skills needed. The Model Sentencing Act, therefore, insists on a state diagnostic clinic, although it may be set up administratively in any one of several ways. A footnote to section 6 states:

> A separate statute is needed to establish the diagnostic facility, which may be a state agency independent of the state correctional system (*e.g.*, the New Jersey Diagnostic Center), a part of a special state treatment (*e.g.*, Patuxent Institution, Maryland), or a part of the correctional system (*e.g.*, as in federal diagnostic referrals). It is important that it be a well-established clinic set up by the state, perhaps with regional branches, but staffed by full-time psychiatric and other necessary personnel. The diagnostic facility statute should authorize referrals of not only the defendants under section 5 but also, in the discretion of the judge, other offenders.

The Baltimore court clinic, for example, meets the specifications of the Model Sentencing Act. Its director, Dr. Manfred S. Guttmacher, writes:

> We do not presume to usurp the court's functions in a sentencing. Our recommendations are based exclusively on our psychiatric findings. We do not pass on such factors as community acceptance nor the deter-

---

12 Kuh, The Insanity Defense—An Effort to Combine Law and Reason, 110 U. Pa. L. Rev. 771, at 803 (1962).

rent effect of a penal sentence. We do, however, make specific recommendations to probation and the conditions of probation, advisability of commitment to Patuxent Institution for Defective Delinquents, etc. Our complete report, which is the result of a social work investigation, a full battery of psychological tests, and the psychiatric examination, is given to the defense counsel and to the prosecutor, as well as to the court, in every case. The report runs from five to forty single-spaced typewritten pages, with a face sheet giving the impression and recommendations.[13]

The Massachusetts Court Clinics[14] and the already mentioned New Jersey Diagnostic Center also illustrate services readily accomodated to the Model Sentencing Act requirements; the same is true, probably, of the reception centers in several state correctional systems,[15] although their present functions are far more limited, being confined to classification for institutional placement purposes.

Therapeutic Correctional Treatment

We earlier said: "The Model Act not only facilitates much more precise sentencing—more than does any existing or other proposed code—especially in detecting dangerous offenders and those who are mentally ill, but also evisages that such defendants shall be given special treatment, following clinical diagnosis, in a suitable therapeutic institution."[16] We subsequently noted that (except for murder in the first degree) life terms are abolished. No longer is it possible for a correctional system to give up the treatment attempt and rely on mere custody.

The Model Sentenching Act authorizes commitment of dangerous offenders for a maximum of thirty years. The judge may fix the maximum at any point less than thirty years also. If an offender cannot be released at the end of a thirty-year term,

---

[13] Guttmacher, The Mind of the Murderer 139 (1962).

[14] The Massachusetts Court Clinic Program, 13 Juvenile Court Judges Journal 3 (1962); Ordway, Adult Diagnostic Court Clinics, 2 Current Psych. Therapies (1962).

[15] Rubin, Weihofen, Edwards & Rosenzweig, The Law of Criminal Correction ch. 8 sec. 9 (1963).

[16] *Supra*, p. 13.

his disorder is almost inevitably the kind that would render him committable to a state mental hospital.

A defendant who is *not* within any of the dangerous offender categories cannot be committed for more than five years. Why only two terms—up to thirty years and up to five years? The situation is comparable to hospital care. There are hospitals for chronically ill people and hospitals for short-term care, where the patient stays for not more than a week, several weeks, or a month. There is no need for an "in-between" institution.

But the abolition of life imprisonment does not produce this result of itself. The more important contribution toward a therapeutic penal apparatus is that long terms under the Model Sentencing Act will coincide with personality disorder. (The one exception is racketeers, who are subject to long terms without reference to personality disorder.) Just as important, the long-term prisoners, it is foreseen, would be relatively few in number, far fewer than their number in state prisons today. Two psychiatrists, experienced in psychiatric service to courts and institutionalized disturbed criminals, have said: "Persons who are clinically, psychiatrically, or psychologically abnormal to any significant degree constitute, all together, only a *minor* segment —about 4 or 5 per cent—of the criminal population as a whole."[17] Instead of institions of 1,000 or more inmates, as today, in which therapeutic programs—certainly psychotherapeutic programs— are impossible, institutions for disturbed long term prisoners could be as small as 100 or 200, in which treatment would be a practical possibility. These prisoners would also be eligible for parole; none would be barred.

We have condemned the commitment of persons acquitted under Durham as punitive, pointing out that under a penal commitment, probation and fine would be considered if the offense is not a grave one, as they are for defendants who are not disturbed. The MSA, it is anticipated, would encourage the expanded use of probation and suspended sentence, as well as fines. The Act does not mandate probation or suspended sentence in any case. However it is reasonable to assume that if a penal code is reduced in punitiveness, judges would be

---

[17] Messinger & Apfelberg, A Quarter Century of Court Psychiatry, 7 Crime and Delinquency 343, at 348 (1961).

more inclined to use community treatment. This is particularly supported by the nondangerous offender category. Aware that the defendant is legally categorized as nondangerous, the judge takes less risk in placing him on probation or suspending sentence.

I have always considered that the failure of probation to expand adequately reflects an anomalous reality. To increase the use of probation we usually push for additional probation staff, better qualified probation officers, and so on, and naturally this is a sound thing to do. Yet improvement in probation service does not necessarily result in an increase in the use of probation. To increase the use of probation we have to push on the *prison* side. In effect, we will have an increased use of probation, suspended sentence, and fine when we curtail the use of imprisonment. Occasionally this has happened without planning when we have had overcrowded institutions, but we ought to approach this problem in a rational way. When we reduce prison commitments, we will increase the use of community dispositions.

With respect to fines—another disposition that avoids imprisonment—the MSA again reaches new levels, and, again, through the separation of dangerous and nondangerous offenders. The Model Act has the usual provisions that the court may impose a fine as provided by law for the offense, and it may be with or without probation or commitment. The Act then goes on to provide as follows: "Where a sentence of fine is not otherwise authorized by law, in lieu or in addition to any of the dispositions authorized in this paragraph, the court may impose a fine of not more than $1,000." What this means is that in any case of a nondangerous offender the judge may, if he wishes, impose a fine as the full sentence or a fine in combination with another disposition. I know of no statute that provides for a fine on an equally sensible system of classification.

Nor is a vast personnel program in correctional institutions indicated. For most jurisdictions, it is true, psychiatrists would have to be added to serve as the core staff for the long-term institutions, and as consultants for the institutions for nondangerous offenders. But the regearing of institutions will have a liberating effect on personnel at present capable of contributing to rehabilitative programs but frustrated by the custodial nature of the correctional institutions, in part the product of the commingling of all kinds of prisoners. Since the long-term institution would be much smaller than the average maximum-security institution today, and camps or other minimum-security institutions would be appropriate for institutionalized nondangerous offenders (with a concomitant increase, as already indicated, in probation, susended sentence, and fines), state correctional budgets would go down.

A Final Word on M'Naghten, Psychiatry, and the Model Sentencing Act

The development of our thesis (the role of sentencing, and particularly the requirements met by the MSA) lends additional insight to our defense of the M'Naghten rule in preference to Durham. The propaganda of psychiatry was intended, after all, not really to change M'Naghten—although that is what they asked for—but to "find the bridge" between law and psychiatry. With the Model Sentencing Act, that bridge is found, and the great sense of a narrow rule, such as M'Naghten, becomes evident. The criticism of M'Naghten must vanish, and the value of the narrow rule—that is, seeing M'Naghten for its meaning in relation to *mens rea* and not to mental illness—becomes clear, we trust, even to psychiatrists who favored a change to a Durham or Durham-type rule.

But there are other new reciprocal advantages in M'Naghten combined with the Model Sentencing Act. Let us first think of the nondangerous offender who is mentally ill but not within M'Naghten. Psychiatry is not looking for, or capable of, a vast program of treatment for all mentally ill criminals.

Under Durham, in the District of Columbia, or in any jurisdiction in which the defense of insanity, if established, results in an indeterminate commitment to a mental hospital, a defendant who is mentally ill but likely to be sentenced to a term of a few years at most will not usually bring forward the defense of mental illness, since the penal disposition would likely be less punitive than the indetermine commitment. Important information about the defendant will therefore be suppressed.

However, in a jurisdiction with the Model Sentencing Act and with M'Naghten, there would be no barrier to the defense's honestly bringing forward the defendant's mental condition. If the defendant was categorized as a nondangerous offender, his term would at the most be five years and he would be eligible for parole. If he was a dangerous offender—that is, if he had committed a crime dangerous to the person and was found to be suffering from a severe personality disorder—the question of his mental condition would not be one for technical debate under the restrictive rules of a trial. The judge or prosecutor would call for a diagnostic workup and the defense could serve its interest best by a full exposure of his condition. All of this would contribute to sounder, individualized sentencing.[18]

Realization of such a plan is supported by provisions for discretionary—not automatic—commitment of those incompetent to stand trial or acquitted for insanity, the discretion to be governed by meaningful criteria, mainly of dangerousness. Even the mandatory commitment is less damaging in a M'Naghten jurisdiction: "Under the M'Naghten rule . . . the automatic commitment is applicable to fewer people; second, a defendant exculpated under the M'Naghten rule probably meets the criteria for civil commitment because his condition, usually psychosis, is much more severe than the 'mental illness or defect' required by the Durham rule."[19]

Now let us turn to the dangerous offender. As we know, in the District of Columbia the Durham decision led to a change in the law to require commitment upon acquittal for mental illness. This was interpreted as needed for protection of the public. We have indicated, however, that many in this group were not dangerous, and much of the outcry against Durham has been its needless punishment of such persons. But the issue of dangerousness is truly important. Whatever rule we use should be one that helps the court in its sentencing and the correctional service in its treatment to protect the public against the dangerous offender.

It is the Model Sentencing Act that places the focus for the psychiatric contribution not merely on mental illness, but on the dangerousness of the offender. Here again we see that with

[18] *Supra*, pp. 38-9.
[19] *Supra*, pp. 35-36.

this view, M'Naghten assumes a new superiority: it is the rule that makes individuals responsible for their crimes, subject to individualized sentencing.

Furthermore, the combined rules (M'Naghten, Model Sentencing Act) make the demand on psychiatry that it can probably meet, in contrast to the demand made by the Durham rule and the sexual psychopath acts it cannot meet. Guttmacher has noted:

> Psychiatrists must agree with the observation made by Zilboorg that "psychoanalysis has no answer as to what it is that makes men succumb or give in to his fantasies so that they become criminal acts." Clinical psychologists assert that projective tests give an indication of the strength of the controlling mechanism, but we must admit that present devices for measuring social control are quite faulty.[20]

The demand of the Model Sentencing Act is a limited one. The MSA calls only for a professionally made study to show whether the defendant is suffering from a severe personality disorder that indicates a propensity toward criminal activity. Here is neither the requirement of establishing causation, nor predicting behavior. A current condition is passed on, and a judgment made that, in the light of the defendant's behavorial history and his condition, further criminal acts are or are not likely. These judgments are made for sentencing purposes. The prisoner will be observed in the institution, and a parole board will judge his coming behavior.

We think some incidental legal advantages in procedure will also accrue. James V. Bennett observed:

> Reliable figures indicate that 40 to 50 per cent of the time of the appeals court is required to review cases which would not be there had a reasonable sentence been pronounced. After giving a number of examples of this type, Chief Judge Simon Sobeloff of the Fourth Circuit Court of Appeals said: "Such fantastic vagaries tear down the mightiest sanction of the law—respect for the courts. We have good and wise men on the bench, but not all are wise and good; and even the best

---

[20] Guttmacher, *op. cit. supra* n. 13 at 11.

and most prudent, being human are like Homer, sometimes likely to nod."[21]

This situation will be overcome, we believe, with application of the Model Sentencing Act and its reasonable sentences.

Bargaining for pleas of guilty against the quid pro quo of reduced charge or an easier sentence has long been an uneasy feature of criminal justice.[22] We believe this activity will be lessened with application of the Model Sentencing Act, for most offenders will in any event face a maximum term of five years or less.

The hardships of exclusionary rules of evidence, applicable on the trial, would be modified with such a sentencing act, to the general advantage of the court, the psychiatrist, and the defendant as well.

These observations are speculative, and cannot be pursued very far. Experience with the application of the Model Sentencing Act will reveal whether these advantages are real and no doubt will also reveal difficulties.

It is an intellectual curiosity, at least to the writer, that the "answer" to the role of the psychiatrist in criminal law administration is provided in a proposed penal reform that set forth to accomplish several things, but none related to psychiatry. The Durham rule has not enabled the psychiatrists to improve their contribution to criminal law administration; but the fault has been in the new legal rule, not in the psychiatrists, although they had an improper expectation of what would follow. If the Model Sentencing Act is adopted, the weight of expectation will be on the other foot: psychiatry would then have the opportunity to meet a clear and important requirement in correctional dispositions and treatment.

---

[21] Bennett, The Sentence—Its Relation to Crime and Rehabilitation, U. of Ill. L. Forum, winter 1960, p. 500 at 506.

[22] Rubin, *op. cit.* n. 15, at ch. 2.

APPENDIX

Text of The Model Sentencing Act*

ARTICLE I. CONSTRUCTION AND PURPOSE OF ACT

§ 1. LIBERAL CONSTRUCTION

This act shall be liberally construed to the end that persons convicted of crime shall be dealt with in accordance with their individual characteristics, circumstances, needs, and potentialities as revealed by case studies; that dangerous offenders shall be correctively treated in custody for long terms as needed; and that other offenders shall be dealt with by probation, suspended sentence, or fine whenever such disposition appears practicable and not detrimental to the needs of public safety and the welfare of the offender, or shall be committed for a limited period.

ARTICLE II. PRESENTENCE INVESTIGATIONS

§ 2. WHEN INVESTIGATION MADE

No defendant convicted of a crime involving moral turpitude, or a crime the sentence for which may include commitment for one year or more, shall be sentenced or otherwise disposed of before a written report of investigation by a probation officer is presented to and considered by the court. The court may, in its discretion, order a presentence investigation for a defendant convicted of any lesser crime or offense or adjudicated a youthful offender.

§ 3. CONTENT OF INVESTIGATION; COOPERATION OF POLICE AGENCIES

Whenever an investigation is required, the probation officer shall promptly inquire into the characteristics, circumstances, needs,

---

* Reproduced with permission of the National Council on Crime and Delinquency from its 1963 publication, which also contains comment on each of the sections.

and potentialities of the defendant; his criminal record and social history; the circumstances of the offense; the time the defendant has been in detention; and the harm to the victim, his immediate family; and the community. All local and state mental and correctional institutions, courts, and police agencies shall furnish to the probation officer on request the defendant's criminal record and other relevant information. The investigation shall include a physical and mental examination of the defendant when it is desirable in the opinion of the court.

§ 4. AVAILABILITY OF REPORT TO DEFENDANTS AND OTHERS

As to defendants sentenced under section 9 of this Act, the judge may, in his discretion, make the investigation report or parts of it available while concealing the identity of persons who provided confidential information. As to defendants sentenced under section 5 or section 7 of this Act, the judge shall make the presentence report, the report of the diagnostic center, and other diagnostic reports available to the attorney for the state and to the defendant or his counsel or other representatives upon request. Subject to the control of the court, the defendant shall be entitled to cross-examine those who have rendered reports to the court. Such reports shall be part of the record but shall be sealed and opened only on order of the court.

If a defendant is committed to a state institution the investigation report shall be sent to the institution at the time of commitment.

ARTICLE III. SENTENCES FOR FELONIES

§ 5. DANGEROUS OFFENDERS

Except for the crime of murder in the first degree, the court may sentence a defendant convicted of a felony to a term of commitment of thirty years, or to a lesser term, if it finds that because of the dangerousness of the defendant, such period of confined correctional treatment or custody is required for the protection of the public, and if it further finds, as provided in section 6, that one or more of the following grounds exist:

(a) The defendant is being sentenced for a felony in which he inflicted or attempted to inflict serious bodily harm, and the court finds that he is suffering from a severe personality disorder indicating a propensity toward criminal activity. (b) The defendant is being sentenced for a crime which seriously endangered the life or safety of another, has been previously convicted of one or more felonies not related to the instant crime as a single criminal episode, and the court finds that he is suffering from a severe personality disorder indicating a propensity toward criminal activity. (c) The defendant is being sentenced for the crime of extortion, compulsory prostitution, selling or knowingly and unlawfully tarnsporting narcotics, or other felony, committed as part of a continuing criminal activity in concert with one or more persons.

The findings required in this section shall be incorporated in the record.

§ 6. PROCEDURE AND FINDINGS

The defendant shall not be sentenced under subdivision (a) or (b) of section 5 unless he is remanded by the judge before sentence to [diagnostic facility] for study and report as to whether he is suffering from a severe personality disorder indicating a propensity toward criminal activity; and the judge, after considering the presentence investigation, the report of the diagnostic facility, and the evidence in the case or on the hearing on the sentence, finds that the defendant comes within the purview of subdivision (a) or (b) of section 5. The defendant shall be remanded to a diagnostic facility whenever, in the opinion of the court, there is reason to believe he falls within the category of subdivision (a) or (b) of section 5. Such remand shall not exceed ninety days, subject to additional extensions not exceeding ninety days on order of the court.

The defendant shall not be sentenced under subdivision (c) of section 5 unless the judge finds, on the basis of the presentence investigation or the evidence in the case or on the hearing on the sentence, that the defendant comes within the purview of the subdivision. In support of such findings it may be shown that the defendant has had in his own name or under his control substantial income or resources not explained to the satisfaction of the court as derived from lawful activities or interests.

§ 7. MURDER

A defendant convicted of murder in the first degree shall be committed for a term of life.

OPTIONAL § 8. ATROCIOUS CRIMES

If a defendant is convicted of one of the following felonies—murder second degree; arson; forcible rape; robbery while armed with a deadly weapon; mayhem; bombing of an airplane, vehicle, vessel, building, or other structure—and is not committed under section 5, the court may commit him for a term of ten years or to a lesser term or may sentence him under section 9.

§ 9. SENTENCING FOR FELONIES GENERALLY

Upon a verdict or plea of guilty but before an adjudication of guilt the court may, without entering a judgment of guilt and with the consent of the defendant, defer further proceedings and place the defendant on probation upon such terms and conditions as it may require. Upon fulfillment of the terms of probation the defendant shall be discharged without court adjudication of guilt. Upon violation of the terms, the court may enter an adjudication of guilt and proceed as otherwise provided.

If a defendant is convicted of a felony and is not committed under section 5 or 7 [or 8] the court shall (a) suspend the imposition or execution of sentence with or without probation, or (b) place the defendant on probation, or (c) impose a fine as provided by law for the offense, with or without probation or commitment, or (d) commit the defendant to the custody of [director of correction] for a term of five years or a lesser term, or to a local correctional facility for a term of one year or a lesser term. Where a sentence of fine is not otherwise authorized by law, in lieu of or in addition to any of the dispositions authorized in this paragraph, the court may impose a fine of not more than $1,000. In imposing a fine the court may authorize its payment in installments. In placing a defendant on probation the court shall direct that he be placed under the supervision of [the probation agency].

§ 10. STATEMENT ON THE SENTENCE

The sentencing judge shall, in addition to making the findings required by this Act, make a brief statement of the basic reasons for the sentence he imposes. If the sentence is a commitment, a copy of the statement shall be forwarded to the department or institution to which the defendant is committed.

§ 11. MODIFICATION OF SENTENCE

The court may reduce a sentence within ninety days after it is imposed, stating the reason therefor for incorporation in the record.

§ 12. WHO IMPOSES SENTENCE

All sentences under this Act shall be imposed exclusively by the judge of the court.

§ 13. PAROLE

Sections .... relating to the powers of the parole board shall be applicable to persons committed under this article.

ARTICLE IV. ALTERNATIVE SENTENCING OF MINORS

§ 14. ARRAIGNMENT AND TRIAL AS YOUTHFUL OFFENDER

A person charged with a crime which was committed in his minority but was not disposed of in juvenile court and which involves moral turpitude or is subject to a sentence of commitment for one year or more shall—and, if charged with a lesser crime, may—be investigated and examined by the court to determine whether he should be tried as a youthful offender, provided he consents to such examination and to trial without a jury where trial by jury would otherwise be available to him. If the defendant consents and the court so decides, no further action shall be taken on the indictment or information unless otherwise ordered by the court as herein provided. After such investigation and examination, the court in its discretion may direct that the defendant be arraigned as a youthful offender, and no further action shall be taken on the indictment or information; or the court may decide that the defendant shall not be arraigned as a youthful offender, whereupon the indictment or information shall be deemed filed.

§ 15. CONDUCT OF TRIAL

If the defendant does not plead guilty, the trial of the charge as youthful offender shall be before the judge without a jury. The trial of youthful offenders and proceedings involving them shall be conducted at court sessions separate from those for adults charged with crime.

§ 16. ADMISSIBILITY OF STATEMENTS

No statement, admission, or confession made by a defendant to the court or to any officer thereof during the examination and investigation referred to in section 14 shall be admissible as evidence against him or his interest, except that the court may take such statement, admission, or confession into consideration at the time of sentencing, after the defendant has been found guilty of a crime or adjudged a youthful offender.

§ 17. DISPOSITION OF YOUTHFUL OFFENDER

If a person is adjudged a youthful offender and the underlying charge is a felony, the court shall (a) suspend the imposition or execution of sentence with or without probation, or (b) place the defendant on probation for a period not to exceed three years, or (c) impose a fine as provided by law for the offense, with or without probation or commitment, or (d) commit the defendant to the custody of [director of correction or youth authority] for a term of three years or a lesser term, or to a local correctional facility for a term of one year or a lesser term. Where a sentence of fine is not otherwise authorized by law, in lieu of or in addition to any of the dispositions authorized in this paragraph the court may impose a fine of not more than $1,000. In imposing a fine the court may authorize its payment in installments. In placing a defendant on probation the court shall direct that he be placed under the supervision of [the probation agency]. If the underlying charge is a misdemeanor, a person adjudged a youthful offender may be given correctional treatment as now provided by law for such misdemeanor.

§ 18. EFFECT OF DETERMINATION AS YOUTHFUL OFFENDER

No determination made under the provisions of Article IV shall disqualify any youth for public office or public employment, or operate as a forfeiture of any right or privilege, or make him ineligible to receive any license granted by public authority; and such determination shall not be deemed a conviction of crime except that, if he is subsequently convicted of crime, the prior adjudication as youthful offender shall be considered. The fingerprints and photographs and other records of a person adjudged a youthful offender shall not be open to public inspection, except that the court may, in its discretion, permit the inspection of papers or records.

ARTICLE V. MULTIPLE CHARGES

§ 19. MERGER OF SENTENCES

Unless the judge otherwise orders, (a) when a person serving a term of commitment imposed by a court in this state is committed for another offense, the shorter term or the shorter remaining term shall be merged in the other term, and (b) when a person under suspended sentence or on probation or parole for an offense committed in this state is sentenced for another offense, the period still to be served on suspended sentence, probation, or parole shall be merged in any new sentence of commitment or probation.

§ 20. TRANSMITTAL OF INFORMATION OF MERGED SENTENCES

The court merging the sentences shall forthwith furnish each of the other courts and the penal institution in which the defendant is confined under sentence with authenticated copies of its sentence, which shall cite the sentences being merged.

§ 21. EFFECT OF MERGER OF SENTENCES

If an unexpired sentence is merged pursuant to Section 19 of this Act, the courts which imposed such sentences shall modify them in accordance with the effect of the merger.

§ 22. CONCURRENT OR CONSECUTIVE SERVICE OF TERMS

Separate sentences of commitment imposed on a defendant for two or more crimes constituting a single criminal episode shall run concurrently unless the judge otherwise orders.

ARTICLE VI. REPEALS

§ 23. SECTIONS REPEALED, AMENDED

The following [chapters, sections] are hereby [repealed, amended] .... All other acts and parts of acts inconsistent with the provisions of this act are hereby repealed.

Index

Index